THE
Vocabulary
Teacher's
BOOK OF LISTS

EDWARD B. FRY, PH.D.

JOSSEY-BASS
A Wiley Imprint
www.josseybass.com

Published by Jossey-Bass
A Wiley Imprint
989 Market Street, San Francisco, CA 94103-1741   www.josseybass.com

Jossey-Bass books and products are available through most bookstores. To contact Jossey-Bass directly call our Customer Care Department within the U.S. at 800-956-7739, outside the U.S. at 317-572-3986 or fax 317-572-4002.

Jossey-Bass also publishes its books in a variety of electronic formats. Some content that appears in print may not be available in electronic books.

ISBN: 0-7879-7101-4

Printed in the United States of America
FIRST EDITION
PB Printing   10 9 8 7 6 5

Contents

1 INTERESTING LISTS

2 ROOTS

3 WORD ORIGINS

4 SUBJECTS

5 WRITING

6 FOREIGN WORDS (EXONYMS)

7   SPELLING, ABBREVIATIONS, and PHONICS

8   MEASUREMENT and GEOGRAPHY

9   METHODS

10 AFFIXES and ROOTS

11 HOMOPHONES

MATH AND SCIENCE LISTS

Most of the lists in this book are suitable for any teacher and perhaps a bit more for English teachers, but a surprising number of the lists are aimed at math and science teachers or those teachers who at least sometimes teach in those areas.

Chapter 8

Chapter 10

INTRODUCTION

Once I went to a teachers' conference and spent some time in a publisher's booth that was showing a copy of a book I co-authored, *The Reading Teacher's Book of Lists*. A teacher came up, leafed through the examination copy, and said, "This is nothing but some lists of words." Well, she didn't buy the book, but some 300,000 other teachers have, so those lists of words, lists of books, lists of teaching strategies, and lists of a lot of other things must be useful to someone.

I hope this book will be useful too. It is written for teachers of a little older audience: upper elementary school, middle school, secondary school, and college freshmen.

Its focus is vocabulary improvement for reading and writing. It is strong on roots and word origins. It brings in a lot of words used in science, psychology, and literary works. Fortunately, or unfortunately, many of these words appear on standardized tests.

A whole chapter on vocabulary teaching methods is included, but the strong point of the book is to give you vocabulary curriculum content so that you can choose the content for your lessons. You decide what is too hard or too easy for your students. You decide how long or short your class lessons should be. Some lists might be great for just one or two bright students to study; other lists might help students with a foreign language background learn more English. Students who want to "cram" for college entrance exams will find some helpful lists.

Good writers tend to have good vocabularies. These lists can help student writers' vocabularies grow. An important part of writing is spelling. There is a whole chapter on spelling (Chapter 7), but spelling can be improved by a lot of other lists, such as homophones (did he mean "site" or "cite"—see Chapter 11).

But this book will only succeed if it is interesting. To that end, we have started out with what might be a new word for you—Capitonyms, in List 1, Chapter 1. Leaf around in that chapter and later chapters. As one friend put it, "If you don't find something interesting, you are brain dead." Well, that is going a bit too far, but a lot of teachers are interested in learning vocabulary for their students and for themselves. I can assure you that I have learned a lot of new words putting this book together and I found it interesting. I hope you will find it interesting too.

February, 2004

Edward B. Fry, Ph.D.
245 Grandview St.
Laguna Beach, CA 92651

ACKNOWLEDGMENTS

First, I would like to thank my diligent editorial assistant, Pat Warren, for helping to keep the manuscript on track, typing, proofreading, and massaging lists. The large homophone chapter was improved by the work of editorial assistant Reta Holmback and my granddaughter (future editor) Jamie Rau.

The contents of this book also were made possible by the earlier scholarship of the sixty-five or more different works of other authors and editors listed in the references, most of which are in my personal library. In particular I found help and inspiration from the works of the late Edgar Dale, professor of education at Ohio State University, and Norman Lewis, longtime author of popular books on vocabulary building.

I would also like to acknowledge the help and motivation of the Jossey-Bass editor, Steve Thompson, who threw me a curve by changing the title and focus of this book from the more narrow "homophones" to the broader focus of "vocabulary." We both hope the readers approve.

E.F.

To my wife, Cathy

ABOUT THE AUTHOR

Edward B. Fry was a professor of education and director of the Reading Center at Rutgers University in New Brunswick, New Jersey, for twenty-six years. Before that, he taught at Loyola University in Los Angeles and in California public schools sixth grade (in La Habra), special education (in Culver City), and high school reading improvement (in Ventura). He is known to a wider audience of reading educators because of his readability formula, the Instant Words high frequency vocabulary, dozens of journal articles, and a dozen or so reading textbooks and curriculum materials.

Dr. Fry is a past president of the National Reading Conference and a member of the International Reading Association (IRA) since its inception. He was elected to the Reading Hall of Fame in 1993 and has had two Fulbright lectureships to Africa.

He received his Ph.D. from the University of Southern California and a B.A. from Occidental College. Dr. Fry currently writes curriculum materials in reading and writing, skis, snorkels, and speaks on occasion.

In the beginning was the Word . . .

John 1:1

INTERESTING LISTS

Some words take on a different meaning when they are capitalized (forming a proper noun). These words are called *capitonyms* (cap = head, nym = name). Here are a couple of examples.

August – month
august – grand, majestic

Polish – citizen of Poland
polish – to make shiny

Job – biblical name
job – an occupation

Pound – money in UK
pound – a unit of weight

Frank – a boy's name
frank – open opinion

Yen – money of Japan
yen – desire

Bob – boy's name
bob – to cut shorter

Crow – an Indian tribe
crow – a bird

Chile – a country
chili – a hot spice
(the spice may be spelled either chile or chili)

Pat – a first name
pat – a light tap

Chow – dog type
chow – food

China – a country
china – fine dishes

Major – army officer
major – important or main thing

Caco and Chiro

You might know that *cacophony* is a harsh sound sometimes produced when the teacher is not in the room (caco = bad, phon = sound) or when an orchestra is tuning up. But bad handwriting from your students or your doctor is *cacography* and bad speech either defective or vulgar is *cacology*. Incidentally, the high-class word for handwriting is *chirography* (chiro = hand).

List 2   Very Hard Words

Can kids learn complicated new words? Here is some proof for you. Simply ask almost any kid you know to tell you what these words mean.

Quidditch	Azkaban
Mirror of Erised	Sneakoscope
Hogwarts	Patronus
Wingardium Leviosa	Voldemort
Remembrall	portkeys
Tarantallegra	Dumbledore

List 3   Fun with Words

Richard Lederer is a linguist who writes newspaper columns and talks on the radio (PBS). He likes to have fun with words. Here are a few from his book, *Crazy English*:

There is no **ham** in a hamburger nor **straw** in a strawberry.

There is no **egg** in eggplant nor **apple** in a pineapple.

A Guinea pig is not a **pig**, and a panda bear is related to a **raccoon** not a bear.

Fireflies are beetles, and **greyhounds** can be any color.

Rush hour lasts longer than an hour, and **boxing rings** are square.

Sweetmeat is made of fruit, and **sweetbread** is a meat.

Hot dogs can be cold, and **homework** can be done in school.

If a **vegetarian** eats vegetables, what does a **humanitarian** eat?

Button and **unbutton** are opposites, but **loosen** and **unloosen** are the same.

You **wind up** a watch to start it, but **wind up** a romance to end it.

Last Names

All last names came from something, and finding out what that something is can be interesting. Last names are also called "surnames" or "family names." For more names, see List 56, Eponyms.

1. Last names from occupations:

Name	Occupation	Name	Occupation
Bannister	crossbowman	Mercer	merchant of silks
Barker	shepherd	Milner	miller, grain grinder
Black	dyer		
Boyer	one who sold bows	Naylor	nail maker
Carter	delivery person	Norris	wet nurse
Chamberlain	personal servant	Ostler	innkeeper
Chandler	candle maker	Packard	peddler
Chaplin	clergyman	Packman	peddler
Chapman	merchant, peddlar	Parker	park keeper
Clark	clerk	Pointer	lace maker
Cooper	barrel maker	Porcher	swineherd
Coward	cowherd	Pottinger	soup maker
Currier	leather worker	Proctor	attorney, tax collector
Deemer	judge		
Faber	smith, metalworker	Sanger	singer
Farman	ferryman	Sawyer	woodworker
Faulkner	hawk keeper	Sellers	saddle maker
Fisher	fisherman	Seward	swineherd
Foster	forester	Smith	metalworker
Fowler	bird hunter	Stone	stoneworker
Fuller	cloth worker	Stringer	bowstring maker
Furber	polisher of armor	Sumner	summoner
Gaylor	jailer	Tiller	farmer
Grover	woodsman	Tucker	cloth worker
Hansard	swordmaker	Turner	woodworker on lathe
Harrower	farmer		
Joiner	carpenter	Wainwright	wagon maker
Kellogg	slaughterer	Wakeman	watchman
Keefer	seller of vats and bands	Wall(er)	mason
		Ward	guard
Kemp	wrestler	Weber	weaver
Ladd	servant	Webster	weaver
Leach, Leech	doctor	Wheeler	wheel maker
Lister	cloth dyer	Woodward	forest warden
Marner	seaman	Wright	mechanic

Plus some of the more obvious occupations such as Hunter, Farmer, Baker, Miner, Carpenter, Potter, Butler, Wheelwright (wright = craftsman), Tyler, Mason, Weaver, Cooke, Gardner, and Parson.

2. **Last names from places: (toponyms)**
   London, York, Blackwell, Melville (ville = city), Buckingham (ham = hamlet), Thorp (= village), Clinton (ton = town), Longfield, Chillcot (cot = cottage)

3. **Variations on smith: ("smith" means metalworker)**
   Goldsmith, Coppersmith, Silversmith, Arrowsmith, Blacksmith (iron) (may be shortened to Gold, Silver, etc.)

4. **Variations on "son of": (patronyms)**
   Mac or Mc as in MacDonald; O' as in O'Donnel; son or sen as in Williamson, Johnson, Olsen

5. **Names based on regal households: (eponyms)**
   King, Duke, Knight, Earl, Pope, Bishop, Baron, Lord, Abbott, Squire, Prince, Noble

6. **Names based on geographical features: (toponyms)**
   Mountain, Lake, Moore, Lowe (lowland), Brooks, Rivers, Meadows, Pond, Field, Clifford, Hill, Glen, Ford

7. **Names based on saints or biblical names: (eponyms)**
   St. Clair, St. Charles, Gabriel, Adam(s), Peters, Paul, Johns (apostles)

8. **Last names based on first names:**
   Williams, Edwards, Arthur, Daniels, Richards, Roberts

9. **Names based on animals:**
   Wolfe, Lyons, Bullock, Bird, Crow, Fox, Lamb

10. **Names based on tribes:**
    English, German, Frank (French), Irish, Scott, Walsh (Welsh), Norse

11. **Names based on colors:**
    White, Black, Brown(e), Grey, Green(e), Blue

12. **Names based on natural things:**
    Stone, Waters, Sands, Rains, Day, Woods, Grove, Forest

13. **Names based on directions:**
    North, Southern, Eastman, West, High, Lowe

14. **Seasonal names:**
    Summers, Winters, Day, Christmas, May

15. **Names based on human characteristics:**
    Small, Black*, Long, Whitehead, Cripwell*, Hand*, Heart*, Goodman, Sharp

16. **Most European surnames are patronymic,** that is, inherited from the father; but some are matronymic, inherited from the mother. They tended to be formed in the 12th to the 14th centuries.

---

*"Black" referred to hair color, whereas "Cripwell," "Hand," and "Heart" referred to defining deformities.

17. Of course, I had to look up the origin of my surname. Fry means "free," as does its related surnames, Frey and Freeman. Those of us who had free ancestors had ancestors somewhere between a serf and a nobleman. Those lucky chaps didn't have to work for the lord of the manor or pay him taxes on the land.

18. **Names based on foreign names** have similar sources as above, for example, Schmidt is German for Smith.

    In the United States, practically every language in the world has contributed last names: Lee (Chinese or Korean), Gonzales (Spanish), Levi (Hebrew), Vandermast (Dutch), Schnitger (German), Czarnecki (Czech), Yamashita (Japanese).

19. **Onomastics is the study of the origin of proper names.** So you are now an amateur onomast. In Europe especially, onomastics is a recognized specialty in a university's history department.

SAT Vocabulary Words

Lots of words in this book are apt to appear on the SAT (Scholastic Aptitude Test), so a good general vocabulary is the best way to get a good score. However, some people actually take the SAT, remember some of the words, write them down, and pass them along to future test-takers. Here are some of those words in case you want to do a quick cram or to have some idea of the type of words encountered on the SAT.

SAT Word	Meaning
aberration	abnormal, highly unusual
abridge	shorten
accessible	available; ready for use
antidote	something that relieves or prevents; a remedy that counteracts the effects of poison
appease	to make tranquil or quiet, especially by giving into demands; to pacify
arable	(land) suitable for farming
arrogant	overbearing; proud; haughty
aspire	to work toward or to have a goal
austere	having great economy; showing self-control when it comes to foregoing luxuries, frills; stern in manner or appearance
autonomous	independent
berate	to rebuke or scold in a harsh tone
bolster	to support; to strengthen
candor	honesty, sincerity
cantankerous	bad-tempered; quarrelsome
cartographer	map maker
cliché	an idea or expression that has become stale due to overuse
coalesce	unite, grow together, combine
cryptic	hidden; hard to understand; mysterious; obscure
cynical	distrusting motives of others, disparaging
effervescent	lively; full of uplifted spirit; vivacious
egotistical	excessively self-absorbed; very conceited
eloquence	artful ease with speaking; speech that can impact people's feelings
expropriated	take (land, etc.) from the owner
exuberant	overflowing with vitality and good spirits
fastidious	very attentive to detail; fussy; meticulous
gratify	to please or indulge
gregarious	sociable, outgoing
hamper	to hinder; to prevent something from happening
hardy	healthy and strong; robust
homogeneous	of the same kind; alike; uniform
integrity	holding firmly to values, such as honesty; completeness
intrepid	fearless

linger	to hang around; to stay
lofty	very high; towering; grand or noble
malinger	pretend illness (to avoid work)
mock	to make fun of; to imitate
modicum	tiny amount
mundane	commonplace; ordinary
nefarious	very mean and wicked
nurture	to care for; to nourish
ominous	related to feeling that something bad or evil is about to happen; foreboding
opportunist	a person who seeks self-gain, even at the expense of others, without regard to values or moral principles
ostentatious	showy, to attract notice
pariah	outcast, unwelcome person
phlegmatic	slow moving, sluggish
placate	to make calm; to soothe
prodigal	wasteful; lavish, "throws money away"
proximity	nearness
querulous	whining; complaining
recount	to tell a story
redundant	unnecessary repetition
rigor	harshness; severity
saturate	to wet or soak completely; to totally fill up
scrutinize	to read or look at very closely and carefully
stealthy	secretive; sly
surpass	to be better than; to excel
swagger	to walk around in a proud, showy manner; to boast in a loud manner
tentative	hesitant; not definite
thrifty	showing care with how money and resources are spent or used; miserly
thrive	to grow strong; to flourish
tranquility	peacefulness; calmness
uniformity	sameness
verbose	using too many words; wordy; long-winded
vilify	to slander or defame someone's name
virulent	extremely poisonous; deadly; full of spiteful hatred
whimsical	fanciful
zenith	highest point (opposite of nadir), a point on the celestial sphere corresponding to a point on earth

List 6   SAT Math Words

Mathematics vocabulary usually relates to mathematical concepts that are acquired by taking math courses or studying a math book. To get a respectable score on the SAT, you really need to know what most of these terms mean and be able to manipulate them in problems. See Chapter 2, lists 23 through 27, and Chapter 8, lists 169, 170, and 173 for more math words.

Averages: mean, median, mode
Integers: prime numbers, negative numbers, common factors, prime factors
Rate: time, distance
Number line: order, betweenness, connective numbers
Ratio: proportion, percentage
Signed numbers: plus or minus, exponents
Algebraic expressions: equations, inequalities
Factoring
Exponents, roots
Quadratic equation
Triangles: right, isosceles, equilateral, areas
Pythagorean theorem
Polygons, angles within, periphery
Decimal, fraction equivalents
Weighted average: some numbers given more weight
Quadrilaterals, parallelograms, perimeter
Circles: diameter, radius, circumference, arc, tangent, pi, area
Graphs: bar chart, frequency polygon, relation to table, grid lines, *x* and *y*, perpendicular
Odometer: distance measurement

Also see List 173.

Music Notation

The **Staff** are the five lines and four spaces, indicating pitch, on which to place the notes. These are preceded by the staff symbol.

Note symbols indicate the amount of time the note is held.

whole note	o	eighth note	♪
half note	♩	sixteenth note	♬
quarter note	♩		

Don't confuse the SAT (Scholastic Aptitude Test) taken by high school seniors for college entrance purposes with the SAT 9 (Stanford Achievement Test, 9th Edition). Unfortunately, they both have the acronym SAT, but the Stanford Achievement Test is usually followed by a number like 9 or 10 that indicates the edition.

The SAT 9 series tests students from Grade 2 to Grade 11. Here are some of the harder words found at about the 7th grade level in the language arts section of a hypothetical test:

acclimatize	fossilize	prologue
acquisition	gastronomic	promote
adverse	gesticulating	propaganda
alliteration	harmony	proponent
amplify	humanitarian	protagonist
annihilate	hysterical	ravenous
avalanche	illustrious	react
brutalize	implode	rebate
biodegradable	incredible	reduce
cacophony	innocuous	redundant
catalyst	insatiable	remembrance
codify	insecticide	restatement
compassionate	irresistible	retaliate
concentric	itemize	revenge
consensus	launch	reverse
conscientious	legalize	semantics
conscious	magnitude	snippet
contagious	metaphor	sporadically
contiguous	millipede	succinct
deface	misconstrued	superfluous
digitize	monoliths	synonyms
discernable	monotheistic	transaction
distraught	monotony	transformation
enormous	nullify	transmit
exfoliate	omen	tumultuous
excommunicate	ominous	typify
extrapolate	omnipotent	unforeseen
forecast	omnivorous	uninhabited
foretell	pessimistic	unmitigated
fortuitous	probability	verify

Minimum U.S. History Terms

abolitionism—The belief that slavery should be abolished.

Alamo—A fort and battle in 1836 where Texans fought Mexicans for independence. Mexicans won the battle. (*Alamo* is also a Spanish word for a cottonwood tree.)

Alien and Sedition Acts—Laws passed during the second presidency (John Adams) that restricted public activities of radicals who sympathized with the French (who were fighting the British in Europe).

antebellum—Things and houses built before the Civil War (ante = before, bellum = war).

Articles of Confederation—The 1782 agreement among the states before the Constitution was signed in 1789.

Battle of Bull Run—The first battle of the Civil War. The Confederates won.

Battle of Bunker Hill—The first battle of the Revolutionary War. The British won.

Bill of Rights—The first ten amendments to the Constitution, giving freedom of speech, press, religion, and assembly and limiting search and criminal laws.

Boston Tea Party—In 1773 colonists threw tea shipment into the harbor, an act moving toward **Revolutionary War**.

Civil War—1861–1865, between the Union (northern states) and the Confederacy (southern states). The Union won.

Declaration of Independence—This declares the U.S. independent of the British king; adopted July 4, 1776.

Emancipation Proclamation—President Lincoln declared all slaves to be free, 1863.

French and Indian War—British fought French in America 1754–1763. The British won and kept Canada. Some French people moved to Louisiana.

Gettysburg—The greatest Civil War battle and a turning point. The Union won.

Jamestown—The first English settlement in America; Virginia, 1607.

Lewis and Clark Expedition—President Jefferson sent two explorers to the northwest (later Washington state) to see what he bought from France.

Mason-Dixon Line—Essentially was the division between northern (free) and southern (slaveholding) states.

New Amsterdam—City founded by the Dutch in 17th century; now called New York.

Plymouth Rock—Landing site for early Pilgrims on the *Mayflower* in 1620.

Revolutionary War—The thirteen American colonies fought the British for independence 1775–1781. The French helped. Official end was the Treaty of Paris in 1783.

War of 1812—U.S. versus the British, a second war of independence. U.S. attacked Canada and lost. British burned the White House, but lost the war.

List 9   Reduplication

Reduplication means to double (re = again, du = two, ply = fold or unit). In any event, reduplications are an interesting class of words that have some doubling of a sound such as *dilly-dally*. Here are some more:

hanky-panky	shilly-shally
itsy-bitsy	claptrap
fiddle-faddle	hubbub
pell-mell	teetotal
namby-pamby	flimflam
hoity-toity	geegaw
bon-bon	

List 10   Test Scores

Standardized tests frequently tell the student how his raw score (the number right) compares with a standardized group, such as all the 8th graders in his district (**local norms**) or of a random sample of 8th graders in the country (**national norms**).

A **percentile** score means how the student ranks with a hundred typical students in her norm group. This is something like **percent**, except it means "rank placement," not amount. For example, a student who receives a percentile score of 43 would be ahead of 42 out of 100 typical 8th graders.

This would place that student in the 4th **decile** (tenth) because that decile covers the range of percentile scores from 40 to 49. And it places that student in the second **quartile** (quarter) or percentile scores 25 to 49; or in the third **quintile** (fifth) percentile scores 40 to 59.

One argument for not using percentile is that most tests are really not accurate enough to say a student who scores 43 is worse than a student who scores 44. So some larger grouping might be fairer; for example, he or she scored in the 4th decile or the middle quintile.

Review:
     percentile   decile   quartile   quintile   local norms

List 11   The Shortest Words

There are only a few regular one-letter words in English, such as **a** as in "a book" or **i** as in "I will."

You will note that **a** and **i** are both vowels because you cannot have a word shorter than a syllable, and a syllable must contain at least one vowel sound.

Occasionally, single letters are used as words as in "make a <u>U</u> turn" or "sit in the <u>M</u> section," but these are not regular words. (See our list of advertising spelling in Chapter 7, List 149.)

Single letters are used in abbreviations with or without a period, as in addresses, such as "403 <u>N</u> Elm Street" or in scientific notations such as temperature "72° <u>F</u>".

Whether or not an abbreviation is capitalized is sometimes arbitrary, sometimes mandatory, based on convention and field of use.

Here are some single-letter abbreviations:

M	Monsieur, male	**P**	page, President
g	gram, gold	**O**	ocean, October, oxygen
N, S, E, W	directions	**C**	centigrade, copper
a	area, acre	**k**	1,000, king

For more abbreviations, see Chapter 7, Spelling, Abbreviations, and Phonics, List 142.

List 12   Set

What English word has the greatest number of different meanings?

The answer is **set**, which has fifty-eight noun meanings or uses, some 126 verb uses, and, finally, ten adjective uses. Here are just a few:

set the table (verb meaning *to arrange*)
a **set** of dishes (noun meaning *group*)
Are you all **set**? (adjective meaning *ready*)
set out = start a journey (beginning)
set in = place into (put)
set = slang for sit (dialect)
set upon = to attack (attack)
set a clock = correct time (correct)
set apart = save (separate)
set a fire = start
set a trap = make ready
set hair = form shape
set the price = determine cost
set a time = appoint, state length
set your mind on = focus
set a fast pace = rate
set a gem = mount

Word Pairs

Some pairs of words we use so often that they act like a separate word. Not only that, but they have a recognized order. For example, we usually say "fun and games," rather than "games and fun." Companies post "profit and loss" statements, rather than "loss and profit" statements.

We ask people to dinner to come "rain or shine," cook it in "pots and pans," season it with "salt and pepper," and use a "knife and fork" to eat it, then have coffee in a "cup and saucer" mixed with "cream and sugar."

The women's movement has certainly given us the freedom to say "girls and boys" versus "boys and girls," but it hasn't changed the master of ceremonies who calls a group to attention by saying "ladies and gentlemen" or the minister who pronounces at a wedding that the happy couple are "man and wife."

Here are a few more word pairs that usually are not pronounced or written in a reverse order:

sooner or later	up and down
wine and cheese	shoes and socks
ham and eggs	life and death
pen and pencil	dead or alive

Perhaps you can add some pairs of your own.

Acrostic—the first letters of words to form a new word or the first letters of lines in a poem to form a new word. You could also use last letters or any designated letter.

S elf
U nderstanding
C an
C reate
E normous
S elf
S atisfaction

Affective Connotation

"A word," says Alice in Wonderland, "means exactly what I intend it to mean." So words have many kinds of meanings. A **connotative** meaning refers to a secondary and often more emotionally charged meaning. For example, a *weed* is an undesirable *plant*. Biologists classify *plants,* and gardeners destroy *weeds*. **Affective**, incidentally, means "emotional" (af = to, fec = make).

The opposite of connotation is **denotation**. It is the primary meaning or more factual and formal definition. So a **plant** is the denotative word to describe that green thing growing at the edge of your garden. You can declare it a **weed** if you want to get rid of it.

Whenever you start dealing with connotative meanings, you are treading on the Alice problem of meaning, so don't expect the dictionary to always help you out. Dictionaries always have denotative meanings and only sometimes have one or more of the connotative meanings.

Most of the examples below are negative connotations, but keep in mind that there can also be positive connotations; for example, a *house* can be a *home,* the same *road* to nowhere can be a *highway* to success.

Here are a few connotative and denotative meanings. You can probably think of a lot more.

Connotative	Denotative
weed	plant
dumb (person)	retarded, speechless
whore	prostitute, sex worker
shack	house
fat (person)	heavy
Hun	German (enemy in WWI)
wreck	used automobile
wasteland	desert, undeveloped
antique	old furniture
clumsy	unskilled, uncoordinated
slime	liquid, viscous
slimy (person)	repulsive
crippled	handicapped

Oxymorons

An **oxymoron** is a pair of two terms that seemingly have opposite or noncompatible meanings. The word *oxymoron* itself is an oxymoron (oxy = sharp or keen, moron = foolish, dull). Some common oxymorons are *pretty ugly, honest crook,* and *awfully good.* To understand oxymorons, you need to concentrate on one half of the pair, usually the second term, and use the other term as a modifier. A *clever fool* is a fool all right, but he has some cleverness. Sometimes one of the terms has a different meaning: A *jumbo shrimp* is a type of animal called a shrimp, but the term *shrimp* often means someone small. Below are a few more oxymorons that are vocabulary terms encountered in reading and used in writing. You can probably add some of your own.

bankrupt millionaire	loud whisper
clearly misunderstood	original copy
global village	random order
graduate student	student teacher
living dead	work party
black light	controlled chaos
Microsoft Works	

Feminism in Suffixes

In the later half of the 20th century the women's movement caused a great awareness of **gender** (male-female) in words. Many women wished that all or most "feminized" words be dropped or changed. A suffix that indicates gender is *–ess,* hence, a *waitress* is a woman, a *waiter* is a man. Today many cafés employ *wait persons* or *food servers;* the post office employs "mail carriers" not just *mailmen.* A woman who flies an airplane is now a *pilot,* no longer an *aviatrix,* but a woman who administers a will could still be an *executrix.*

Feminizing Suffixes	Examples
-ess	waitress, actress
-ina	ballerina, Wilhelmina, czarina
-ine	heroine, Josephine
-trix	aviatrix, executrix
-enne	comedienne, equestrienne

For more person suffixes, see Chapter 10, List 189. Also see lists 192, 193, and 194.

A **synonym** (syn = together, nym = name) is a word that means the same or nearly the same as another word. Conversely, an **antonym** (ant = against) means the opposite or nearly the opposite as another word. However, there is a large catch in the word "nearly" the same or opposite. They tend to mean the same or opposite in just one meaning of the word.

For example, if a synonym for *exercise* is *activity,* then an antonym might be *rest.* But using another meaning, a synonym for *exercise* might be *employment* as in the "exercise of a contract," to put it into effect, then the antonym might be *withhold.* Hence, just what is a *synonym,* or just what is an *antonym,* is often not just about finding a word, but can be a rather complicated or confusing concept.

However, in general, the concept of synonyms and antonyms is a valid and a useful concept for writers. It is also useful in defining, trying to understand, or learning the meaning of new words. Many tests or standardized examinations use a knowledge of synonyms and/or antonyms to test vocabulary or reading skills.

The list of synonyms and antonyms below is by no means exhaustive. There are many whole dictionaries of synonyms and antonyms. The best-known reference books of synonyms and often antonyms are called thesauruses. The original thesaurus was compiled by Peter Roget, an English physician, in 1852. Later editions were done by his son and grandson and today *Roget's Thesaurus* is a rather generic term, something like *Webster's Dictionary.* To give you an idea of the number of synonyms for individual words, the Norman Lewis modernized version of Roget's Thesaurus has over 17,000 entries, plus over 1,000 general categories like Love, Death, and so forth. And that is why this vocabulary book does not attempt to compete with a thesaurus by having a large list of synonyms and antonyms, but here are a few to get you started:

appeal—to ask with special earnestness

Synonyms:	*address*	*call (out or upon)*	*refer (to)*
	apply (for or to)	*entreat*	*request*
	ask	*invoke*	*request strongly*
	beseech	*urge*	*resort (to)*
Antonyms:	*abjure, defy, deny, disavow, refuse, repudiate*		

convey—delivery to a destination; in law or real estate convey means transferring title

Synonyms:	*carry*	*move*	*shift*	*transmit*
	change	*remove*	*transfer*	*transport*
	give	*sell*		
Antonyms:	*cling to, hold, keep, possess, preserve, retain*			

extemporaneous—done or made with little (if any) preparation

Synonyms:	*extemporary*	*impromptu*	*offhand*
	extempore	*improvised*	*unpremeditated*
Antonyms:	*elaborated, premeditated, prepared, read, recited, studied, written*		

impatience—lack of patience or intolerance of opposition

| Synonyms: | fretfulness | peevishness | petulance |
| | irritation | pettishness | vexation |

Antonyms: amiability, benignity, forbearance, gentleness, leniency, lenity, mildness, patience, peace, peaceableness, peacefulness, self-control, self-restraint

propogate—to have offspring

Synonyms:	beget	generate	originate	sire
	breed	increase	procreate	spread
	engender	multiply	reproduce	

Antonyms: annihilate, destroy, eradicate, exterminate, extirpate, root out, root up, uproot

renounce—declare against and give up formally and definitively

Synonyms:	abandon	disavow	disown	recant	repudiate
	abjure	discard	forswear	refuse	retract
	deny	disclaim	recall	reject	revoke

Antonyms: acknowledge, adopt, assert, avow, cherish, claim, defend, hold, maintain, own, proclaim, retain, uphold, vindicate

subsidy—monetary aid directly granted by government to an individual or commercial enterprise

Synonyms:	aid	bounty	pension	subvention
	allowance	gift	premium	support
	appropriation	grant	reward	tribute
	bonus	indemnity		

Antonyms: (none)

George Orwell wrote an important satirical novel entitled *1984* in which a mythical country controlled by The Party told lies for the truth and used language to control and obfuscate. For example, the Department of War was called the Department of Peace. The United States is not quite that bad, but some decades ago the U.S. government did change the War Department to the Defense Department. In Orwell's cynical view, "Political language . . . is designed to make lies sound truthful and murder respectable, and to give an appearance of solidity to pure wind."

William Lutz, a professor of English at Rutgers University, has made quite a career out of Orwell's doublespeak language used in the novel and has encouraged the National Council of Teachers of English (NCTE) to co-sponsor publications on this issue. Lutz has his own comment, "The great enemy of clear language is insincerity. When there is a gap between one's real and one's declared aim, one turns instinctively to long words."

Doublespeak

killing = arbitrary deprivation of life, The Final Solution, capital punishment
car mechanic = automotive internist, member of the vertical transportation corps
used cars = pre-owned, experienced cars
clerks = scanning professionals
product improvement = zero defect goal
budget cut = downward adjustment, efficiency action
lie = misspeak, inoperative statement, nuanced answers
bombing = protective reaction strike
starting a war = preemptive counterattack
tax increase = revenue enhancement, tax base broadening
neutron bomb = enhanced radiation device
invasion = rescue mission, incursion
civilian deaths = collateral damage
parachute = aerodynamic personnel decelerator
jailing = protective custody
retreating = straightening the front, regrouping
recession = period of accelerated negative growth
gambling = gaming
bullet hole = ballistically induced aperture
bad product = mechanical deficiencies
fired = nonretained, placed out, dehired, nonrenewed
cutback = cost reduction action, eliminate marginal outlets, divestment program
stock market fall = retreat, eased, technical adjustment, correction
library = learning resource center
desks = work stations, pupil stations
sea sickness = motion discomfort
overbooking = space planning, capacity management, revenue control
slaughterhouse = meat processor
junk yards = recycle centers, dismantlers
teachers = classroom managers, learning facilitators
testing = evaluation, assessment, analysis, feedback

<u>Oxymorons</u> (Impossible Combinations)

> **genuine draft beer in a can**
> **new antiques**
> **natural preservatives**
> **genuine imitation leather**
> **virgin vinyl**
> (Also see Oxymorons in List 15 in this chapter.)

<u>Weasel Words</u> (Mean Hardly Anything)

> **Helps** relieve cold symptoms (how much? maybe a tiny bit)
> **Relieve** cold symptoms (not cure)
> cold **symptoms** (not the cold itself)
> **Nothing better** (it's the same as others)
> **Nothing faster** (perhaps it is equal)
> **Fights** dandruff (but does it do anything?)
> **Virtually** spotless (so there are some spots)
> **New** product (perhaps not better, maybe worse)
> Acts **fast** (how fast? ten minutes, two days?)
> **More** flavor (more than what?)

Popular Science Vocabulary

If you read the newspapers, or a news magazine, or maybe take a test, here are some critical terms:

Fission versus Fusion

Fission refers to splitting, such as the splitting of the nucleus of an atom (uranium), as in the atom bomb. Atomic power plants use controlled fission.

Fusion refers to fusing, such as putting two nuclei (hydrogen) together to form a new, heavier element (helium) as in the hydrogen bomb.

Both processes release extremely large amounts of energy in explosions.

Atom Bomb versus Hydrogen Bomb

The **atom bomb** uses fission and was as powerful as 20,000 tons of TNT. It flattened a city and killed 75,000 people in Hiroshima in 1945.

The **hydrogen bomb** (H-bomb) is a thousand times more powerful. It blew a crater a mile wide and two hundred feet deep in a test on the Pacific Atoll in 1952.

Kiloton versus Megaton

A **kiloton** is a thousand tons.

A **megaton** is a million tons.

Linear versus Nonlinear Mathematics

Linear mathematics essentially means problems that refer to straight line, sequential, numerical modeling; for example, formulas for the orbits of planets, the bouncing of billiard balls, the trajectory of a rifle bullet.

Nonlinear mathematics is much more complicated and has numerous inputs and less certain results; for example, weather patterns, the stock market, and many biological and mental functions.

Nanotechnology

A **nanometer** is one billionth of a meter. A human hair is about 100,000 nanometers wide, or ten hydrogen atoms side-by-side equal one nanometer.

Nanoscience is the study of anything on a scale of one to one hundred nanometers.

Nanotechnology is using nanoscience to make things. A typical application is in chips (tiny circuits) used in computers or other electronic applications.

Sizes change yearly, but the smallest practical wires using photolithographic lenses (conventional) technology can make wires that are ninety nanometers in diameter. Future smaller wires made by combining atoms may shrink the diameter to three nanometers.

For more science words, see Chapter 3, lists 56 and 65.

Type	Atomic Bomb	Hydrogen Bomb (H Bomb)
Atomic Reaction	Fission split atoms Thermonuclear	Fusion
First Exploded	July 16, 1945 White Sands in New Mexico (Almogordo)	November 1, 1952 Elugelab Island in Eniwetok Atoll (Pacific Ocean)
Nickname	Trinity	Ivy Mike
Size	20 kilotons (1 kiloton = 1,000 tons of TNT)	10 megatons (1 megaton = 1 million tons of TNT) (1,000 times Trinity)
Necessary Computers	Friden Calculators IBM punch cards 1942 Herman Hollerath 1890	ENIAC (Electronic Numerical Integrator and Computer) 18,000 vacuum tubes 1945 U of PA John Von Neumann, Princeton
Project Director	Robert Oppenheimer	George Cowan
Basic Scientists	Edward Tellar Enrico Fermi	Edward Tellar Enrico Fermi
Results	1st bomb flattened Hiroshima; killed 75,000 people	Eliminated an island, made a crater a mile wide, 200 feet deep and a cloud 100,000 feet high, 100 miles wide
	Nuclei of heavier element (Uranium 235)	Nuclei of lighter element (hydrogen)
	Split into nuclei of lighter elements	Fuse together to form heavier element (helium)

First controlled atomic chain reaction 1942
Enrico Fermi, University of Chicago

Palindromes

Palindromes are fun words because they can be read forward or backward, like "mom." Some palindromes are different words when read backward, like "rats" spelled backward is "star." Here are a few single-word palindromes:

eve	did	sees	Bob
civic	madam	radar	Anna
deed	racecar	noon	Otto

Some people even try to find whole phrases or sentences that can be read backwards. Here are a few:

Rise to vote sir.

net ten

Never odd or even.

Was it a car or a cat I saw?

Flee to me remote elf.

Be on the lookout to see if you can find or think up a few more.

Paronomasia

Paronomasia has to do with fooling around with words, like making puns or clever remarks using words of similar sounds, like the poor rancher who bragged about having several "cattle acts." Jokes using homophones would also fall into the paronomasia category.

ROOTS

Here is an absolutely insane list of phobias. A phobia simply means a fear. It might be a little fear that you can joke about, or a fear that leads to avoidance, or it might be a blood-chilling, serious fear that leads to panic that you ought to see a doctor about.

In any event, it seems like you can take almost any Greek word and add phobia to it. And yes, human beings are so strange that probably somebody, someplace, really does have one of these phobias. However, there is another Greek root you can substitute for *phobia,* and that is *philia,* meaning love. So for every person who has *cynophobia,* a fear of dogs, there are probably ten persons who have *cynophilia,* or a love of dogs. Look at that! We have just doubled the list, but more than that, you can use this list as a list of roots.

Once we have a root like *cyno* for dogs, we can add any number of roots (or combining forms) to make up all sorts of technical-sounding terms. See the following table:

Root	Meaning	Example	Meaning
-phobia	fear	**cynophobia**	fear of dogs
-philia	love	**cynophilia**	love of dogs
-ology	study of, science of	**cynology**	study of dogs
-ologist	one who studies	**cynologist**	specialist on dogs
-cide	killing	**cynocide**	killing of dogs
-mania	madness (for)	**cynomania**	madness of dogs

Bathophobia, which is the fear of depth, is used in **bathysphere**, which is a round-shaped submarine used in exploring the extreme ocean depths. Although the ancient Greeks certainly did not have a bathysphere, as it wasn't invented until 1930, we see that those marine explorers did what scientists do all the time—invent new words from Greek roots when they need a new word for something. So these roots are useful for naming anything from bugs to drugs and all sorts of diseases and phenomena in between.

Phobias: A

acaraphobia: mites
acrophobia: heights
acustiophobia: noise
aerophobia: air, flying
aichurophobia: being touched
by pointed objects
algophobia: pain
aleurophobia: cats
alychiphobia: failure
amathophobia: dust
amaxophobia: riding in vehicles
ambulophobia: walking
androphobia: men
anemophobia: cyclones, wind

Anglophobia: the English
anthophobia: plants, flowers
anthropophobia: people
antlophobia: floods
anuptaphobia: staying single
aplophobia: bees
arachnophobia: spiders
asthenophobia: weakness
astraphobia: lightning, thunder
astrophobia: stars
ataxiophobia: disorder
automysophobia: being dirty
auroraphobia: northern lights
aquaphobia: water

Phobias: B–L

bacilliphobia: bacilli
bacteriaphobia: bacteria
ballistrophobia: being shot
basophobia: standing (for fear of falling)
batarachophobia: frogs and toads
bathophobia: depth
bibliophobia: books
blenophobia: pins and needles
blennophobia: slime
bogyphobia: demons and goblins
bromidrosophobia: body smells
brontophobia: thunderstorms
cainophobia: novelty
cardiophobia: heart disease
cathisophobia: sitting
catophtrophobia: mirrors
cheimaphobia: cold
cherophobia: gaiety
chionophobia: snow
chrematophobia: wealth
chromophobia: colors
chronophobia: time
cibophobia: food
claustrophobia: enclosed spaces
climacophobia: staircases
cometophobia: comets
coitophobia: sexual intercourse
coprophobia: excrement
cremnophobia: precipices
cryophobia: frost, ice
crystallophobia: glass
cynophobia: dogs
deipnophobia: dining and dining conversation
dementophobia: insanity
demophobia: crowds
dendrophobia: trees
dentophobia: dentists
dinophobia: whirlpools
diplopiaphobia: double vision
diplychiphobia: accidents
domatophobia: being in a house
dromophobia: crossing streets
dysmorphophobia: deformity
ecophobia: home

eisoptrophobia: termites
emetophobia: vomiting
entophobia: insects
elektrophobia: electricity
ergasophobia: work
erotophobia: sexual feelings
erythrophobia: blushing, the color red
eosophobia: dawn
eurotophobia: female genitals
febriphobia: fever
galeophobia: sharks
Galophobia: the French
gamophobia: marriage
gephyrophobia: crossing bridges
gerontophobia: growing old
glossophobia: speaking in public
graphophobia: writing
gymnophobia: nudity
gynephobia: women
hagiophobia: saints and the holy
halophobia: speaking
hamartophobia: error or sin
haphephobia: touching, being touched
hedenophobia: pleasure
heliophobia: sun
hematophobia: the sight of blood
herpetophobia: snakes
hippophobia: horses
hodophobia: travel
homichlophobia: fog
homilophobia: sermons
hylophobia: forests, wood
ichthyophobia: fish
kenophobia: large, empty spaces
kinesophobia: motion
kleptophobia: thieves
kopophobia: mental or physical examination
lachanophobia: vegetables
laliophobia: talking
lepraphobia: leprosy
lilapsophobia: tornadoes
linonophobia: string
lygophobia: dark
lyssiophobia: becoming mad

Phobias: M–Z

macrophobia: long waits	**ponophobia:** fatigue
maieusiophobia: child birth	**potumophobia:** rivers
mehalophobia: large things	**pyrophobia:** fire
merinthophobia: being bound	**rhabdophobia:** criticism, punishment, being beaten
metereophobia: weather	
metrophobia: poetry	**rhytiphobia:** getting wrinkles
mikrophobia: microbes, germs	**Russophobia:** Russians
molysomophobia: infection	**scriptophobia:** writing
monophobia: being alone	**selaphobia:** flashing light
motorphobia: motor vehicles	**siderodromophobia:** train travel
musicophobia: music	**skiaphobia:** shadows
musophobia: mice	**sociophobia:** friendship, society
myrecophobia: lice	**soleciphobia:** worms
necrophobia: death	**sophophobia:** knowledge
nephophobia: clouds	**spectrophobia:** looking in the mirror
nosophobia: becoming ill	**stasiphobia:** standing
numberophobia: numbers	**staurophobia:** cross or crucifix
nyctophobia: darkness, night	**stenophobia:** narrow places
odontophobia: teeth, especially those of animals	**stygiophobia:** hell
	swinophobia: swine, pigs
ochlophobia: crowds	**syngenesophobia:** relatives
odynophobia: pain	**tacophobia:** speed
oenophobia: wine	**taeniophobia:** tapeworms
olfactophobia: smells	**taphephobia:** cemeteries, being buried alive
ombrophobia: rain	
onomatophobia: a certain word or name	**tapinophobia:** small things
	taurophobia: bulls
ophthalmophobia: being stared at	**teleophobia:** religious ceremonies
ornithophobia: birds	**telephonophobia:** using the telephone
pantophobia: everything	**thalassophobia:** the sea
papaphobia: the pope or the papacy	**thanatophobia:** death, dying
paralipophobia: responsibility	**thassophobia:** sitting idle
paraphobia: sexual perversion	**theatrophobia:** theaters
parthenophobia: young girls	**theophobia:** God
peccatiphobia: sinning	**thermophobia:** heat
pedophobia: dolls	**Teutophobia:** Germans
peniaphobia: poverty	**tomophobia:** surgical operations
pentheraphobia: mother-in-law	**topophobia:** certain places
phagophobia: eating or swallowing	**trichophobia:** hair
pharmacophobia: drugs	**triskaidekaphobia:** number 13
phobophobia: afraid	**tropophobia:** changes
phengophobia: daylight	**uranophobia:** homosexuality
philophobia: falling in love or being loved	**vaccinophobia:** vaccines
	verbaphobia: words
photophobia: light	**xenophobia:** foreigners
pnigophobia: choking	**xerophobia:** dry places, desert
politicophobia: politicians	**zoophobia:** animals

You probably know what **suicide** means—killing yourself (self + kill). This is usually caused by some form of temporary mental problem; so if you know of someone talking about suicide, get that person to talk to a counselor or psychologist.

The -cide root means killing, and we see it in a lot of words like **pesticide** (pest + kill), which is a substance used by gardeners to get rid of plant-destroying pests. But the gardener better be careful and not get an **herbicide** (plant + kill) because that is a substance that will kill plants. Fortunately, herbicides are mostly used on weeds that the gardener wants to get rid of.

Regicide (king + kill) means the killing of the king, but it has come to have a broader meaning of killing any ruler. That's why the president always has to have the Secret Service around him; there is always some unstable person who wants to take a pot shot at the head of state, and unfortunately sometimes they are good shots. Regicide occurred throughout history, in ancient Rome, in the European kingdoms of the middle ages, and you can read about regicide in modern newspapers.

The opposite of regicide is even more tragic; when the head of state or a government decides to kill off a whole race, it is called **genocide** (race + kill). The classic case of genocide was the Nazi dictator killing Jews in World War II, but we see elements of genocide in continuing smaller wars.

A number of -cide words apply to family members killing each other. If you kill your brother, it is **fratricide** (brother + kill), and if you kill your sister, it is called **sororicide** (sister + kill). You might remember this because in college some young men join social organizations called **fraternities** and young women join **sororities**.

Getting rid of your parents is also classified. Killing your father is **patricide** (father + kill) and getting rid of your mother is **matricide** (mother + kill). It will help you to remember these words if you remember that "maternal" instinct is the warm, loving, mothering instinct. And on the other side, a **patriarch** is the father or head of a family or a clan. You have to be a pretty crazy family member to practice patricide or matricide.

The killing of any human is generally wrong and illegal, but one legal term for killing any human is **homicide** (man + kill). However, we should end with a better type of killing, and that is **bactericide** (bacteria + kill), which means killing bacteria. When you get a cut, you can often avoid getting an infection by using a bactericide.

Review:

suicide (self)
herbicide (plants, weeds)
regicide (king, ruler)
genocide (race, tribe)
homicide (man, human)
fratricide (brother)
sororicide (sister)
patricide (father)
matricide (mother)
bactericide (bacteria)

Numbers (uni-, bi-, tri-)

A lot of prefixes tell you "how much" or a number. A **bicycle** tells you that it has two wheels (cycles) because the prefix **bi-** means two . A **unicycle** has only one wheel; the prefix **uni-** means one. Now it is easy to know that a **tricycle** has three wheels because **tri-** means three.

A unicycle (one + cycle) is the one-wheeled trick cycle that clowns ride in the circus. Sometimes jugglers or even ordinary kids have unicycles. But if you know that "uni" means "one," then it is fairly easy to get the meaning of **uniform**, which means one form. Band uniforms are all the same, and uniform houses all look the same. Ah, but a **unicorn** (one + corn) might be unknown to you. But by now you know that it has something to do with one—actually it is a mythical one-horned animal. Unicorns don't really exist, but writers of myths and fairy tales talk about them.

We see "**bi-**" in a lot of other words like **binocular**, which literally means "two" eyes. Binoculars are field glasses or something that you use to see well in the distance. You might contrast it with a **monocular**, which is only for one eye (like half a binocular).

The prefix "**mono-**" also means "one" (like "uni-"), and it is used in other words like **monarch**, or a rule by one. A queen is a monarch because she is the only one who rules. We also see mono- in **monogamy**, which means that a man can only have one wife. You could contrast this with some cultures where **polygamy**, or many wives, are permitted.

The prefix "**tri-**" occurs in a lot of words longer than *tricycle*. It also appears in **trillion**, which is a very big number. In fact a trillion has three sets of three zeroes in addition to the base set of three zeroes (1,000,000,000,000). You can contrast this with a million, which has only one set in addition to the base (1,000,000), and a billion, which has nine places after the number (1,000,000,000).

If you want a little help in remembering how many zeroes are in a million, billion, or trillion, just remember to omit the first set of zeroes; then the prefix will help to tell you how many other sets of three zeroes to use.

Million	1,000,000
Billion	1,000,000,000
Trillion	1,000,000,000,000

Exponents also tell you the number of zeroes.

Ten = 10^1	Million = 10^6
Hundred = 10^2	Billion = 10^9
Thousand = 10^3	Trillion = 10^{12}

"Tri-" also occurs in **triplex**, a building with three apartments, or **triplets**, for three children all born at the same time.

A triplex has one more apartment than a **duplex** because "du-" means "two." If you are asked to fill out a form in **duplicate**, you must make two copies. The root words of "-**ply**" or "-**plex**" means "fold" or "layers."

Review:

mono- and uni- mean one	uni- = 1:	**unicycle**	bi- = 2:	**bicycle**
bi- and du- mean two		**unicorn**		**binocular**
tri- means three	mono- = 1:	**monocular**	tri- = 3:	**tricycle**
		monogamy		**triplex**
				triplet

million	duplex	unicycle	monogram
billion	triplex	unicorn	polygamy
trillion	duplicate	monocular	binocular

List 25 — More Numbers

Prefixes that count in the low numbers (1, 2, and 3) are fairly easy, but there are a number of other prefixes that indicate number. For example, the prefix "**semi-**" means half. We see it in some easy words like semicircle, which means half a circle. Some theaters might have seats arranged in a **semicircle**. But **semiannual** (half + year) means half a year. A magazine that is published **semiannually** comes out every six months. A **semicolon** is a punctuation mark (;) that is half comma (,) and half colon (:). So "semi-" has the general meaning of less than the whole, and this is how it is used in **semiprecious** (half + precious). A diamond is precious and very valuable, while a garnet or turquoise is semiprecious and worth much less by weight.

Another prefix that means half is "**hemi-**." A **hemisphere** (half + sphere) is half a sphere. The Western Hemisphere is half the earth, consisting of the continents of North and South America. And **hemiplegia** (half + stroke) is paralysis on one side of the body. A hemiplegic can't move one leg and one arm.

Well, if prefixes can mean part of a whole, they can also mean very large numbers. For example, "**milli-**" means thousand. A **milligram** (thousand + small weight) is a thousandth of a gram, a very small weight indeed, at only about 1/30th of an ounce. A milligram is a metric unit of measure used in weighing the active ingredients of vitamins and mineral pills, or in scientific measurement. But since "milli-" means thousand, it can also represent bigger things, like a **millennium** (thousand + years), which is 1,000 years. We are now in the third millennium A.D. "Milli-" is also used inexactly as in **millipede**, which is a little insect that is supposed to have a thousand feet. I've never counted them, but I doubt that they really have a thousand feet.

Another prefix that means thousand is "**kilo-**." We see it in the European distance measure **kilometer** (thousand + measures), which is 1,000 meters or about 6/10ths of a mile. A **kilogram** (thousand + grams) is 1,000 grams or about 2.2 pounds. In Europe many foods like bread and cheese are sold by the kilogram.

Perhaps an easy prefix is "**cent-**," which means a hundred. A penny or a cent is one hundredth of a dollar. So then you should easily remember that a **century** is a hundred years and a **centennial** is the hundredth anniversary of something. If your town is having a centennial, it is celebrating its founding one hundred years ago. A person who has lived a hundred years is called a **centenarian** (hundred + person).

A lesser used prefix **demi-** also means "half" as in: **demitasse** (half cup) or **demigod**, a mythological lesser god.

Review:

semi (half)	**mili** (thousand)	**cent** (hundred)
hemi (half)	**kilo** (thousand)	**demi** (half)

Remuneration! O! That's the Latin word for three farthings.

— Shakespeare, *Taming of the Shrew*

Even More Numbers

All right, so you think you can count with prefixes. Let's see how you do with these toughies.

Quad- means four. You can easily remember this because you already know that a **quarter** is one fourth of a dollar or a quarter of a piece of pie is one fourth of the pie. Or maybe you remember that a **quadrangle** has four right angles (four + angles). This knowledge should help you to understand what an expensive stereo with **quadraphonic** (four + sounds) sound is all about. That's right, it has four separate channels of sound so that it really sounds good. Also you shouldn't have much trouble with **quadrennial** (four + years). You might remember that **centennial** is 100 years so quadrennial is every four years.

The next prefix is **penta**- meaning five. Probably it's most popular use is for **pentagon** (five + sides), which is a five-sided geometric figure. But when it is spelled with a capital, Pentagon means the five-sided building near Washington, D.C., which houses the U.S. military chiefs. However, in the Olympic Games there is a relatively new grueling event called the **pentathlon** (five + contest), which combines five different skills: horseback riding, swimming, running, fencing, and shooting.

Okay, the next prefix for five is **quint**-. Maybe you have heard of the mother who has five children all at the same time; these are called **quintuplets** (five + units). It's rare but possible. Or again you might go to hear a small musical group with only five musicians, that's a **quintet** (five + diminutive). There are both classical music and jazz quintets.

We are up to six, and that prefix is **hex**-. In geometry a **hexagon** is a six-sided figure. Auto mechanics sometimes use **hexagonal** (six + angle) nuts, and those are nuts with six sides and hence, six angles. Poets sometimes write verses in **hexameter** (six + measure), which means that each line or verse has six metrical feet (something like six beats).

And finally we are up to sex, not the kind of sex you see in X-rated movies but **sex**-, the combining form, meaning six. We see this in the navigation instrument called a **sextant**, which measures the angle between the horizon and a star or sun. It is called a sextant because it uses one sixth of a circle in its scale. Someone who is in his or her sixties can properly be called a **sexagenarian** (sixty + person).

Review:

> **quad** (four)
> **penta** (five)
> **quint** (five)
> **hex** (six)
> **sex** (six)

Also see List 27.

Counting in Latin and Greek

Number	Prefix	Examples
1	**mono-, mon-** (Gk.)	**monogamy** (having one wife)
		monocular (having one eye)
		monorail (having one rail)
		monk (a single friar)
	uni- (L.)	**unicameral** (single chamber, legislative assembly)
		uniform (one form)
		unicycle (one wheel)
		unite (put together as one)
2	**di-** (Gk.)	**dioxide** (two atoms of oxygen)
		diphthong (vowel with two sounds)
		diploma (originally a letter folded double)
	bi-, bin- (L.)	**biennial** (happening every two years)
		bicycle (two wheels)
	du-, duo-, dup- (L.)	**duplex** (two-fold, two units)
		double (two of, twice)
		duple (twice, two-fold)
3	**tri-** (L., Gk.)	**triangle** (figure having three angles)
		triathlon (three athletic events)
		trillion (three groups of thousands before a thousand—1,000,000,000,000)
		triplet (simultaneous birth of three)
4	**tetra-, tetr-** (Gk.)	**tetrahedron** (four plane sides, a cube)
		tetrameter (poem with four feet)
	quadri-, quadr- (L.)	**quadrilateral** (figure having four sides)
		quadrangle (figure having four angles)
5	**penta-, pent-** (Gk.)	**Pentateuch** (first five books of the Old Testament)
		pentathlon (athletic contest comprising five events)
		pentagram (five-pointed star)
		Pentagon (the five-sided Defense Department building)
	quinque- (L.)	**quinquereme** (galley with five banks of oars)
	quint- (L.)	**quintuplet** (five children born at the same time)
		quintet (a group of five, often musicians)

Counting in Latin and Greek *(continued)*

Number	Prefix	Examples
6	**hexa-**, **hex-** (Gk.)	**hexagon** (figure having six faces) **hexameter** (verse with six feet) **hexagram** (six-pointed star)
	sex- (L.)	**sextuple** (six-fold) **sextet** (company of six singers or players) **sextant** (an instrument for measuring angles using one sixth of a circle)
7	**hepta-**, **hept-** (Gk.)	**heptagon** (figure with seven angles) **heptamerous** (divided into seven parts) **heptathlon** (athletic event of seven parts)
	sept-, **septem-**, **septe-**, **septi-** (L.)	**September** (seventh month of the ancient Roman calendar) **septuagenarian** (70-year-old) **septennial** (seven years)
8	**oct-**, **octo-**, **octa-** (L.)	**octet** (company of eight singers or players) **October** (eighth month of the ancient Roman calendar) **octopus** (eight-armed sea animal) **octave** (set of eight notes)
9	**nove-** (L., Gk.)	**novena** (prayers or services on nine days) **November** (ninth month of the ancient Roman calendar)
10	**deca-**, **deka-**, **dec-** (Gk.)	**Decalogue** (the Ten Commandments) **decathlon** (athletic event with ten events) **decade** (ten years)
	deci- (L.)	**December** (the tenth month of the ancient Roman calendar) **decimal** (one tenth)
100	**centi-**, **cent-** (L.)	**centenarian** (one who has reached the age of 100) **century** (one hundred years) **cent** (one hundredth)
1,000	**milli-** (L.)	**millimeter** (one thousandth of a meter) **million** (a thousand thousand)
	kilo- (Gk.)	**kilometer** (a thousand meters) **kilogram** (a thousand grams)

Amounts Non-Numerical

Meaning	Root	Examples
Many	**poly-** (Gk.)	**polyglot** (knowing many languages) **polyester** (fiber with complex molecule) **polygon** (many angled figure)
	multi-, mult- (L.)	**multiplication** (many folds or units) **multifloral** (compound flower head) **multifold** (numerous)
First	**proto-, prot-** (Gk.)	**protagonist** (the leading character in a play) **protohistory** (between non-recorded and recorded history)
	prime- (L.)	**primer** (first reading book) **primer** (first coat of paint)
Half	**hemi-** (Gk.)	**hemisphere** (the half of a sphere) **hemicycle** (half of a cycle)
	semi- (L.)	**semicircle** (the half of a circle) **semiannual** (half a year, twice a year) **semiliterate** (barely able to read or write)
	demi- (L.)	**demitasse** (half a cup, small cup) **demigod** (a lesser god)
Almost	**para-** (Gk., L.)	**paramedic** (almost a doctor) **paralegal** (almost an attorney)
Few	**olig-** (Gk.)	**oligarchy** (rule by a few) **oligopoly** (market control by a few)
Quarter	**quarter-** (L.)	**quarter** (1/4 of a dollar) **quarters** (housing of military) **quartermaster** (person in charge of housing) **quarterfinal** (round preceding semifinal) **quarter note** (one fourth of a whole note)
Very Many		**legion** (a large amount, multitude) **bushel** (means a lot of something, measure unit) **myriad** (very many or over 10,000)

List 29 ▸ Ruling (-crat, -cracy, -archy)

Here are some words based on the -**crat** root, meaning "rule." Note that -**cracy** and -**archy** mean the same thing, while -**crat** refers to the person. For example, we can have a **democracy** and some of the people are **democrats**. The -*y* ending is similarly dropped when shifting from **monarchy** to **monarch**.

plutocracy	rule by wealthy people
genecocracy	rule by women
democracy	rule by people (all citizens)
aristocracy	rule by nobility
autocracy	rule by one person
theocracy	rule by God or priests
oligarchy	rule by a few people
monarchy	rule by a monarch (king or queen)

List 30 ▸ Antidote (anti-, dis-, don-, con-)

An **antidote** is usually a remedy for pain or a counteraction for poison. For example, aspirin is an antidote for a headache. But **antidote** can also be used in a more general sense as something that counteracts something bad. For example, "money is an *antidote* for poverty!"

Anti- is a very widely used root (or prefix) meaning "against." We see it in hundreds of uses like **anti-guns**, **anti-German**, **anti-feminism**, and what was once thought to be the longest word in the English language (it's not), **antidisestablishmentarianism**.

Break it into parts (**morphemes**), and you will see that it has double negative prefixes (**anti-** + **dis-**), so it means "the movement for the establishment of an official national religion," which was a big conflict in England a few centuries ago. The antidisestablishmentarians won, so the Anglican Church is now the established religion of the United Kingdom.

Watch out for those double negatives: **non-reoccurring** means that it does occur, but it just does not reoccur.

The second part of **antidote** is related to all sorts of roots like **don-**, which means to give. We see it in **donation,** a gift frequently for a charitable or religious cause. It also has some related words: for example, a **donor donates** to the **donee**.

We also see **don-** in **pardon** (par-don) (for + give), so to pardon is to forgive or excuse. And a related word is **condone** (con-done) (with + give), which is to give, often *tacit* (silent), approval of some action (that might be illegal or objectionable).

Review:

antidote	condone	non-reoccurring
anti-guns	donation	pardon
anti-German	donor	
anti-feminism	donee	
antidisestablishmentarianism		

          The Vocabulary Teacher's Book of Lists

List 31   Twa- (twa-)

The old English word **twa**, meaning *two*, has survived in modern English with the number **two**, **twenty** (two tens), and **twice** (two times). **Twine** is a cord made of two or more strands. **Entwine** (also spelled properly as **intwine**) means all mixed up with or tangled up with.

When the old river boats were approaching the dock, the boatman might cry out "**mark twain**," which was the second mark on the lead line used in measuring water depth. It is interesting that Samuel Clemens, who grew up near the river boats, took Mark Twain as a pen name.

The same prefix probably accounts for the *tw* in **between** (by + two) and in **twilight** (between the two worlds of day and night).

Review:

two	entwine	between
twenty	intwine	twilight
twice	mark twain	

List 32   Beget (gen-)

Gen- is a tricky root because it means several different things. Here is the first meaning: from *ginere,* to beget = **procreate**, or cause to produce (children).

gene	tiny element that transmits heredity
genetics	part of biology that studies heredity
eugenics	attempts to improve heredity (eu- means good)
gender	male or female
generic	a general class (not a specific)
genesis	creation, beginning
generation	a group conceived about the same time
regenerate	start again
progeny	children, offspring
progenitor	ancestor

Kind (gen-)

Gen- also means *kind*. Here are some words from the second meaning:

generous	willing to share
genial	kindly personality
congenial	friendly
gentle	soft, easy going
genteel	well bred, good manners
gentleman	a genteel man
benign	kind, generous, good
malign	bad, harmful
homogeneous	same kind, alike

Good and Bad (bene-, mal-)

Here we have two prefixes (roots) with opposite meanings: **bene**, which means "good," and **mal**, which means "bad." We see these in many words.

benediction	a blessing (bene-dic-tion) (good + say + noun)
malediction	a curse (male-dic-tion) (bad + say + noun)
beneficent	kindly acts (bene-fic-ent) (good + do + adjective)
maleficent	harmful acts (male-fic-ent) (bad + do + adjective)

A **benefactor** (good + doer) **benefits** you, like your rich uncle who leaves you a million dollars, but a **malefactor** (bad + doer) is a crook who tries to steal it.

When you visit your doctor for a strange lump, you hope it is **benign** (good or non-cancerous) rather than **malignant** (bad or cancerous). Worse yet it could spread with **malignancies** (bad growths).

We also see these opposites in **malevolent** (bad + wish), which means to wish harm or evil toward someone, versus **benevolent**, which is to show mercy or compassion.

Review:

benediction	benefactor	benign
malediction	benevolent	malignant
beneficent	malevolent	
maleficent		

List 35 — Say (dic-)

Here is a root we can have some fun with; **dic-** means "say," and we find it in all sorts of words like **benediction** (good + saying). A benediction is a verbal blessing.

Bosses **dictate** (say) letters to their secretaries and **dictators** dictate orders that are not to be **contradicted** (contra = against) or changed.

A **dictionary** says what a word means, which is rather friendly compared to an **edict** (e- means from), which is not just a saying but a firm order spoken by an authority. A **dictum** means about the same as *edict*.

If you study well and have good **diction** (pronunciation), you could become the **valedictorian** (vale + dict + orian) (farewell + say + person), who usually has the best grades and has the honor of making the **valedictory** speech saying farewell to the school for the class.

Review:

benediction	dictionary	diction
dictate	contradict	valedictorian
dictator	dictum	edict

List 36 — Death (necro-)

You remember that a **necropolis** is a city of the dead or cemetery, but the root **necro-** (meaning dead) crops up in a number of other Greek words. Organizations sometimes publish a list of members who have died during the year and this list is a **necrology** (necro-ology) (dead + study of). If you are really afraid to get on that list, you may have **necrophobia** (necro-phobia) (dead + fear). There is a worse psychological problem, and that is **necromimesis**, where you think that you are already dead (necro-mimesis) (dead + imitation). Well, maybe there is something worse than that, and that is **necrophilia**, where you fall in love with corpses (necro-philia) (dead + love).

Necrosis (necro-osis) (death + state) is a sad condition in which a part of a plant or animal dies, but if that happens a gardener or surgeon can perform a **necrotomy** (necro-tomy) (death + cut), which removes the dead part.

Review:

necropolis	necrology	necrophobia
necrophilia	necromimesis	necrosis
necrotomy		

Climbing (sen-, scend-)

The root **sen-** (or **scend-**) means to "climb," and we see it in an interesting family of words. To **ascend** you climb up, as in ascend a mountain or ascend to power like becoming king (a-scend) (to + climb). But conversely you **descend** a mountain when you go down or descend from power (de-scend) (down + climb). You can make these verbs into nouns by changing the suffix, as in **ascension** or **descent**.

A **descendant** is somebody or something that comes directly from something else. You are a descendant of your grandfather (de-scend-ant) (from + climb + one who). Computers are a descendant of an adding machine.

When you **condescend** you accept something, usually a little grudgingly or by changing your opinion. If you *condescend* to take a lower-paid job you might not be so happy, but you are doing it because you prefer to eat regularly.

Somewhat the opposite is **transcend,** which means you go beyond some established belief or obstacle. People with disabilities often *transcend* what is expected of them. Or you might hear a story that *transcends* your belief in how the world works (transcend) (across + climb).

Review:

ascend	**ascension**	**condescend**
descend	**descent**	**transcend**
descendant		

Your Diploma

In ancient Greece, a letter folded twice (di- = 2) was given to a person when he traveled and was sent to represent his city (nation). He presented this *diploma* to show who he was. Today graduating students receive a *diploma* to show their accomplishment, and we have *diplomats* who still present credentials when they arrive at foreign countries and join the *diplomatic corps.*

Knowledge Areas (-ology)

Scientists, and those who specialize in particular subjects, like to use more formal words to describe their areas of study or specialty. These words frequently end in the root "**-logy**," which means "science of" or "study of." The letter "o" is a common form used in combining roots.

Most schools have a course in **biology** (bio-logy) (life + science), which is the study of life or living things, as opposed to **geology** (geo-logy) (earth + science), which is the study of the earth and nonliving things like rocks and the formation of mountains.

Medical doctors have a lot of terms that describe what the doctor specializes in. A **cardiologist** (cardio-logist) (heart + science) specializes in hearts, the cure and prevention of heart diseases. Just down the hall is a **radiology** (radio-logy) (radiation + science) department, which takes pictures by radiation using X-rays or curing diseases by giving radiation treatment.

But if radiology doesn't cure you, maybe the doctor can use **pharmacology** (pharmaco-logy) (drug + science), which is the science of drugs. That's easy to remember because a pharmacy is also a drug store.

If the disease is only skin deep, then the doctor better know something about **dermatology** (dermat-ology) (skin + science), which is the study of skin and its diseases.

Meanwhile, over at the university they have all sorts of "ology" departments. They not only have a biology department, they even have a **microbiology** (microbio-logy) (microbes + science) department, which is a subsection of biology. Microbiology studies very small things like microbes (tiny organisms). Another subsection of biology is **entomology** (entomo-logy) (insect + science), which studies a little bigger things like bugs and insects. If the biologist is interested in certain types of animals, he or she might take up something like **ornithology** (ornitho-logy) (bird + science), which is the study of birds.

Biologists are also interested in bigger things like **ecology** (eco-logy) (environment + science), the system of how all living things interact and are dependent on each other. So all kinds of biologists, such as microbiologists, entomologists, and ornithologists, are interested in ecology. In fact, everybody in the world should be interested in ecology because we are all living organisms and part of the system.

Review:

biology (life)	**dermatology** (skin)
geology (earth)	**microbiology** (small life)
cardiology (heart)	**entomology** (insects)
radiology (radiation)	**ornithology** (birds)
pharmacology (drugs)	**ecology** (environment)

One word frees us from all the weight and pain of life:
That word is love.

—Sophocles, *Oedipus at Colonus*

More Knowledge Areas (-ology)

But "-**ologies**" are not just used for the exact "sciences." They are also for many other subjects, like **musicology**, which, as you might guess, is the formal study of music, or **theology**, the study of God. So ministers must study theology, but the choir director studies musicology. It would help both of them if they studied a little **psychology**, which is the study of the mind. Usually psychology means the human mind, but there are those who study *animal psychology*. Maybe you should do this to understand your pet a little better.

Someone might be interested in **cosmetology**, which is the study of cosmetics. But this department in a community college might also include hairdressing, nails, and grooming.

When you watch weather forecasters on TV, they are applying the science of **meteorology**, which is the general study of weather, including storms, clouds, and temperature. And the weather forecasters usually come after the report of crimes like murder or arson (illegal fires). The formal study of these bad things is called, appropriately, **criminology**.

Studying your ancestors is called **genealogy**. Perhaps you will recall from biology that genes are the tiny bits of protein that determine your basic characteristics such as hair color or size. Don't confuse genealogy (origins) with **gerontology**, which is the study of aging. Those interested in older aged humans are interested in gerontology.

While we are on confusions, you will not find an **astrology** department in most universities because *astrology*, which literally means the study of stars, is really an ancient practice of trying to figure out how stars influence your life. In a university the scientific study of stars will be found in the **astronomy** department. The "aster-" root means star (an aster flower is a star-shaped flower) and the "-nomy" means "measure." So the university department claims to measure stars scientifically, while **astrology** is more apt to be found in a fortune-teller's shop.

Review:

musicology (music)	**meteorology** (weather)
theology (God)	**criminology** (crime)
psychology (mind)	**genealogy** (genes)
cosmetology (cosmetics)	**gerontology** (aging)
astronomy (stars)	**astrology** (stars)

Ontology

The word ontology refers to the science of or study of being (onto = being). It is used in theology (god + study) when discussing proof of the existence of God. When used in other contexts, it refers to the very beginning.

List 40   Too Much Knowledge (-ology)

Can you stand even a few more -ologies?

anthropology	(humans)	ophthalmology	(eyes)
archaeology	(ancient)	otology	(ears)
enterology	(intestines)	petrology	(stones)
homology	(laws)	pterodology	(ferns)
hydrology	(water)	sociology	(society)
ichythyology	(fish)	thantology	(death)
morphology	(shapes)	thaumatology	(miracles)
mythology	(myths)	toxicology	(poisons)
neurology	(nerves)	urology	(urine [tract])
ontology	(existence)	zoology	(animals)

Also see the list of phobias in List 22 in this chapter for more possible roots to combine with *-ology*.

List 41   More or Less (hyper-, hypo-, equi-)

Hyper- means "excessive." Someone who is **hyperactive** (over + active) is always running around doing things. In contrast **hypo-** means "too little." Someone who is **hypoactive** (under + active) doesn't really move very much—a real couch potato. Likewise, someone who is **hypercritical** (over + critical) goes around criticizing everything too much. But watch out for this: someone who is **hypocritical** (under + play a part) (note different pronunciation) is not someone who doesn't criticize but rather someone who says one thing but does something else. Perhaps you know somebody who is a real **hypocrite** (under + play a part), who tells you she is your friend but does something to show you that it is not true or tells you she will vote one way then votes the opposite.

The prefix **equi-** means "equal"—you could sort of guess that, couldn't you? We see this prefix in such words as **equidistant** (equal + distant), which means equal distance. If Bob lives two miles east of school and Pedro lives two miles west of school, they are equidistant from school. **Equilibrium** (equal + balance) means that things are in balance. Two weights on a simple scale are in equilibrium when the scale is balanced. In nature animals tend to be in balance in the long run. If there are too many rabbits, for example, more coyotes and hawks will develop to become predators.

Review:

hyperactive	equidistant
hypoactive	equilibrium
hypercritical	equal
hypocritical	hypocrite

Order is an interesting word with several related meanings. Sometimes it refers to proper sequence. If the words in this sentence were jumbled it would not make much sense; they have to be in a proper *order* to be meaningful. So order is related to meaning. When an authority gives an order, it is frequently to put something into a meaningful pattern.

Generals *order* their troops around and teachers try to keep order in their classrooms. If this doesn't work, they have **disorder**. But with luck things can be **reordered**.

If a student is especially good at something, he or she might be **extraordinary** rather than just **ordinary**.

Priests or ministers are **ordained** so that they can perform the **holy orders** (sacraments) and the work of the church after their **ordination**.

In mathematics we have **ordinal numbers**, which denote a sequence such as first, second, third, etc. The **cardinal** (principal) **numbers** are the more commonly used such as one, two, three, etc.

To **coordinate** means to have order with something such as doing something at the same time (co- is part of the prefix con- meaning *with*). But a set of **coordinates** are usually parallel lines, with intersecting parallel lines used in defining location. The most common coordinates are **latitude** and **longitude**, used in describing a place on the globe; but less formal maps such as city maps often have their own system of coordinates. **Coordination** refers to having your body or some things work in an orderly fashion.

Inordinate refers to something out of the ordinary (in- sometimes means *not*). Phobias are inordinate fears.

To **subordinate** means to place something under the established order (sub- means *under*). A **lieutenant** is *subordinate* to a captain. If he does not follow orders, he is **insubordinate**. A lieutenant holds the command **in lieu of** the captain (tenant = holder).

Note that the base word *order* can accept many of the common prefixes: in = not, sub = under, dis = not or opposite, co = with, and re = back.

Review:

order	orderliness	disorder	ordinary
ordained	ordinance	coordinate	coordinates
inordinate	subordinate	suborder	insubordination
ordinal numbers	reorder		

List 43   Carry (port-)

The root **port-** means to bear or carry, and it is readily adaptable to many prefixes.

To **support** someone or something means to bear it up from underneath (sub = under). A foundation *supports* a house and money *supports* a college student. If you don't want to support something, you can declare it **unsupportable**.

In time of war, the officer wanted to know if his orders were carried out or what the spies found out about the enemy, so they sent a **report** to carry back the information (re = back). Today *report* is used more generally for any kind of verbal information. A **reporter** writes or says those reports, which collectively are known as **reportage**.

If we take off the prefix, a **porter** carries bags in a hotel. A **portage** is a place where you carry or **transport** your canoe around a waterfall in a stream (trans = across), whereas just a plain **port** is a place where ships go to carry things. Perhaps they carry things in, **imports**, or they carry things out, **exports** (im = in and ex = out). If it is a person being kicked out, he or she is being **deported** (de = from).

If a subject carries a lot of weight, it is **important**; but if not, it is lightweight fluff and it is **unimportant** (un = not). If it is only **purported**, it means that it is perhaps a rumor. Both **purportedly** and **reportedly** mean that you are not going to vouch for it yourself, you are just giving what is rumored or what has been reported.

Review:

support	report	import
unsupportable	unreportable	export
important	reportage	transport
unimportant	reportedly	deported
purportedly	portage	porter

> *He can compress the most words into the smallest idea of any man I ever met.*
>
> —Abraham Lincoln

Suffering (-path)

The root -**path** refers to suffering or disease; hence we have various systems of medicine that attempt to cure or alleviate disease. **Homeopathy** attempts to alleviate the suffering by giving you something that decreases the symptoms (homo = same, path = suffering), while most people go to the doctor or medicine cabinet for **allopathy**, something to get rid of the pain (allo = other). Most modern doctors are descendents of allopathic medicine. If you take an aspirin for a headache, you are practicing allopathy.

However, if you really don't like drugs, you might go to a **naturopath,** one who uses a lot of herbs or nature's cures. The system of **chiropathy** literally means using hands to cure illness (chiro = hand). But in the evolution of things, a chiropractic doctor practices medicine by using his or her hands for spinal adjustments or massage to cure suffering but not drugs.

Osteopathic doctors historically used manipulation of the bones and muscles to cure suffering (osteo = bone). Modern osteopaths may still use some manipulation, but also most of the modern scientific techniques of diagnosis and treatment.

Historically, **chiropodists** worked on both hands and feet (chiro = hand, pod = foot). But nowadays this medical practice is usually called **podiatry**, and the **podiatrist** works on just foot problems.

Review:

path = suffering, disease	**homo** = same
allo = other	**chiro** = hand
osteo = bone	**pod** = foot

We see these roots cropping up in all sorts of words like:

pathology—the study of diseases

osteoarthritis—arthritis in the bones

homosexual—preference for the same sex

podium—a stand for a lecturer

allocation—putting things into other locations

Man does not live by words alone, despite the fact that sometimes he has to eat them.

—Adlai Stevenson

List 45 — Writing (scribe-)

There are a lot of Latin-based words that are based on the root **scribe-** meaning "write."

When we first started to write, we used a **script**, which means any kind of writing; but now a script often refers to the written directions for a play or movie. If we wrote it by hand, then actually it is a **manuscript** (manu = hand), but now a manuscript is often a pre-published book, while **manuscript handwriting** is separated letters as opposed to **cursive writing** with connected letters.

Doctors often write a **prescription**, which is a written order to the pharmacists for medicine. More generally, to **prescribe** is to set down an order. Don't confuse this with a **proscription**, which is an order against something (pre = for, pro = put forward). **Pro-** also means "in favor of," as in **pro-education**.

To **subscribe** to something is to approve of it, and one way is to sign your name such as at the end of the petition (sub = under). A common use of subscription is a written approval for sending a magazine to your home.

When you write down something that has occurred, like the testimony in court, it is a **transcript** of the trial. When you graduate from school you might want a copy of your grades sent someplace in a transcript. Also, a **transcription** might be rewriting something in another language; in this use transcription and **translation** mean the same (trans = across).

Review:

script	manuscript	subscription
prescription	proscription	transcript
subscribe	subscription	

List 46 — More Writing (scribe-)

When you try to tell about something in writing, you are **describing** it (de = from, away) and what you have written is a **description**. But what you have seen might be so fantastic that it is **indescribable** (in = not). This is a little different from **nondescript**, which merely means that it is hard to classify (non = not).

Someone who is called up for military service in a draft is a **conscript**; he or she received a written letter with the news (con = with).

To **circumscribe** is to draw a line around something or to state the limits (circum + ring around). Police are circumscribed from entering your house without your permission or a court order. Someone being **circumscript** is someone dancing around the subject not wanting to approach it directly, and perhaps withholding something.

Assigning the source of something is to **ascribe** it (a = to). For example, the development of our alphabet is ascribed to the Phoenicians. (That's why our alphabet is largely phonetic.)

Monuments frequently have an **inscription** on them giving a name or a brief dedication (in = in). You can also inscribe a book given to a friend by writing your own carefully chosen words in it.

Review:

description	indescribable	nondescript
circumscribe	ascribe	conscript
inscription	circumscript	

Send (mit-)

The Latin verb *mitere* gives us a lot of English words The simple root **mit-** can be found in **admit** (ad = to, mit = send). Someone who is **admitted** to college is given permission to enter or be sent in.

You have to work a little harder to see that **commit** has to do with sending, but a **commitment** is a guarantee that some action or trust will be taken. Marriage is a commitment. If you commit to finishing a project, you are giving your personal assurance that it will be done. Perhaps you are pledging your assurance along with the action (com = with).

A **committee** is a group that has been elected or selected to do some task. It is a group sent with a purpose. You might say that they have a **commission** or authorization to do something.

To **imet** is to interject something. You might imit some comments to the discussion (im = in). Note that this is the opposite of **emit**, which means to send out (e = out). Some people emit happiness, or radio waves are emitted from the tower.

If you have a lot of static on the radio, the music might be sent out only **intermittently** between the crackling (inter = between).

If you are an author, you might **submit** your manuscript to a publisher (sub = under). To submit generally means to place something under the will of another. Just maybe your dog will submit to your command and the publisher will wish to publish your manuscript. And if you **permit** (per = through) him to publish it by signing a royalty contract, he will **remit** (re = back) to you a percentage of the sales.

Review:

admit	admission	commit	commitment
committee	commission	imit	emit
intermittently	submit	permit	remit

Send (miss-)

Due to the irregularities of Latin verbs, both **mit-** and **miss-** come from the same verb. This causes some spelling shifts. Note that you are **admitted** by the **admission** office and that a **committee** has a **commission**. They all have the same root.

A *commission* is authorization to perform certain tasks (com = with). An ambassador might get a commission to sign a treaty, and a ship that is *commissioned* is now ready to perform services like going to sea. The person giving this **permission** might be the **commissioner**.

The ambassador is also called an **emissary**, one who is sent out to perform a task (e = out). But if he does not do a very good job, he could be **dismissed** (dis = not).

Then he could not perform his **mission** (-ion is a noun-forming suffix, so *mission* is really a "sending"). If his mission (task) was a failure, then the two countries might send **missiles** against each other (-les is also a noun suffix).

This could cause a lot of difficulty in **transmitting missives** (trans = across). A missive is simply a high-class way of saying "a letter" or message.

Review:

admission	commission	commissioned	missives
emissary	dismissed	mission	permission
missiles	transmitting		

List 49   To Hold (ten-)

We see the root **ten-** in a lot of English words. A **tenant** (-ant = person) is someone who holds on to something, like an apartment renter or a farmer who does not own the land but can hold on to it and use it. A **tenement** house is a place full of tenants.

A **lieutenant** is a lower ranking officer who holds the position of leadership in *lieu* of a more senior officer. Maybe one of his jobs is to hold somebody in *detention*. **Detention**, as some students know, is being held after school as punishment for some infraction and **house of detention** is a nice way to say prison.

If you are **content** (con = with), you are happy and want to hold on to that feeling. It implies no change. The opposite is **discontented** (dis = not). You could also say that the discontented person is **malcontented** (mal = bad), but a malcontented person also means that he or she is apt to cause trouble.

Contention, unfortunately, does not have much to do with happiness, but rather has to do with controversy. A **contentious** person is argumentative and tends to oppose others. He or she is much more apt to be *discontented*.

Review:

tenant	tenement house	lieutenant
detention	house of detention	contention
content	discontented	malcontented
contentious		

List 50   To Hold (-tain)

The root **-tain** is just another way of spelling **ten-**; it means "to hold." We see it in a lot of relatively common words:

contain (con = with): to hold, to enclose
detain (de = away): to hold back, withhold, keep from
abstain (ab = from): to refrain or not do something
obtain (ob = to): to get possession of something, get hold of
pertain (per = through): to be related to the topic
retain (re = back): to hold on to something, hold back something
maintain (manu = hand): to keep up, carry on, hold steady
sustain (sus = under): to support, keep in existence, continue
appertain (ap = to + pertain): to relate to, part of a function
entertain (enter = among): to amuse or treat with hospitality

Word Names (-nyms)

People who study words (linguists or philologists) have all sorts of words to describe words. Here are some of them.

-nym word	Definition	Root	Example (Chapter:List)
synonyms	different words/ same meaning	syn = same	pretty – beautiful (1:17)
antonyms	different words/ opposite meaning	anti = against	up – down (1:17)
eponym	word based on a person's name	epi = upon	America – Amerigo Vespucci (3:56)
toponym	word based on place	top = place	frankfurter – Frankfurt, Germany (3:57)
capitonym	capitalization changes meaning	cap = head	August – august (1:1)
contronym	same word that has opposite meaning	contra = opposed	left = departed "I left" left = remain "How many left?"
anatonyms	body parts used as verbs	from anatomy	"hand me a spoon"
acronym	a word formed by initial letters	acro = end	AIDS = Acquired Immune Deficiency Syndrome (7:140)
heteronyms	different pronunciation/ same spelling	hetero = different	bass = a fish (7:158) bass = low male voice
homonyms	sound the same but have a different spelling	homo = same	beat = hit repeatedly (11:195) beet = a vegetable
patronym	surname taken from father	patri = father	common in Western culture; Williamson (1:4)
matronym	surname taken from mother	matro = mother	common in some cultures (1:4)
metonym	a word that stands for another	met = along with	count heads = people on the bottle = strong drink, drunk
exonym	foreign word that becomes common in America	exo = outside	safari, ciao, bon voyage (6:all)

Easy Root Lessons

Here are some common roots with relatively common examples. Each root and its examples might be about right for a single vocabulary lesson. See the simple old-fashioned vocabulary lesson at the end of Chapter 9. Also see the Master List of Roots, List 191 in Chapter 10.

audi = hear

audible	audibly	audience
audiometer	audit	audition
auditor	auditorium	auditory
inaudible		

bon, bonus = good

bona fide	bonanza	bonbon
bonny	bon voyage	boon
bounteous	bountiful	bounty
debonair		

cap = head

capital	capitalism	capitalist
capitalize	capitol	capitulate
captain	decapitate	per capita
recapitulate		

cor = heart

accord	accordance	cordial
courage	discord	discourage
encourage	record	

corp = body

corporate	corporation	corps
corpse	corpulent	corpuscle
incorporate	unincorporated	

dec = ten

decaliter	Decalogue	decameter
decathlon	decagon	December
decibel	decimal	decimate
decimation	decimeter	

dic = say

addict	benediction	condition
contradict	dictate	dictator
diction	dictionary	edict
indict	interdict	judiciary
judicious	jurisdiction	malediction
predict	verdict	vindicate
vindictive		

duc = lead

abduct	adduce	aqueduct
conducive	conduct	conduit
deduce	deduct	deductive
ducal	duchess	duchy
ductile	duke	induce
induct	inductive	introduce
produce	product	reduce
reproduce	reproduction	seduce
subdue	traduce	viaduct

equ = even, just

adequate	equable	equality
equanimity	equate	equation
equator	equidistant	equilateral
equilibrium	equinox	equipoise
equitable	equity	equivalent
equivocal	unequated	

fin = end

affinity	confine	define
definite	finale	finance
fine	finery	finesse
finicky	finish	finite
infinite	infinitesimal	infinity
paraffin	refine	

fus = pour, melt

confuse	diffuse	effusive
fusion	infuse	profuse
refuse	transfusion	

gen = birth, race

degenerate	gender	general
generate	generation	generator
generic	generous	regenerate

hab = have, hold

habeas corpus	habitat	habitual
inhabit	rehabilitate	uninhabited

hem = bloodlike

hematite	hemoglobin
hemophilia	hemorrhage

host = guest, host

hostage   hostel
hostess   hostile

hydr = water

dehydrate   hydrant   hydra
hydrangea   hydrate   hydraulic
hydrocarbon   hydrochloric   hydroelectric
hydrofoil   hydrogen   hydrogenate
hydrometer   hydrophobia   hydroplane
hydroponics   hydrosphere

just = right, law

adjust   just   justice
justify   maladjusted

man = hand

command   commandeer   commando
demand   emancipate   manacle
mandate   maneuver   manicure
manifest   manipulate   manual
manufacture   manure   manuscript

mit = send

admit   commit   emit
intermittent   omit   permit
remit   submit   transmit

nat = born

natal   innate   international
nation   nationality   native
natural   naturalize   nature
prenatal   supernatural

naut = ship, sail

nautical   aeronautical   astronaut
cosmonaut   nautilus
nom = name
denomination   denominator   misnomer
nom de plume   nomenclature   nominal
nominate

oper = work

cooperate	inoperative	operate	operation

re = thing

(Note: the prefix re- means "back," this is a root.)

real	reality	realize
realtor	reality	surrealism
unrealistic		

reg = rule, guide

regime	regent	regiment
region	regular	regulate
regulatory		

vert = turn

advertise	avert	convert
convertible	divert	extrovert
introvert	invert	invertebrate
pervert	vertebra	

rupt = break

rupture	abrupt	corrupt
disrupt	erupt	interrupt

script = write

conscription	description	inscription
manuscript	nondescript	postscript
prescription	proscription	script
scriptural	Scripture	subscript
subscription	superscript	superscription
transcription	typescript	unscriptural

soc = companion

antisocial	social	associate
association	dissociate	sociability
socialism	socialize	socialite
society	sociological	sociology
unsociable		

tain = hold

contain	container	detain
entertain	maintain	obtain
pertain	retain	retainer
sustain		

tract = pull, drag

attract	attractive	contract
contraction	detract	distract
extract	intractable	protract
protractor	retract	subtract
tract	traction	

uni = one

unicellular	unity	unicorn
uniform	unify	unilateral
union	unique	unison
unit	unite	univalve
universal	universe	university

val = strong

devalue	equivalent	evaluate
invalid	invalidate	invaluable
prevalent	valedictorian	valence
valiant	valid	valuable
value		

ven = come

advent	adventure	avenue
convene	convenient	convent
convention	conventional	covenant
intervene	invent	inventory
misadventure	prevent	revenue
souvenir	supervene	venture

voc = call

advocate	avocation	convocation
equivocal	equivocate	invocation
irrevocable	provocation	provocative
vocation		

There is a weird power in the spoken word . . . and a word carries far—very far. . .

—Joseph Conrad, *Lord Jim*

WORD ORIGINS

Greek and Roman Mythology

Many English words come from Greek and Roman mythology.

Greek Mythology	*English Words*
Phos (god of Light)	photo, phosphorus, photon
Cyclops (three giants each with one big round eye)	cyclical, bicycle, encyclopedia, cycle, optical, optician, optometrist, myopia
Hekatoncheires (monster kids with one hundred hands)	hectometer (100 meters)
Oceanus (god of oceans, also the name of a river that circled the earth)	ocean, oceanic
Furies (monsters)	furious, furor (anger)
Giants (monsters)	giant, gigantic
Aphrodite (goddess of love)	aphrodisiac
Eros (god of love, sex)	erotic
Mount Olympus (home of the gods)	Olympic Games
Crete (a Greek island)	cretin (deformed person)
Atlas (he held up the earth)	atlas (map book)
Typhon (monster)	typhoon
Pandora (so pretty that gods gave her gifts, a box with many things—mostly bad)	Pandora's box
Europa (princess carried off by Zeus)	Europe
Hippius (horse-tending god)	hippopotamus, hippodrome
Athena (promised olive trees to people)	Athens, Greece
Phobus (god of panic)	claustrophobia, acrophobia, and others
Trojan (warrior)	popular mascot name
Paris (judge of beauty)	city in France
Amazons (women warriors)	Amazon River
Mentor (teacher of Odysseus' son)	mentor, mentoring
Electra (daughter of Agamemnon)	electricity
Hygeia (goddess of health)	hygiene
Echo (nymph with only voice left)	echo
Morpheus (god of dreams)	morphine

Roman Mythology	*English Words*
Ceres (goddess of grain)	cereal
Egypt (a land to the south)	gypsies, gypped (Note: Gypsies are originally from India, not Egypt.)
Morta (goddess of death)	mortician, mortuary, mortal
Venus (goddess of love)	venereal disease
Pluto (king of the underworld)	plutonium (used in nuclear bombs)
Mars (god of war)	martial arts, court martial
Mercury (winged messenger)	mercurial temperament
Di Penates (gods of indoors)	dependents
Janus (god of doors and gates, two-faced, beginners)	January
Arachne (a great weaver)	arachnid (scientific name for spiders)
Hermaphroditus (the gods put a male and female together)	hermaphrodite (part of both sexes in one)
Orcus (god of the underworld)	ogre (monster), orgy (unrestrained indulgence)
Panacea (goddess of health)	panacea
Vulcan (god of fire)	volcano, vulcanize
Pantheon (temple to all gods)	Pantheism (sees God in all things)
Maia (mother of Mercury)	May
Luna (goddess of the moon)	lunacy, lunatic, lunar month
Romulus (son of Mars)	Rome, Roman

The Vocabulary Teacher's Book of Lists

Roman Gods Are Greek Gods

The Romans copied a lot of Greek mythology but changed the gods' names.

Greek Name	Roman Name	Sphere or Position
Aphrodite	Venus*	Goddess of Love
Apollo	Apollo	God of Music and Medicine
Ares	Mars*	God of War
Artemis	Diana	Goddess of the Hunt
Athena	Minerva	Goddess of Wisdom
Cronos	Saturn*	Titans' Ruler
Demeter	Ceres	Goddess of the Harvest
Dionysus	Bacchus	God of Wine
Eros	Cupid	God of Love (sex)
Gaia	Gaea	Goddess of Earth
Hades	Pluto*	God of the Underworld
Hephaestos	Vulcan	God of the Forge
Hera	Juno	Goddess of Marriage
Hermes	Mercury*	Messenger of the Gods
Hestia	Vesta	Goddess of the Hearth
Persephone	Proserpina	Goddess of the Underworld
Poseidon	Neptune*	God of the Sea
Uranus	Uranus*	God of the Heavens, Sky
Zeus	Jupiter*	King of Gods

*Also planet names.

Paradigm

A paradigm is a model or a pattern (para = almost, digm = show). This word is used in discussing theory or psychological mechanisms. A paradigm for maturity might be a tree that has reached its maximum height.

Onomatopoeia

Words that represent a sound or animal noise are called onomatopoeia.

bang—small gun	**bark**—dog
bong—big gong	**boom**—thunder
burp—air from stomach	**buzz**—bee
chirp—small bird	**choo choo**—steam engine
clatter—banging dishes	**click**—camera shutter
clip clop—horse hooves	**cluck**—hen
crack—breaking egg	**crash**—auto accident
ding dong—bell	**drip**—leaking faucet
fizz—soda water	**flap**—flag in breeze
giggle—silly child	**growl**—mad dog
hee haw—donkey	**hiss**—snake
honk—goose	**hoot**—owl
howl—wolf	**hum**—electric motor
kerchoo—sneeze	**meow**—cat
moan—person in pain	**moo**—cow
murmur—brook	**oink oink**—pig
quack—duck	**ring**—phone
rip—tearing cloth	**roar**—lion
sigh—tired person	**sizzle**—frying pan
slurp—dog drinking water	**snap**—breaking twig
squeak—rusty door	**squeal**—baby pig
tick tock—clock	**toot**—small horn
twang—bow string	**tweet**—bird
whoopee—joy	**zoom**—race car

An **eponym** is a word based on person, real or imaginary, from whom something (tribe, nation, place, and so forth) takes its name. For example, the eponym for America is Amerigo Vespucci (Italian navigator). For more names, see List 4.

bloomers	Amelia Bloomer, a pioneer feminist who made the women's undergarment popular
bowie knife	James Bowie, an American frontiersman who made this type of knife famous
boycott	Charles Boycott, an English land agent who refused to lower rents and tenants refused to produce
braille	Louis Braille, a French teacher who invented an alphabet for the blind
Bunsen burner	Robert Bunsen, who invented a methane gas burner, a heat source for his laboratory experiments
cardigan	Earl of Cardigan, a British officer whose soldiers wore the knitted sweaters during the Crimean War
chauvinist	Nicolas Chauvin, a soldier who worshipped France and Napoleon uncritically
Colt revolver	One of the best-known handguns, named for Samuel Colt, an American firearms designer in the 1800s
diesel	Rudolf Diesel, a German automotive engineer who designed an engine without spark plugs
dunce	Johannes Duns Scotus, a theologian whose followers were called Dunsmen and who were thought to be wrong or stupid
erotic	Eros, the Greek god of love
Ferris wheel	G. M. Ferris, an American engineer who invented the large wheel ride
Frisbee	William Frisbie, a pie company owner in Connecticut in 1871; Yale students played catch with the pie tins
fudge	Supposedly named after Captain Fudge, a 17th-century seaman, who had a reputation for not telling the truth
galvanize	Luigi Galvani, an Italian physicist who discovered electricity in a metal-chemical reaction
gerrymander	Elbridge Gerry, a Massachusetts governor in 1810 who redrew election districts to favor his party
graham crackers	Sylvester Graham, an American reformer in dietetics and a vegetarian who developed a healthy cracker
guillotine	Joseph Guillotin, a French physician who developed an efficient machine for beheadings
Leninism	Nikolai Lenin, a Russian revolutionary who had a particular type of communism
leotard	Jules Leotard, a French acrobat who designed a close-fitting costume for his trapeze act
loganberry	J. H. Logan, a judge and a gardener who developed a berry similar to a raspberry
Luddite	Ned Ludd, an Englishman who led a group of people opposed to mechanization
Lutheran	Martin Luther, a German who started a Protestant Christian church

lutz	Gustave Lussi, a Swiss ice skater who was the first to do this jump
lynch	William Lynch, an American vigilante who organized mobs to supposedly administer justice by hanging
macadam	John Loudon McAdam, a Scottish engineer who invented this road-building material composed of gravel and tar
mackintosh	Charles Macintosh, a Scottish chemist who invented rainproof material of rubberized cloth
malapropism	Mrs. Malaprop, a character in Sheridan's *The Rivals,* who made speech errors
martinet	Jean Martinet, a very harsh French army drill master
Marxism	Karl Marx, a German philosopher of communist economics
maverick	Samuel Maverick, a Texan who didn't brand his cattle and was considered very unconventional
mesmerize	Frederich Mesmer, an Austrian physician who practiced hypnotism (mesmerize is a synonym for hypnotism)
Morse Code	Communication code using dots and dashes invented by Samuel Morse
napoleon	Emperor Napoleon I of France, a pastry with cream filling
nicotine	Jean Nicot, a French diplomat who introduced the tobacco plant to France about 1561
odyssey	Ancient Greek god (also called Ulysses)
panic	Pan, Greek forest god who feared travelers
pasteurize	Louis Pasteur, a French bacteriologist who found heating milk killed germs
platonic	Plato, the Greek philosopher who talked of love without physical sex
praline	A nut and sugar candy named for Marshal Duplessis-Praslin, whose cook invented it
pullman	George M. Pullman, railroad designer of sleeping cars
quixotic	Don Quixote, a Spanish novel character, who was excessively polite or foolish
sandwich	John Montagu, fourth Earl of Sandwich, who invented it so he could gamble without stopping for a regular meal
saxophone	Anton Sax, Belgian instrument maker who combined a clarinet's reed with oboe fingering
Sequoia	A Cherokee Indian chief who invented an alphabet; the trees were named for him by a Hungarian botanist
shrapnel	Henry Shrapnel, an English artillery officer who developed an exploding shell that sent out bits of metal
sideburns	Ambrose Burnside, a Civil War general and governor of Rhode Island, who had thick side whiskers
silhouette	Etienne de Silhouette, a French finance minister of Louis XV whose fiscal policies and amateurish portraits (by him) were regarded as inept (it now means a profile cut from black paper)
spoonerism	William A. Spooner, an English clergyman who transposed initial sounds of two or more words, such as *tons of soil* for *sons of toil.*
Stalinism	The political beliefs of Joseph Stalin, a Russian political leader

Stetson	John Stetson, an American who owned a hat factory in Philadelphia that featured western-style hats
tawdry	St. Audrey, queen of Northumbria; used to describe lace sold at her fair (it now means cheap and gaudy)
teddy bear	Teddy Roosevelt, president of the United States, who spared the life of a bear cub on a hunting trip in Mississippi
valentine	St. Valentine, a Christian martyr whose feast day is February 14, the same date, according to Roman tradition, that birds pair off to nest
vandal	Vandals, the Germanic tribe that sacked Rome
Winchester rifle	Oliver F. Winchester, an American gun manufacturer
zeppelin	German Count Von Zeppelin, who developed a gas-filled, lighter-than-air ship

Science Unit Eponyms

ampere (electricity)	Andre Ampere, a French physicist
baud (computer speed)	Jean Baudot, French engineer
Beaufort scale (wind speed)	Francis Beaufort, English naval officer
celsius (temperature)	Anders Celsius, a Swedish astronomer and inventor
decibel (sound loudness)	Alexander Bell, a Scottish-American inventor of the telephone
Fahrenheit (temperature)	Gabriel Fahrenheit, a German physicist
hertz (electromagnetic wave)	Gustav Hertz, German physicist; one hertz = one cycle per second
mach number (speed)	Ernst Mach, an Austrian philosopher and physicist; ratio of the speed of sound to the speed of an object; for example, an airplane going mach 2 is going twice the speed of sound
ohm (electricity)	Georg Simon Ohm, a German physicist
Richter scale (earthquakes)	Charles Richter, an American seismologist
volt (electricity)	Alessandro Volta, an Italian physicist
watt (electricity)	James Watt, a Scottish engineer and inventor

Flower Name Eponyms

begonia	Michel Begon, French governor of Santo Domingo and a patron of science
camellia	George Kamel, European Jesuit missionary to the Far East
dahlia	Andreas Dahl, a Swedish botanist
forsythia	William Forsyth, a British botanist
fuchsia	Leonhard Fuchsia, a German botanist
gardenia	Alexander Garden, a Scottish-American botanist
hyacinth	Hyacinth, mythical Spartan youth, changed into a flower
iris	Iris, Greek messenger of the gods
magnolia	Pierre Magnol, a French botanist
poinsettia	Joel Poinsett, U.S. ambassador to Mexico
wisteria	Caspar Wistar, an American anatomist
zinnia	Johann G. Zinn, a German botanist

Words Coined from Place Names (Toponyms)

academy	Academeia, a garden where Plato taught his students
calico	Calicut, India
cashmere	Kashmir, India
cologne	Cologne, Germany
cheddar	Cheddar, England
damask	Damascus, Syria
denim	Nimes, France; serge de Nimes (fabric of Nimes)
frankfurter	Frankfurt, Germany
gauze	Gaza, Palestine
hamburger	Hamburg, Germany
laconic	Laconia (Sparta, Greece)
Leyden jar	Leyden, Holland
limousine	Limousin, an old French province
mackinaw	Mackinac City, Michigan
manila paper	Manila, the Philippines
muslin	Mosul, Iraq
Panama hat	Panama, Central America
rhinestone	Rhine, river that flows from Switzerland through Germany and the Netherlands
Roquefort cheese	Roquefort, France
Tabasco sauce	Tabasco, Mexico
tangerine	Tangier, Morocco
worsted wool	Worsted, England

Sound Words

It is a cruel twist of words that *oral* and *aural* sound the same (they are homophones) and that they have similar meanings. But *oral* means spoken, as in *oral history*, which is spoken or non-written history. And *aural* means hearing, as in *binaural*, which is hearing with both (two) ears.

Days

Sunday	The sun's day
Monday	The moon's day
Tuesday	Tiw's day (Tiw was the Teutonic god of war)
Wednesday	Woden's day (Woden was the Norse god of the hunt)
Thursday	Thor's day (Thor was the Norse god of the sky, order, thunder)
Friday	Fria's day (Fria, the wife of Thor, was the Norse goddess of love and beauty, plenty)
Saturday	Saturn's day (Saturn was the Roman god of agriculture)

Months

January	In honor of Janus, the Roman god with two faces, one looking forward and one looking backward
February	In honor of *februa,* the Roman feast of purification
March	In honor of Mars, the Roman god of war
April	A reference to spring, *aprilis,* the Latin word for opening
May	In honor of Maia, a Roman goddess and mother of Mercury
June	In honor of Juno, the Roman goddess of marriage
July	In honor of the Roman general and statesman Julius Caesar
August	In honor of the Roman emperor Augustus Caesar
September	In reference to *septem,* the Latin word for seven; September was the seventh month of the Roman calendar
October	In reference to *octo,* the Latin word for eight; October was the eighth Roman month
November	In reference to *novem,* the Latin word for nine; November was the ninth Roman month
December	In reference to *decem,* the Latin word for ten; December was the tenth Roman month
month	From the Anglo-Saxon *mona* (moon)

Shakespearean Phrases

Maybe you think Shakespeare hasn't much to do with modern speech, but just take a look at the colorful phrases that you hear or read all the time. Maybe Shakespeare didn't invent them all, but he did use each of them.

short shrift	laughing stock
cold comfort	"It's Greek to me!"
too much of a good thing	sinned against than sinning
seen better days	act more in sorrow than in anger
fool's paradise	vanished into thin air
foregone conclusion	refused to budge an inch
bag and baggage	green-eyed jealousy
high time	played fast and loose
your own flesh and blood	tongue-tied
crack of dawn	hoodwinked
suspect foul play	fair play
without rhyme or reason	slept not one wink
dead as a doornail	

Demimonde

In the later half of the 19th century the French applied **demimonde** to a woman who lost her social standing, usually because of indiscreet behavior. **Demi-** means half and **monde** means world. If social standing was the world, the poor lady lost half her world. Later it became a polite word for *whore*. Demimonde also means the shadowy, almost underworld of questionably legal society—perhaps a polite word for crooks.

Demi-, meaning half, is found in many words such as **demitasse** (half cup), **demigod** (half god, or a lesser god in the pantheon), **demijohn** (a large narrow-necked bottle usually enclosed in wickerwork), and **demi-sec** (moderately sweet champagne).

The Vocabulary Teacher's Book of Lists

List 61   Old English Counting System

We have some nice old English words for small amounts. They are **once, twice, thrice**. But interestingly enough there are no more; we have to jump to modern numbers or perhaps *four-fold, fivefold,* and so on.

It is easy to recognize that *once* transformed into **one**, *twice* transformed into **two**, and *thrice* transformed into **three**. Related words are also interesting; *once* is related to **only** and *twice* is related to **twin**.

Thirteen is three more than ten, while **thirty** is three tens.

1	once	only
2	twice	twin
3	thrice	
13 = 10 + 3		
30 = 10 + 10 + 10		

List 62   Pen

A **pen**, the common instrument that we write with, really evolved from a feather (*penna* in Latin). A feather or *quill* from a large bird like a duck was slashed at the base and dipped in ink. This was the major writing tool for over thirteen centuries in Europe. And to slash the quill or sharpen it after much use you needed a **pen knife**—we still call small pocket knives *pen knives,* although people have forgotten their historical use.

Baseball fans who so desperately want their team to have a **pennant** will be interested to know that it is shaped a little like a feather (long and triangular) and probably is a direct descendant from the pennants carried by knights on their lances to identify their loyalty in jousting matches.

If the knight was a little stylish, he stuck some colored feathers in his helmet. The feathers were called a **panache**. Today *panache* means style with a colorful flair.

Review:

pen	**pen knives**	**panache**	**pennant**

The prefix **du-** meaning *two* and its variants (**dou-**, **duo-**) give us some insights.

We all know that a **duplex** is a two-unit building, and duplex can apply to a lot of other things such as a double electrical outlet.

But we see this prefix in **doubt**, which could mean of two minds or two opinions. So **doubtful** or **dubious** are a little shaky.

The opposite is **doubtless** or **indubitably**, which is sure or certain (in- means *not*).

A **duo** refers to two things, often a performance by two musicians. And if they are good, they **duplicate** the performance.

Review:

duplex	dubious	duo
doubt	doubtless	duplicate
doubtful	indubitably	

Many words in English come directly from old or classical Greek. Many of the English words are based on Latin words, which themselves came from Greek.

catastrophe (cata-strophe) (against + overturn) means sudden bad happening

criterion (cri-terion) (separate + means) means standard for comparison

misanthrope (mis-anthrope) (bad + man) means person who hates humans

anonymous (an-onym-ous) (without + name + adjective) means name withheld

List 65 Modern Science Words

Modern scientists faced with the problem of naming something new choose to make up new words (neologisms) based on Greek roots.

electronics (elec-tron-ics) (amber + device + science) means science of electrons

> The ancient Greeks didn't have electricity, of course, but the ancient scientists did know that if you rubbed a piece of amber with a wool cloth it picked up static electricity.

thermodynamics (thermo-dynam-ics) (heat + power + science) means science of heat

> The relationship between heat, such as steam and power, was not discovered until centuries later.

gyroscope (gyro-scope) (revolve + view) means a compass based on a spinning wheel

> Navigators, such as Columbus, found direction by a magnet floating in water (magnetic compass). Modern compasses use a rapidly spinning wheel.

chlorophyll (chloro-phyl) (green + leaf) means green substance in plants

> Ancient Greeks did not know the importance of chlorophyll, the green in most plants, but modern biologists certainly do. Chlorophyll converts the energy of the sun into growth of all plants.

psychoneurosis (psycho-neur-osis) (mind + nerve + condition) means a lesser mental disorder, also called a *neurosis*
An interesting older term for mental disorder is **lunacy**, because the moon was thought to cause insanity (lune = moon).

For more science words, see Chapter 1, List 19.

Wine

Viniculture is the science of making wine (vini = wine). Vinification or vinify is the process of making wine which is done by a *vintner.*

Vinegar is wine gone sour, as the alcohol changes to acetic acid.

Our alphabet is called the Roman alphabet or the Latin alphabet because that is where it came from. Remember the ancient Romans spoke Latin. Modern citizens of Rome speak a direct descendent of Latin called Italian. The early inhabitants of Britain spoke Celtic and various tribal languages. In about 43 B.C. the Roman conquerors arrived and they spoke Latin, so the government ran in Latin. But four hundred years later the Romans left Britain and the Angles and Saxons, two Germanic tribes, moved in. Old English became the Anglo-Saxon with a few Latin words left in. Later, in 1066, a French king became the king of what is now England (Angles + land) and the learned peoples spoke and/or wrote in Latin or French. Hence, in modern English, our common words are often from Anglo-Saxon and our larger science, philosophy, and literary words are often from Latin. French is a Latin derivative and a so-called "Romance Language."

Old English was originally written with an alphabet called Runes, which came from northern Europe (what are now Scandinavia and Germany). Here is the Rune alphabet.* If you want to have some scholarly fun, try writing your name or a short message in Runes.

Rune	Anglo-Saxon	Name	Meaning (where known)
ᚠ	f	feoh	cattle, wealth
ᚾ	u	ür	bison (aurochs)
ᚦ	b	born	thorn
ᚡ	o	ōs	god/mouth
ᚱ	r	rād	journey/riding
ᚲ	c	cen	torch
✕	g[i]	giefu	gift
ᚹ	w	wyn	joy
ᚺ	h	hægl	hail
✝	n	nied	necessity/trouble
⎮	i	is	ice
ᚼ	j	gear	year
ᛃ	ʒ	ēoh	yew
ᛈ	p	peor	?
ᛉ	x	eolh	?sedge
ᛋ	s	sigel	sun
↑	t	tiw/tir	Tiw (a god)
ᛒ	b	beprc	birch
ᛗ	e	eoh	horse
ᛘ	m	man	man
ᚴ	l	lagu	water/sea
ᛝ	ng	ing	ing (a hero)
ᛟ	oe	epel	land/estate
ᛗ	d	dæg	day
ᚨ	a	ac	oak
ᚠ	x	æsc	ash
ᛘ	y	yr	bow
ᛏ	ea	ear	?earth
✕	g [γ]	gar	spear
ᚼ	k	calc	?sandal/chalice/chalk
✳	k̄	(name unknown)	

*Source: D. Crystal, *The Cambridge Encyclopedia of the English Language.* Cambridge, UK: Cambridge University Press, 1995, p. 9.

The Vocabulary Teacher's Book of Lists

List 67 — Voice (voc-)

Sure you know what voice means, but its root **voc-** (which means voice) crops up in all sorts of words. Let's take **equivocal**, for instance (equi-vocal) (equal + voice). So in your **equivocation** you are hearing equal voices on different sides and it is tough to make up your mind. When you do, you can give an **unequivocal** answer (un-equi-vocal) (not + equal + voice), which means a final I-won't-change-my-mind answer.

A **vocation** is a "calling," the main thing you do in life, while an **avocation** is something you do on the side (a-vocation) (not + vocation). Your vocation might be rocket science, but your avocation is surfing.

A **convocation** (with + vocation) is where people get together to talk—not just at graduation, while to **evoke** is to call up something such as memories or feelings (e-voke) (out + call). Historically, an **evocator** called forth the spirits.

An **advocate** is a person who supports you or some cause. Martin Luther King Jr. advocated civil rights (ad-vocate) (to + call). An advocate is a good guy so don't **provoke** him or make him mad (pro-voke) (forth + call).

Review:

equivocal	vocation	advocate
equivocation	avocation	provoke
unequivocal	convocation	evocator

List 68 — Love (ama-)

For some strange reason lots of people are interested in love. It's not a new idea; it was quite popular in ancient Rome. The Latin verb **amare** means to love, and the two roots **ama-** and **-amare** are in a number of English words.

An **amateur** (ama-eur) (love + one who) is quite a respectable word to describe one who does something for the love of it, not money. But to say that something is **amateurish** is a bit of a putdown, meaning the work is sloppy or certainly not up to professional standards.

An **amorous** person (amor-ous) (love + full of) is one who likes to fall in love and maybe read **amatory** literature like love stories or poems.

An **amour**, however, is not a person but a "love affair," hence you can have an amour but it has to be with an **inamorata** (in-amor-ata) (in + love + female) or with an **inamorato** (in-amor-ato)(in + love + male).

Be careful if it is a **paramour**, which is an illicit lover, frequently the woman lover of a married man.

Watch out that **amorphous** doesn't fall into the love category because the root **morph-** means "form" so *amorphous* (a-morph-ous) (without + form) means that something does not have any shape or form. It is hard to pin down, be it an idea or a drop of oil on water.

Review:

amateur	amorous	paramour
amateurish	amatory	amorphous
amour	inamorata	inamorato

Did you ever lose your *temper*? Well, the root **temper-** means to regulate, so getting mad is a loss of self-regulation. It might be better to be *even tempered* or else your friends will consider you **ill tempered** (ill-temper-ed) (bad + regulate + state). Both **even tempered** and *ill tempered* refer to your **temperament**. If you are ill tempered very often you will be considered **temperamental** or apt to have strong feelings. In a slang idiom, you get "hot under the collar."

Now a piece of metal can be **tempered**, which usually means hardened by a *treatment* of heat, or a judge who **tempers** (regulates) a sentence and usually makes it a little less.

Some years ago the **temperance movement** tried to regulate the consumption of alcohol, so **intemperance** means you drink too much.

Temperature refers to the heat in something, so a **temperate** climate is well regulated; it is neither too hot nor too cold.

Your dog might get **distemper** (an illness like a cold).

Review:

temper	tempered	temperature
even tempered	tempers	distemper
ill tempered	temperance movement	
temperamental	intemperance	

If you want to start with a real Greek word, it would be **acropolis**, which you would know if you have ever been to Athens, an ancient city (which is still there) high on a hill (**acro** = high, **polis** = city).

The root *polis-* is indeed interesting because it is the basis of **politics**, which is the art or science of government (poli-ics) (city + science). This science is practiced by **politicians** (politicians)(city + persons) and their **policies** are enforced by **police officers**.

Over the years being **politic** has come to mean discrete or a smooth operator and **impolitic** is just the opposite (im-poletic) (not + city). If you wish to avoid the *body politic* you can become **apolitical** and have nothing to do with politics (a-poletic) (not + city).

Perhaps you don't live in the city but in the suburbs, which are part of the **metropolitan** area (metro-politan) (mother + city), but to travel around you might use the **metro**, which is a train or subway. The word **metroplex** usually refers to several cities forming one area (metroplex) (mother + units).

If you travel far from your city and are at home in many distant places, you are **cosmopolitan** (cosmo-polit-an) (world + city + person). And when you come home to die they will bury you in a **necropolis** or cemetery (necro-polis) (dead + city).

Review:

politics	politician	political
acropolis	metropolitan	cosmopolitan
politic	apolitical	impolitic
policy	police	necropolis

Since most people live in cities or at least villages, here are a few words associated with those groupings:

Example	Definition
arrondissement	administrative district of city (France)
borough	one of five political divisions of New York City; a small municipality
bourg	town; market town (France)
burg	city or town (German) (as in Pittsburgh)
ciudad	city (Spanish)
exurb	area outside a city and beyond the suburbs, often inhabited by wealthy families
hamlet	small village (shortened to –ham, as in Buckingham)
kampong	small native village (Southeast Asia)
kraal	native village (South Africa)
megalopolis	very large city; heavily populated region encompassing several cities
metropolis	large or important city, often a capital or center of business or cultural activity
polis	city-state (ancient Greece)
shtetl	formerly a small Jewish village in Eastern Europe (Yiddish)
suburb	an area on the fringe of a city
thorp	village or hamlet
town	any group of structures considered a distinct place with a distinguishing place name (shortened to -ton, as in Stockton)
ville	city (French)

Avalon—a magical island where King Arthur went, where his wounds would heal and he could stay until the time was ripe for his return.

List 72   City (cit-, civ-)

In ancient times, a **city** was a step up from the primitive hunting and gathering way of life, and even today a **citified** way of life is viewed by some as a more civilized way of life than farming.

In ancient Rome, the definition of a **citizen** was someone who lived in the city (cit = city). He or she was considered more **civilized** (civ = city). In fact the word **civilization** refers to the culture of cities. Even today in a general way, larger cities have more *civilization:* more museums, more large universities, complicated music, more art and architecture, and more commerce.

A **civic office** holder, like a mayor, presides over a city from the **civic center** (city hall) and hopefully has **civility** (politeness) and wears **civilian** (city) clothes. Certainly **uncivilized** behavior might get you thrown in jail if it is against **civil law**.

Here are some other civils:

civil engineering	civil servant	civil rights
civics	civil liberty	civil marriage

List 73   Gym and Women

It might shock today's students to learn the root **gymno-** means "naked" because in ancient Greece physical exercise and sports, including the original Olympic Games, were done in the nude. Hence our word **gymnasium** historically meant a place for nude exercise. **Gym** is just a shortening of gymnasium, **gymnastics** refers to the exercises, and a **gymnast** is one who performs the exercise.

Gymno- is a prefix often used in biology also, and a **gymnogynous** refers to a naked plant ovary (gymno = naked + gyn = woman or female).

The **gyn-** in that word is really part of the prefix **gyneco-** meaning "woman," and we see it in some relatively common words like **gynecologist**, who is a doctor specializing in the reproductive system of women, and a lot of other women words like **gynecocracy** (cracy = rule), a government ruled by women, or **gynephobia**, which is a fear of women (phobia = fear).

Review:

gymnasium	gymnastics	gymnast
gynecologist	gynecocracy	gynephobia

     The Vocabulary Teacher's Book of Lists

The Difference Between a Labyrinth and a Maze

	Labyrinth	**Maze**
Basic Layout	Linear—single path	Bifurcated—many choice points
Purpose	Develop personal insight or spiritual development	Amusement
Requires	Concentration	Cleverness, luck

Chapter 4

SUBJECTS

Driver's License Terms

"Breathes there a teenager so dead
That has not approached the legal age and said
I want my DRIVER'S LICENSE."

accidents	alcohol impairment
Department of Motor Vehicles	emergency signals
hazardous loads	identification
interim license	intersection
lanes for passing	legal U-turns
legal vehicles	license classes
license examination	minor
mobility and gridlock	pedestrian signals
provisional permit	railroad crossings
resident	right-of-way laws
special parking rules	speed limits
suspended or revoked license	traffic control
transfer	vehicle registration
warning signs	yield

Collectors*

Some people would collect anything, or so it seems, for a hobby and sometimes an occupation. Here are a few common types of collections and some high-class Latin names for them.

Collector	Collection
Archtophilist	teddy bears
Bandophilist	cigar bands
Bestiarist	medieval books on animals
Bibliophilist	books
Conchologist	shells
Copoclephilist	key rings
Deltiologist	postcards
Dologist	bird's eggs
Lepidopterist	butterflies
Numismatist	coins
Philatelist	stamps
Philographist	autographs
Phonophile	phonograph records
Plangonologist	dolls
Receptarist	recipes
Vecturist	subway tokens
Vexillologist	banners or flags

*Also see List 89, Hobbies, in this chapter.

In many lessons in this book and in our Master List of Roots, List 191, there are quite a few different general language roots. But this list is a subsection of roots used in science. This is a very useful list for budding scientists.

Root	Meaning	Example Word
aero-	relating to air	aerodynamics
ante-	before	antenatal
anti-	against	antibiotics
arche-	ancient	archaeology
arthr-	relating to joints	arthritis
auto-	self	automobile
-blast	bud	osteoblast
brachi-	arm	brachiopod
bronch-	windpipe	bronchitis
bryo-	moss	bryophytes
-cardo	relating to the heart	pericardial cavity
cephalo-	relating to the head	cephalopod
cerebro-	of the brain	cerebrospinal
chemo-	drug	chemotherapy
chrom-	colored	chromotography
cortico-	outer part	corticoid
cyto-, -cyte	relating to cells	cytoplasm
-derm	skin or outer covering	dermatology
dent-, dont-	relating to teeth	dentist, orthodontist
ecto-	outside	ectoderm
-ectomy	removal	hysterectomy
-emia	blood condition	anemia
endo-	inside	endoderm
epi-	upon or on the outside	epidermis
eu-	true	eusocial animal
-fer, -fers	bearing	conifer
gam-	breeding, mating	gamete
gastro-	relating to the stomach	gastroenteritis
-gen	producing, growing	pathogen
geo-	to do with the earth	geography
-germ	relating to reproduction	germination
gyne-	relating to women	gynecology
hemo-	to do with blood	hemoglobin
herbi-	relating to plants	herbivore
hetero-	others	heterotroph
homeo-	similar	homeostasis
hydro-	to do with water	hydrology
hyper-	excessive	hyperbaric chamber
hypo-	below, deficient	hypothalamus
-itis	inflammation	neuritis
-karyo	cell	prokaryote
lact-	to do with milk	lactation
laparo-	abdomen	laparoscopy
litho-	stone	lithosphere
meso-	middle	mesoderm
micro-	small	microscope

Root	Meaning	Example Word
mono-	one	monocotyledon
morpho-	shape	morphology
myo-	muscle	myocardium
necro-	death	necrosis
neuro-	nerve	neurotransmitter
oculo-	of the eye	binocular vision
oligo-	few	oligochaete
oo-	relating to egg or ovum	oomycete
ophthalm-	of the eye	ophthalmology
ornith-	of birds	ornithology
ortho-	correct	orthodontics
osteo-	of the bone	osteomalacis
paleo-	ancient	paleomagnetism
path-	relating to disease	pathology
pedi-	juvenile	pediatrics
peri-	around	perihelion
phage-	consumor destroyer	bacteriophage
photo-	to do with light	photometry
-plasm, -plasty	growth, living matter	protoplasm
phyto-, phyte-	of plants	epiphyte
poly-	many	polyethylene
pro-	before	prokaryote
proto-	first	protozoa
-rrhage, -rrhea	flow	hemorrhage
-sclero	hard	atherosclerosia
-scope	view	endoscope
-stomy	hole	colostomy
sym-, syn-	alike, together	symbiosis
tachy-	fast	tachycardia
tele-	far off	telescope
therm-, thermo-	temperature, heat	thermodynamica
-tomy	cut	tonsillectomy
tox-	poison	toxemia
-troph, -trophy	of feeding, growing	autotroph
vaso-	tube	vasodilation
-vore	eater	carnivore
xero-	dry	xerophyte

Biology Vocabulary

Swedish biologist Karl Linneaus, in the 1700s, developed a binomial (two-name) nomenclature for all living things, a generic designation + a specific name. For example: Carpodacus + Mexicanus (House Finch) and Zinnia + grandifloria (Golden Zinnia).

Chemical Vocabulary

Some chemicals use binomial nomenclature, for example: argentum + nitratum (silver nitrate) developed by Torbern Bergman in 1775. This system was extended in the early 1800s to use the first letter or two of the Latin name for the atoms plus a subscript for the amount of the atoms. For example, argentum nitratum is $AgNO_3$.

Scientific Measurement Units

In addition to the metric system of measurement, there is the International System of Units (SI Units), which has units for measuring physical phenomena other than just length, volume, and area. Some of these measurement units are rather common, such as electrical resistance (ohm), and some are not in everyday conversation, such as the unit for absorbed dose of radiation (gray). So just in case you want to improve your measurement vocabulary, here are the SI units.

Quality	Unit	Symbol
length	meter	m
mass	kilogram	kg
time	second	s
electric current	ampere	A
temperature	kelvin	K
luminous intensity	candela	cd
amount of substance	mole	mol
frequency	hertz	Hz
force	newton	N
work, energy	joule	J
power	watt	W
pressure	pascal	Pa
quantity of electricity	coulomb	C
potential difference	volt	V
electric resistance	ohm	Ω
capacitance	farad	F
conductance	siemens	S
magnetic flux	weber	Wb
flux density	tesla	T
inductance	henry	H
luminous flux	lumen	lm
illuminance	lux	lx
activity	becquerel	Bq
absorbed dose	gray	Gy
dose equivalent	sievert	Sv
plane angle	radian	rad
solid angle	steradian	sr

Here are some non-SI units in common use.

Quality	Unit	Symbol
plane angle	degree	°
plane angle	minute	′
plane angle	second	″
time	minute	min
time	hour	h
time	day	d
volume	liter	l
mass	ton	t
energy	electron volt	eV
mass	atomic mass unit	u
length	astronomical unit	AU
length	parsec	pc

American Indian Tribes

Apache	Algonquin	Blackfoot	Caddo
Cherokee (1st)	Cheyenne	Chickasaw	Chinook
Chippewa (4th)	Chitimacha	Choctaw (5th)	Cree
Crow	Dakota	Delaware	Hopi
Illinois	Iowa	Iroquois	Kansas
Kickapoo	Lummi	Missouri	Mesquakie
Mohawk	Narragansett	Natchez	Navajo (2nd)
Nipmunk	Oneida	Osage	Paiute
Passamaquoddy	Pawnee	Pequod	Potawatomi
Pueblo	Quapaw	Salish	Sauk
Seminole	Seneca	Shawnee	Sioux (3rd)
Ute	Winnebago	Yuma	Zuni

Note: This list does not include all American Indian tribes. The five largest tribes are indicated by the numbers in parentheses.

Words of the Old West

bronco	buckboard	cavalry
cowpoke	desperado	dude
ghost town	gringo	gunslinger
hombre	lariat	lasso
lynch	marshal	maverick
pony express	posse	reward
rodeo	saloon	six-gun
stagecoach	trail boss	tumbleweed
wagon train		

List 81 Whodunit

blackmail	bloodstain	break-in
bug	corpse	evidence
execution	fingerprint	gangster
getaway	heist	hustler
innocent	judge	loan shark
mob	motive	murder
payoff	prison	private eye
revolver	robbery	sentence
suicide	syndicate	theft
trial	victim	

List 82 Sci-Fi

android	astronauts	bionic
black hole	blast off	clone
cyborg	death ray	flying saucer
force field	galactic empires	humanoid
intergalactic	interplanetary	interstellar
laser	lunar colony	mind swap
mission	mutant	parallel world
ray-gun	robot	rocket
scientist		

The Stage

actress/actor	audience	comedy
costumes	dialogue	director
melodrama	monologue	playwright
plot	producer	protagonist
rehearsal	scene	script
soliloquy	star	suspense
tragedy	villain	

Myths*

amulet	centaur	cult
Cyclops	demigod	dragon
dwarf	elf	fate
genie	gremlin	griffin
incantation	leprechaun	mermaid
nemesis	nymph	odyssey
oracle	quest	sea monster
shaman	siren	sorceress
taboo	titan	troll
unicorn	wizard	

*Also see Chapter 3, lists 53 and 54.

List 85 Emotions

anxiety	betray	breakup	crafty
cruel	cry	danger	desire
ecstasy	evil	flirt	forbidden
forgiven	grief	grin	heartless
hug	ignore	jilt	kiss
lie	love	marry	melancholy
mourn	peril	pout	regret
remorse	revenge	scorn	sneaky
snuggle	tears	tease	tender
tragic	trust	tryst	wicked

List 86 Sports*

archery	auto racing	badminton
ballooning	baseball	basketball
bicycling	billiards	bowling
boxing	bullfighting	canoeing
fencing	field hockey	fishing
football	golf	gymnastics
handball	hang gliding	horseback riding
horseshoes	hunting	ice hockey
ice skating	judo	karate
kayaking	lacrosse	motorcycle racing
mountain climbing	rafting	rowing
running	scuba diving	skiing
sky diving	soccer	softball
speed boating	squash	surfing
swimming	tennis	track and field
volleyball	water-skiing	weight lifting
wrestling	yachting	

*Also see Sports Words, List 86.

List 87 Illnesses

alcoholism	appendicitis	arthritis
bronchitis	cancer	colds
cough	deafness	depression
diabetes	flu	headache
heart disease	hypertension	infection
kidney disease	leukemia	pneumonia

List 88 Moving Around

airplane	bed and breakfast	booking
bus	cancellation	car
cruise	customs	gratuity
immunization	itinerary	package tour
passport	reservations	resort
sightseeing	tourist	train
travel brochure	visa	

I try to catch every sentence, every word you and I say, and quickly lock all these sentences and words away in my literary storehouse because they might come in handy.

—Anton Chekhov, *The Seagull*

List 89 Hobbies*

antique collecting
butterfly collecting
coin collecting
gardening
pets
sailing
working on cars

bird watching
camping
doll collecting
hiking
photography
stamp collecting
writing

book collecting
card collecting
flower collecting
magic
puppetry
volunteering

*Also see List 76, Collectors, in this chapter.

List 90 Musical Instruments*

accordion
banjo
bugle
clarinet
dulcimer
fife
gong
harmonica
horn
lute
oboe
pennywhistle
recorder
triangle
tuba
violin
xylophone

balalaika
bass
castanet
cymbal
drum
flute
Greek lyre
harp
kazoo
mandolin
ocarina
piano
saxophone
trumpet
tympani
viola
zither

bagpipe
bassoon
cello
didgeridoo
fiddle
French horn
guitar
harpsichord
koto
maracas
panpipes
piccolo
tambourine
trombone
ukelele
washboard

*Also see List 91 in this chapter for some illustrations.

More Musical Instruments

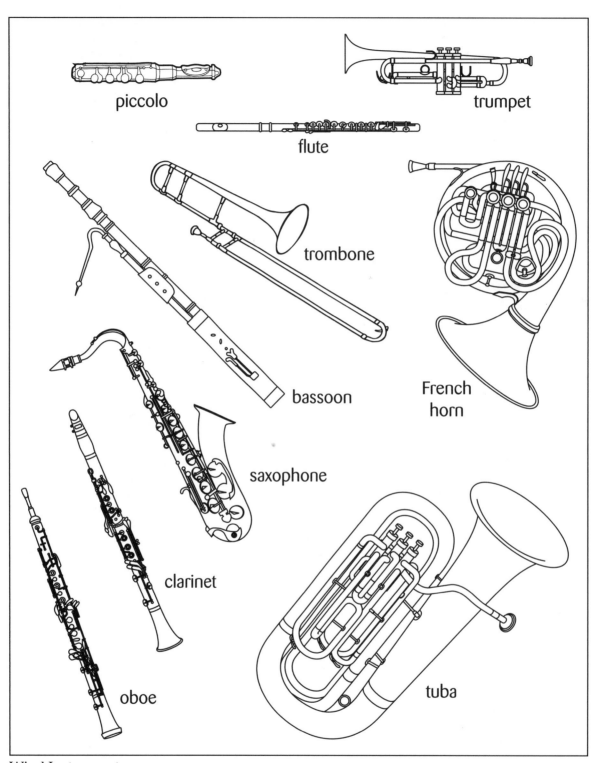

piccolo

trumpet

flute

trombone

French
horn

bassoon

saxophone

clarinet

tuba

oboe

Wind Instruments

More Musical Instruments *(continued)*

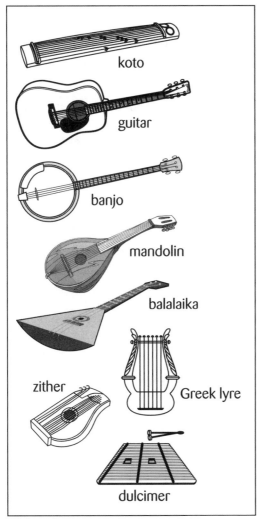

String Instruments

Drums

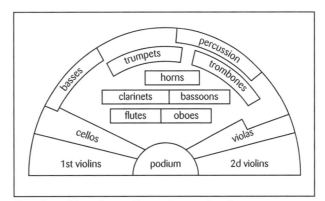

Seating Plan for a Symphony Orchestra

bake—cook in oven with dry heat

barbecue—cook on a grill over charcoal or other heat (*broil*) (*grill*)

boil—cook in boiling liquid

braise—first brown in fat, then cook covered with a small amount of liquid

broil—cook food close to the heat source, such as under a gas flame or over charcoal (*barbecue*) (*grill*)

deep fry—submerge food in hot fat or oil (*French fry*)

fry—cook in hot fat or oil over moderate to high heat

grill—cook on a grill over charcoal or other heat (*barbecue*) (*broil*)

marinate—soak food in a seasoned liquid

parboil—partially cook food in boiling water

pickle—soak in salt water or vinegar mixture to preserve

poach—lightly cook in liquid just below the boiling point

pressure cook—cook in high pressure steam pot

roast—cook in oven in uncovered pan

sauté—fry quickly in small amount of oil

scald—dip fruit into boiling water to loosen the skin; same as blanch

smoke—lightly cook in low heat and smoke

steam—cook in steam above boiling water

Plato used to meet and discuss philosophy with his followers in a place in ancient Athens known as the Groves of Academe. And from this comes our word *academic* meaning "learned" or "scholarly" and related words of *academy* and *nonacademic*.

Animal	Offspring	Animal	Offspring
bear	cub	**goose** (f)	gosling
beaver	kit	gander (m)	
bird	nestling, fledgling	**hawk**	eyas
cock (m)		**horse**	foal, colt (m)
hen (f)		stallion (m)	
cat	kitten	mare (f) (filly)	
tom (m)		gelding (n)	
sire (m) (breeding)		pony (small)	
dame (f) (breeding)		**kangaroo**	joey
grimalkin (old f)		buck (m)	
cattle	calf	doe (f)	
cow (f)		**lion**	cub
bull (m)		lioness (f)	
heifer (young f)		**otter**	whelp
steer (nm)		**oyster**	spat
bullock (nm)		**pig**	piglet, farrow, shoal
chicken	chick, pullet (f),	hog (m) (boar)	shoat
rooster (m) (cock)	cockerel (m)	sow (f)	
hen (f) (biddy)		**rabbit**	bunny
poulard (nf)		buck (m)	
capon (nm)		doe (f)	
deer	fawn	**rhinoceros**	calf
stag (m)		**seal**	pup
buck (m) (hart)		bull (m)	
doe (f) (hind)		cow (f)	
dog (m)	pup, puppy	**sheep**	lamb
bitch (f)		ram (m)	
donkey	jack (m)	ewe (f)	
	jenny (f)	**swan**	cygnet
duck	duckling	cod (m)	
drake (m)		pen (f)	
eagle	eaglet	**tiger**	cub
eel	elver	tigress (f)	
elephant	calf	**turkey**	poult
bull (m)		gobbler (m)	
cow (f)		cock (m)	
fox	cub, kit	hen (f)	
vixen (f)		**whale**	calf
giraffe	calf	**wolf**	cub
goat	kid		
billy (m)			
nanny (f) (doe)			

---

n = neutered or castrated

Unusual Animals

liger = lion (m) + tiger (f)
tiglon = tiger (m) + lion (f)
mule (n) = horse (f) + donkey (m)

Animals in Groups

Animal	Group Name	Animal	Group Name
apes	shrewdness	hogs	drift
asses	pace	horses	herd, team
badgers	cete	kangaroos	troop, mob
bears	sleuth	leopards	leap
beavers	colony	lions	pride, sault
bees	swarm	mallards	sord
birds	flock	monkeys	troop
buffalo	gang	partridge	covey
cats	clowder, clutter	peacocks	muster
chickens	flock	pheasants	nide, nest
chicks	clutch, brood	pigs	drove, litter
cows, cattle	herd	quail	bevy, covey
dogs	pack, kennel	rabbits	colony, nest, trace
ducks	brace, team	seals	pod
elephants	herd	sheep	drove, flock
elk	gang, herd	snakes	bed, nest
fish	school, shoal	toads	knot
foxes	skulk	turkeys	rafter, gang
frogs	army	turtles	bale
geese	flock, gaggle	whales	gam, pod
goats	tribe, trip	wolves	pack, rout
hawks	cast		

Animal Groups by Behavior

Covey is a group of quail on the ground.
Doggie is a motherless calf in a herd.
Drove is a group of animals moving together.
Herd is a group of animals grazing.
Hounds are a group of dogs used for hunting.
Pack is a group of wild animals moving together.
Skein is a group of geese in flight.
Whelp is the young of dogs, wolves, bears, lions, tigers, or seals.

American Military Ranks

Army and Air Force

General
Lieutenant General
Major General
Brigadier General
Colonel
Lieutenant Colonel
Major
Captain
First Lieutenant
Second Lieutenant
Warrant Officers (5 grades)
Noncomissioned Officers
Specialists
Enlisted Personnel

Navy and Coast Guard

Fleet Admiral
Admiral
Vice Admiral
Rear Admiral (upper half)
Rear Admiral (lower half)
Captain
Commander
Lieutenant Commander
Lieutenant
Lieutenant (j.g.)
Ensign
Warrant Officers (3 grades)
Enlisted Personnel

Marine Corps

General
Lieutenant General
Major General
Brigadier General
Colonel
Lieutenant Colonel
Major
Captain
First Lieutenant
Second Lieutenant
Warrant Officers (5 grades)
Enlisted Personnel

Space Names

Gemini (twins)	two-person space vehicle
Titan	powerful rocket
Mercury (messenger)	project name
Poseidon (god of the sea)	submarine class
Nike (a winged god)	missile

Sports Words

Baseball

balk	mitt
bases	mound
batting average	outfield
bloop	pinch hitter
bullpen	pitch
bunt	RBIs
count	relief pitcher
dugout	shortstop
error	sinker
foul tip	strike out
fungo	switch hitter
glove	triple
home run	wind up
infield	World Series

Football

end zone	quarterback
field goal	scrimmage
fumble	snap
huddle	Super Bowl
incomplete pass	tackle
line of scrimmage	touchdown
punt	

Basketball

assists	free throw
backboard	hoop
back court	jump shot
blocking	layup
bucket	NBA Finals
center	rebound
charging	traveling
foul	

Lawyer Words

The law is written with a number of Latin words. Just in case you get in trouble, here are a few words that might help you understand what is happening.

plaintiff   the person who is *complaining* (with + sorrow); in a suit, he or she is the one who wants the money from the *defendant*. The old Romans showed great sorrow by beating their breast, hence the Latin verb *plactus* gives us the root *plant,* which means "sorrow," as in *complaint.*

intestate   (in-test-ate) (not + witness + noun) if you die without making a will, that is *intestate* and that's trouble. You can see that the *test* appears in many other words like *testimony* and *testing* (witnessing what you know). If you *detest* something you can't stand looking at it (de-test) (not + witness).

acquittal—not-guilty verdict

adjourn—suspend court proceedings until later

affidavit—written statement sworn under oath

allegation—contention or accusation; statement

appeal—procedure by which case is brought from lower to higher court for revised ruling

arbitration—settling dispute without formal court trial

arraignment—calling of accused before court to hear charges and enter plea

bail—payment of bond that is forfeited if one fails to appear in court

bench warrant—arrest order issued by judge

bequest—gift by will of personal property

capital punishment—execution as criminal sentence

cessation—temporary adjournment of case

civil case—lawsuit between private parties, as distinguished from criminal case

clemency—reduction of sentence, usually by executive branch

codicil—amendment or addition to will

constitution—fundamental law by which state governs

court-martial—judicial court proceeding in armed forces

declaratory judgment—determination stating legal rights or duties or interpretation

default judgment—judicial decision rendered without trial proceedings

defendant—a person required to answer a legal action or suit (the accused)

deposition—sworn testimony of witness taken outside court proceedings

disbarment—expulsion of attorney from legal profession

double jeopardy—repeat prosecution for same criminal offense, prohibited by U.S. Constitution

ex post facto—"after the fact": fixing or changing punishment for act after it was committed, now forbidden by U.S. Constitution

extradition—transfer of accused fugitive from state where arrested to state where charged

habeas corpus—"have the body"; court order requiring that detained prisoner be produced in court to inquire into legality of detention

indictment—criminal charge made by grand jury

inquest—official inquiry or examination before jury; coroner's investigation of cause of death

interrogatories—written questions answered under oath

jury trial—consideration of case by jury, as opposed to by judge or arbitrator

litigation—legal case contested in court

moratorium—legally authorized period of delay

nolo contendere—"I do not wish to contest"

own recognizance—condition of release of accused person without payment of bail

plea—defendant's answer to plaintiff's declaration; accused's answer to criminal charge

power of attorney—written authority allowing one person to act for another

preventive detention—holding of prisoner without bail

punitive damages—damages in excess of actual loss awarded to wronged plaintiff to punish defendant

replevin—action to recover actual item of personal property rather than its value

revoke—annul or rescind a document decision or offer

sequester—isolate jury

statute of limitations—legislative act limiting time in which plaintiff may bring civil suit or state may bring criminal action

subpoena—command to appear in court and testify

tender—offer money or property to fulfill an obligation

testimony—oral evidence given by witness

waiver—intentional abandonment of right

warrant—court order authorizing action by public officer, usually arrest or search and seizure

writ—written court order issued to serve administration of justice; usually stipulating that something be done or not be done

Sooner or later most people go to a doctor, but what kind? Many people go to what is called a **General Practitioner**, which means no particular specialty. This has merged into something called **Family Practice**. But as specialties develop, the old General Practitioner is becoming an **Internist**. All of these doctors look at you, handle some things, and—for serious things—often call in a specialist because the amount of knowledge required is so large and changing so fast that doctors specialize in just one area. In fact, some even have subspecialties; for example, *surgeons* who only operate on hands, or *oncologists* who only deal with breast cancer, and so on. Below are some of the specialties that you might run into in most hospitals or large clinics. Note that each word ends in the suffix *–ist* which means "someone who practices." You can easily substitute different suffixes like **–ology**, which means "the study or science of," hence a *cardiologist* who treats your heart practices *cardiology*. For more medical words, see List 99.

Physician/M.D.	Root	Area
Allergist	aller = other	allergies
Anesthesiologist	an = without	at operations
	esthe = feeling	
Cardiologist	cardio = heart	heart
Dermatologist	derma = skin	skin
Endocrinologist	endo = within	glands
Gastroenterologist	gastro = stomach	stomach and bowel
Gynecologist	gyne = woman	women
Internist	inter = inner	diagnosis and general medicine
Neurologist	neuro = nerve	nerves
Obstetrician	ob = to, ste = stand	childbirth
Oncologist	onco = tumor	cancer
Opthalmologist	opthalmo = eye	eyes
Orthopedic Surgeon	ortho = straight	surgery of bone, muscle
	ped = child	
Otolaryngologist	oto = ear	ear, nose, and throat
	laryngo = larynx = throat	
Pediatrician	pedia = child	children
Psychiatrist	psych = mind	psychotherapy
Radiologist	radio = radiant energy	X ray and nuclear
Urologist	uro = urine	kidneys and bladder

Other Medical Specialists	Root	Area
Chiropractor (D.C.)	chiro = hand	adjusts spine
Dentist (D.D.S.)	dent = teeth	teeth
Optician	opt = see	grinds lenses
Optometrist (O.D.)	opt = see	vision, glasses
Physical therapist	physic = nature	muscles

Other Medical Specialties

Acupuncture—Chinese medical procedure using needles
Bariatrics—weight control
Endoscopy—scope of the stomach
Hematology—blood
Orthodontia—teeth straightening
Prosthetics—artificial limbs
Vascular—veins

Most of the body parts have a Latin or Greek root name. In a doctor's office you don't have a finger, you have a *digit*. How can she charge you so much money for curing a skin rash? Because you have *dermatitis*. Your doctor for heart problems is no ordinary doctor; he's a *cardiologist*.

    Besides doctors, a lot of functions of life derive from body parts. If you are scared, you are *nervous*; the process of breathing in and out is *respiration* (spir = breath). If you speak two languages, you are *bilingual* (bi = two, lingu = tongue).

    Here are a few more body parts and example words:

Root	Body Part	Example Word
auri	ear	auricular
bronch	windpipe	bronchitis
capit	head	decapitate
card, cord	heart	cardiac
corp	body	corpuscle
dent	tooth	dentist
derm	skin	dermatitis
digit	finger	digital
emia	blood	anemia
gastro	stomach	gastronomy
glos	tongue	glossary
hal	breathing	inhale
hema, sang	blood	hemorrhage
lingu	tongue	bilingual
man	hand	manufacture
neur	nerve	neuron
ocul	eye	binocular
osteo	bone	osteoarthritis
ped, pod	foot	pedal, tripod
pneuma	breathing	pneumonia
psych	mind	psychosis
spir	breathing	respiration

For more words, see List 98.

List 100   Body Parts—Expressions

You may never have thought about it, but a lot of our common expressions use names of body parts, perhaps to make the expression more vivid, perhaps it's just an old habit. Sometimes the expression is an adjective that makes the verb more exact; for example, to "win by a hair." Sometimes the body part becomes a verb, as in "hand me a book" or "toe the line." A few reflect mythology; for example, in olden times, the heart was thought to be the seat of emotion, so to be "warm hearted" meant emotionally warm.

Be ankle deep	Have a big mouth
Be hot blooded	Have a nose for news
Be knee high	Have a warm heart
Don't be an ass	Have sticky fingers
Fight tooth and nail	Head down the road
Get a cold shoulder	Head's up!
Get a foot in the door	Run neck and neck
Get a tongue lashing	See eyeball to eyeball
Get elbow room	To get an earful
Go arm-in-arm	To have guts
Hand me a book	Toe the line
Hang on by a fingernail	Win by a hair

> *A word is a microcosm of human consciousness.*
>
> —Vygotsky

Chapter 5

WRITING

Words for Letters

Sooner or later most people need (or should) write letters for various occasions or to friends. Save money, don't buy a card, write your own.

Here are a few words that might inspire you to rise above the norm:

Sympathy (Death or Misfortune)

anguish	appalling	bleak
compassion	concerned	condolences
disaster	faith	healing
heavyhearted	hope	mourn
pain	regret	saddened
shocked	sympathy	

Congratulations (Graduation, Awards, Accomplishment)

achievement	admire	appreciate
celebration	compliment	contribution
delighted	distinguished	excellent
feat	impressed	inspiring
milestone	perseverance	pleased
proud	special	superb
superlative	triumph	unique
well-deserved		

Apologies (You Forgot, Goofed, Can't Come)

absentmindedly	accidental	amends
blame	blooper	botched
careless	disconcerting	embarrassed
erroneous	fault	forgive
imperfect	inadvertent	lax
misdirected	misquote	misunderstanding
offended	overlooked	pardon
red-faced	remiss	sheepish
tactless	troublesome	unaware

Get Well (Lots of Hope, a Little Sympathy, Humor)

accident	affection	cheer
comfort	concerned	convalescence
experience	heal	health
hope	indisposed	optimistic
ordeal	painful	recovery
sorry	suffering	treatment
trouble	uncomfortable	unwelcome

Reference and Résumé (You're good, I'm good)

accurate	approve	capable
competent	congenial	conscientious
cooperative	creative	dependable
discreet	efficient	energetic
ethical	first-rate	friendly
hardworking	honest	ingenious
intelligent	loyal	outstanding
productive	professional	promising
resourceful	responsible	successful
suitable	superior	trustworthy

Holidays (Cards, Notes, Letters)

blessings	celebration	happiness
Happy Anniversary	Happy Birthday	Happy Hanukkah
health	holiday greetings	holidays
Merry Christmas	peace	prosperity
rejoice	remembrances	season
season's greetings	success	
well-being	wishes	

Holiday	Date
New Year's Day	January 1
Martin Luther King Jr. Day	Third Monday in January
Presidents' Day	Third Monday in February
Memorial Day	Last Monday in May
Independence Day	July 4
Labor Day	First Monday in September
Veterans' Day	November 11
Thanksgiving	Fourth Thursday in November
Hanukkah	Eight days in December
Christmas	December 25
Kwanzaa	Seven days in December

Avoid looking semi-literate; use the right word, not *almost* the right word. This list is also the basis of some important spelling lessons.

accede (v.) – to comply with
exceed (v.) – to surpass

accent (n.) – stress in speech or writing
ascent (n.) – act of going up
assent (v., n.) – consent

accept (v.) – to agree or take what is offered
except (prep.) – leaving out or excluding

access (n.) – admittance
excess (n., adj.) – surplus

adapt (v.) – to adjust
adept (adj.) – proficient
adopt (v.) – to take by choice

adverse (adj.) – opposing
averse (adj.) – disinclined

advice (n.) – recommendation
advise (v.) – to recommend

affect (v.) – to influence
effect (n.) – feeling

alley (n.) – narrow street
ally (n.) – supporter

allude (v.) – to refer
elude (v.) – to avoid

allusion (n.) – indirect reference
delusion (n.) – mistaken belief
illusion (n.) – mistaken vision

all ready (adj.) – completely ready
already (adv.) – even now or by this time

altitude (n.) – elevation
attitude (n.) – outlook

all together (pron., adj.) – everything or everyone in one place
altogether (adv.) – entirely

anecdote (n.) – short amusing story
antidote (n.) – something to counter the effect of poison

angel (n.) – heavenly body
angle (n.) – space between two lines that meet in a point

annual (adj.) – yearly
annul (v.) – to make void

ante – prefix meaning before
anti – prefix meaning against

any way (adj., n.) – in whatever manner
anyway (adj.) – regardless

appraise (v.) – to set a value on
apprise (v.) – to inform

area (n.) – surface
aria (n.) – melody

ascent (n.) – climb
asset (n.) – value

avocation (n.) – hobby
vocation (n.) – job

biannual (adj.) – occurring twice per year
biennial (adj.) – occurring every other year

bibliography (n.) – list of writings on a particular topic, references
biography (n.) – written history of a person's life

bizarre (adj.) – odd
bazaar (n.) – market, fair

breadth (n.) – width
breath (n.) – respiration
breathe (v.) – to inhale and exhale

calendar (n.) – a chart of days and months
colander (n.) – a strainer

casual (adj.) – informal
causal (adj.) – relating to cause

catch (v.) – to grab
ketch (n.) – type of boat

cease (v.) – to stop
seize (v.) – to grasp

click (n.) – short, sharp sound
clique (n.) – small exclusive subgroup

collision (n.) – a clashing
collusion (n.) – a scheme to cheat

coma (n.) – an unconscious state
comma (n.) – a punctuation mark

command (n., v.) – an order, to order
commend (v.) – to praise, to entrust

complement (n.) – completeness
compliment (n., v.) – flattery, to flatter

comprehensible (adj.) – understandable
comprehensive (adj.) – extensive

confidant (n.) – friend or advisor
confident (adj.) – sure

confidentially (adv.) – privately
confidently (adv.) – certainly

conscience (n.) – sense of right and wrong
conscious (adj.) – aware

contagious (adj.) – spread by contact
contiguous (adj.) – touching or nearby

continual (adj.) – repeated, happening again and again
continuous (adj.) – uninterrupted, without stopping

cooperation (n.) – the art of working together
corporation (n.) – a business organization

cornet (n.) – musical instrument
coronet (n.) – crown

costume (n.) – special way of dressing
custom (n.) – usual practice or habit

council (n.) – an official group
counsel (v., n.) – to give advice, advice

credible (adj.) – believable
creditable (adj.) – deserving praise

deceased (adj.) – dead
diseased (adj.) – ill

decent (adj., adv.) – proper
descent (n.) – way down
dissent (n., v.) – disagreement, to disagree

deference (n.) – respect
difference (n.) – dissimilarity

deposition (n.) – a formal written document
disposition (n.) – temperament

depraved (adj.) – morally corrupt
deprived (adj.) – taken away from

deprecate (v.) – to disapprove
depreciate (v.) – to lessen in value

desert (n.) – arid land
desert (v.) – to abandon
dessert (n.) – course served at the end of a meal

desolate (adj.) – lonely, sad
dissolute (adj.) – loose in morals

detract (v.) – to take away from
distract (v.) – to divert attention away from

device (n.) – a contrivance
devise (v.) – to plan

disapprove (v.) – to withhold approval
disprove (v.) – to prove something false

disassemble (v.) – to take something apart
dissemble (v.) – to disguise

disburse (v.) – to pay out
disperse (v.) – to scatter

discomfort (n.) – distress
discomfit (v.) – to frustrate or embarrass

disinterested (adj.) – impartial
uninterested (adj.) – not interested

effect (n.) – result of a cause
effect (v.) – to make happen

elapse (v.) – to pass
lapse (v.) – to become void
relapse (v.) – to fall back to previous condition

elicit (v.) – to draw out
illicit (adj.) – unlawful

eligible (adj.) – ready
illegible (adj.) – can't be read

elusive (adj.) – hard to catch
illusive (adj.) – misleading
emanate (v.) – to rise out of
eminent (adj.) – prominent
imminent (adj.) – impending

emerge (v.) – to rise out of
immerge (v.) – to plunge into

emigrate (v.) – to leave a country and take up residence elsewhere
immigrate (v.) – to enter a country for the purpose of taking up residence

empire (n.) – government
umpire (n., v.) – game official, to referee

envelop (v.) – to surround
envelope (n.) – a wrapper for a letter

erasable (adj.) – capable of being erased
irascible (adj.) – easily provoked to anger

expand (v.) – to increase in size
expend (v.) – to spend

expect (v.) – to suppose; to look forward
suspect (v.) – to mistrust

extant (adj.) – still existing
extent (n.) – amount

facility (n.) – ease
felicity (n.) – happiness

farther (adj.) – more distant (refers to space)
further (adj.) – extending beyond a point (refers to time, quantity, or degree)

finale (n.) – the end
finally (adv.) – at the end
finely (adv.) – in a fine manner

fiscal (adj.) – relating to finance
physical (adj.) – relating to the body

formal (adj.) – solemn
former (adj.) – prior

formally (adv.) – with rigid ceremony
formerly (adv.) – previously

hardy (adj.) – rugged
hardly (adv.) – barely

human (adj.) – relating to people
humane (adv.) – kind

hypercritical (adj.) – very critical
hypocritical (adj.) – pretending to be virtuous

imitate (v.) – to mimic
intimate (v.) – to hint or make known; familiar, close

incredible (adj.) – too extraordinary to be believed
incredulous (adj.) – unbelieving, skeptical

indigenous (adj.) – native
indigent (adj.) – needy
indignant (adj.) – angry

infer (v.) – to arrive at by reason
imply (v.) – to suggest meaning indirectly

ingenious (adj.) – clever
ingenuous (adj.) – straightforward

later (adj.) – more late
latter (adj.) – second in a series of two

lay (v.) – to set something down or place something
lie (v.) – to recline; to tell an untruth

least (adj.) – at the minimum
lest (conj.) – for fear that

lend (v.) – to give for a time
loan (n.) – received to use for a time

loose (adj.) – not tight
lose (v.) – to not win; to misplace

magnet (n.) – iron bar with power to attract iron
magnate (n.) – person in prominent position in large industry

mediate (v.) – to negotiate
meditate (v.) – to ponder

message (n.) – communication
massage (v.) – to rub the body

moral (n., adj.) – lesson, ethic
morale (n.) – mental condition

morality (n.) – virtue
mortality (n.) – the state of being mortal; death rate

of (prep.) – having to do with; indicating possession
off (adv.) – not on

official (adj.) – authorized
officious (adj.) – offering services where they are neither wanted nor needed

oral (adj.) – verbal
aural (adj.) – listening

pasture (n.) – grass field
pastor (n.) – minister

perfect (adj.) – without fault
prefect (n.) – an official

perpetrate (v.) – to be guilty of; to commit
perpetuate (v.) – to make perpetual

perquisite (n.) – a privilege or profit in addition to salary
prerequisite (n.) – a preliminary requirement

persecute (v.) – to harass, annoy, or injure
prosecute (v.) – to press for punishment of crime

personal (adj.) – private
personnel (n.) – a body of people, usually employed in some organization

peruse (v.) – to read
pursue (v.) – to follow in order to overtake

picture (n.) – drawing or photograph
pitcher (n.) – container for liquid; baseball player

precede (v.) – to go before
proceed (v.) – to advance

preposition (n.) – a part of speech
proposition (n.) – a proposal or suggestion

prescribe (v.) – to order for a remedy
proscribe (v.) – to ban

pretend (v.) – to make believe
portend (v.) – to give a sign of something that will happen

quiet (adj.) – not noisy
quit (v.) – to stop
quite (adv.) – very

receipt (n.) – proof of purchase
recipe (n.) – cooking directions

recent (adj.) – not long ago
resent (v.) – to feel indignant

respectably (adv.) – in a respectable manner
respectively (adv.) – in order indicated
respectfully (adv.) – in a respectful manner

restless (adj.) – constantly moving, uneasy
restive (adj.) – contrary, resisting control

suppose (v.) – assume or imagine
supposed (adj.) – expected

than (conj.) – used in comparison
then (adv.) – at that time; next in order of time

through (prep.) – by means of; from beginning to end
thorough (adj.) – complete

use (v.) – to employ something
used (adj.) – secondhand

veracious (adj.) – truthful
voracious (adj.) – greedy

> *Colors fade, temples crumble, empires fall, but wise words endure.*
>
> — Edward Thorndike

There is an interesting kind of vocabulary that uses other words as one word. We are talking about similes and metaphors. A simile uses *like* or *as* in a phrase, and the whole phrase must be read as if it were one word (an adjective that modifies a noun). For example, in the sentence "She was busy as a bee," the *as a bee* is the simile and it simply means *very*. The sentence could be written "She was very busy."

The problem is that the second sentence is a little boring and so the writer could choose to use a simile to liven up the writing. Below are a few more common similes. Look for others in your reading and use some when you write.

Similes Using "As"	Similes Using "Like"
as cold as ice	acts like a bull in a china shop
as dark as night	cry like a baby
as dry as a bone	eat like it's going out of style
as fat as a pig	eyes like stars
as green as grass	fits like a glove
as hard as a rock	fought like cats and dogs
as innocent as a newborn baby	moves like a snail
as light as a feather	sit there like a bump on a log
as rough as sandpaper	slept like a dog
as slow as molasses in January	stood out like a sore thumb
as smart as a whip	works like a charm

There is a tendency, not a rule, for the "as" similes to function as adjectives (modifying a noun) and the "like" similes to function as adverbs (modifying a verb). For example: "He was *fat as a pig* and he *moved like a snail.*"

Metaphors are "figures of speech" that use comparisons, but unlike similes, they do not use "as" or "like." A metaphor modifies a verb or a noun by inferring that it is similar to the quality of something else. For example, if you "bottle up an idea" you don't literally put an idea into a bottle, but the basic quality that a bottle contains liquid means that your ideas are contained and not available for discussion.

If your teenager has a *bottomless pit* as a stomach, the basic quality of the bottomlessness or inability to be filled up conveys the real meaning of the metaphor.

Here is a metaphor acting like an adjective: "The teenager's stomach was *a bottomless pit.*"
Here is a metaphor acting like an adverb: "He ran *faster than an antelope with his tail on fire.*"

You can have a lot of fun with metaphors, try a few like: "She learned to cook *in cement mixing school.*"

Here are a few other metaphors in use:

The boss's bark is worse than his bite.

The sunset painted the sky orange.

My legs turned to rubber.

The calculator became a crutch.

The sun peeked over the horizon.

Metaphors apply to more than just a word or a phrase. Stories, poems, and even works of art use metaphors. For example, a ship leaving the dock might be a metaphor for a lover leaving his beloved.

Achilles Heel — This is named for the mythical Greek warrior, magically protected from wounds over all of his body except for one spot—his heel. Hence "Achilles Heel" now means a person's one vulnerable spot.

Idioms are phrases or a group of words that are much like a single word. In short they are a vocabulary term and must be seen as a whole meaning unit. For example, if a person *blows up* he usually does not come apart in pieces, but he does show anger. If you *catch someone's eye* there is not an eyeball floating through the air, but it means that you have caught that person's attention.

Idioms are most often used in informal oral conversation. They are sometimes used in informal writing, but seldom in more formal writing. Some idioms are so often used that they appear in dictionaries as a separate entry, just like a single word, but most idioms are not in dictionaries.

Idioms are the bane of people who are just learning English as a second language (ESL) because those people often treat them as though each word had its more common meaning. If it is raining cats and dogs, it does not have much to do with animals.

It takes years of familiarity with the language and culture to learn the idioms. Native speakers, like little children, just learn them "naturally," in the way that they learn the meaning of any word. ESL students need to know that idioms exist, and they need a little help from any native language speaker to get the meaning.

Some idioms become *clichés*. That means they are so overused that they become boring. Creative writing classes frown on the use of clichés. Thus, a cliché does not have an exact definition. Whether or not a phrase is a cliché is a matter of judgment.

Here are some common idioms:

all wet	keep the world from the door
blow a fuse	lay your hand on something
come clean	make heads or tails of something
do the honors	play the field
fall head over heels	pull strings
get one's feet wet	run in
go fly a kite	sit on the fence
have a heart	throw one's hat in the ring
hit the road	

Alliteration — repetition of a sound in a string of words or in a poem, such as Little Lucy Longnose.

List 106 Old Derogatory Terms

Apparently people have always had plenty of unkind things to say about their fellow humans. A derogatory term is one intended to lower the reputation of someone or just to show that you have a little hate in your heart (de = from, rog = ask). Here are some derogatory terms that date back to the Middle Ages.

Simpleton—someone who makes plenty of dumb mistakes or is just plain stupid.

Lackey—somebody who is obsequious, also called a **boot licker**, or, in ancient Greece, a **fig shower** (sycophant). A lackey is someone who does lowly jobs for somebody who thinks he or she is high and mighty. Don't use lackey for a nice person who is helping you.

Rogue—a dishonest **scoundrel** who would steal your purse or your damsel while you weren't looking, then hide in the forest with outlaws. You might sometimes use it to describe a mischievous little boy you know.

Knave—this is a sort of low-class rogue; every castle had a few.

Caitiff—simply a base, despicable person.

Scurvy—this is used to describe a mean, nasty, contemptible person who is probably ugly besides. Scurvy is also a disease caused by lack of Vitamin C that causes skin spots. But unless you are a doctor, you don't want to be around a scurvy person.

Vassal—a vassal is not a derogatory term; it simply describes a servant—but certainly someone without a legitimate drop of royal blood.

In case you need a few more derogatory terms, here is how you can make up a few of your own. Start with "thou" and a term each from column A, B, and C. So look your opponent right in the eye and say, "Thou naughty, sour-faced, hedge pig."

Column A	Column B	Column C
naughty	sour-faced	hedge pig
lewd	pale-hearted	rabbit sucker
reeky	onion-eyed	hemp seed
waggish	lily-livered	dogfish
wrenching	ill-nurtured	cut purse
distempered	rug-headed	miscreant
bawdy	evil-eyed	ruffian
hideous	rump-fed	scallion
queasy	clay-brained	water fly
peevish	hunch-backed	malignancy

Here is a list of terms related to words or actions related to writing. It does not pretend to be exhaustive; there are certainly more, particularly terms related to poetry and drama. This list also tends to favor words composed of Latin or Greek roots. Sometimes just one or two of these terms make an interesting writing lesson.

Allegory—an allusion that often has a moral point; representation of an abstract idea by concrete language (allo = other).

Allusion—writing about a person or thing that often represents or alludes to a generalization about life (al = to, lud = play).

Analogy—a comparison of two ideas or events that show an interesting similarity (ana = against, logy = reason).

Anecdote—a short story, maybe humorous (an = not, ecdot = give out).

Antagonist—a person or thing in a play or story who is working against the hero or protagonist (an = not).

Antithesis—interesting use of opposing ideas, often using similar words in a sentence or nearby; for example, "We have nothing to fear, but fear itself" (anti = against, thesis = something set down).

Autobiography—the author's account of his or her own life (auto = self, bio = life, graph = write).

Biography—a story of a life written by somebody else (bio = life, graph = write).

Colloquial—language or sayings used in informal, familiar speech, such as "Hi, y'all" (col = with, loqu = speech).

Dialogue—conversation between characters (dia = across, log = word).

Diction—author's choice of words, clear pronunciation (dict = speak).

Didactic—writing that teaches something (didakt = taught).

Empathy—imagining how you would feel if you were in someone else's place (em = in, path = feeling).

Epigram—a brief or witty saying or poem (epi = upon, gram = write).

Exaggeration—an overstatement to emphasize a point, a hyperbole (ex = from, agger = heap).

Hyperbole—an obvious exaggeration (hyper = excess, bol = throw).

Juxtaposition—placing two words or ideas close together for contrast or interest (juxta = side).

Malapropism—a pun, play on words, or mistake, such as "I like that period," meant to say "person" (mal = bad, prop = near).

Metaphor—a figure of speech comparing two things without using *as* or *like* (meta = beyond, phor = part).

Metonymy—substituting one word for another; for example, "The White House has decided. . . ." (White House = President).

Oxymoron—two words of near opposite meaning put together for a special effect, such as "glorious pain," "clearly misunderstood" (oxy = sharp or keen, moron = dull or stupid).

Paradox—a statement that seems contradictory but actually expresses a truth (para = almost, dox = belief).

Personification—having a non-person speak; "The hills were singing" (persona = role).

Protagonist—the main character or hero in a story (pro = in front of).

Pseudonym—a pen name or false name (pseudo = false, nym = name).

Soliloquy—speaking when you think you are alone (sol = alone, loqu = speech).

Symbol—a concrete object to represent an idea, such as the dove as a symbol of peace (sym = together, bol = throw).

Synecdoche—using part of something to represent the whole. When you "count heads," "heads" represents the whole person (syn = with, together, ec = out of, from, doche = receive).

onymous—with author's name
anonymous—without author's name

euphony—pleasant sound
cacophony—harsh, discordant sound

prologue—before the body of text
postscript—added after the text was finished

header—top of the page, not part of the text
footer—bottom of the page, not part of the text

climax—important or most dramatic point in the story
anticlimax—minor point, misread as the climax

introduction—beginning remarks about the text; separate or included
coda—concluding remarks or summary

protagonist—the main character, hero
antagonist—character opposed to the protagonist, rival

biographer—person who writes the story of someone else's life
autobiographer—person who writes the story of his or her own life

author—person who creates a literary work
critic—person who writes about an author's work
editor—person who cleans up an author's work

Punctuation

Symbol	Name	Purpose
.	Period, Full Stop	1. At the end of a complete sentence. *Birds fly.* (noun + verb or subject + predicate)
		2. At the end of a command sentence. *Go home. Stop.* (no subject or subject inferred)
		3. After most abbreviations. *Mr., Co., Ave.*
		4. In money or to show decimal fractions. *$2.50, .05*
?	Question Mark (Interrogation mark)	1. At the end of a question. *Who is he?*
		2. To express doubt. *He ate fourteen doughnuts? 1933?*
!	Exclamation Point	1. To show strong emotion with a word. *Great!*
" "	Quotation Marks	1. To show a direct quote. *She said, "May I help you?"*
		2. To set off a story title. *He read "A Visit from Saint Nicholas."*
		3. To imply sarcasm or someone else's use of a term. *The "hero" was not at home.*
' '	Single Quotation Marks	1. Used inside quotation marks. *Sally said, "I hope I never see that 'jerk' again."*
'	Apostrophe	1. To form the possessive. *Bill's bike*
		2. In contractions, to show missing letters. *Isn't*
		3. To form the plural of symbols. *Two A's*
,	Comma	1. To set off a descriptive or parenthetical word or phrase. *Tina, the announcer, read her lines.*
		2. Between a dependent and independent clause. *After the game, we went home.*
		3. To separate independent clauses. *I like him, and he likes me.*
		4. To set off incidental words. *I saw it, too. Naturally, I went along. Oh, I didn't see you.*
		5. To separate items in a series. *one, two, three*

Copyright © 2004 by John Wiley & Sons, Inc.

Symbol	Name	Purpose
,	Comma	6. To separate things in a list. *bread, milk, cheese*
		7. To separate parts of a date. *February 22, 2003*
		8. After the greeting in a friendly letter. *Dear Gerry,*
		9. After the closing in a letter. *Sincerely,*
		10. To separate the city and state in an address. *New York, New York*
		11. To separate a name and a degree title. *Jenn Stock, M.D.*
		12. Between inverted names. *Smith, Joe*
		13. In written dialogue between the quotation and the rest of the sentence. *She said, "Stop it." "Okay," he replied.*
		14. Between more than one adjective or adverb. *The big, bad wolf.*
( )	Parentheses	1. To show supplementary material. *The map (see below) is new.*
		2. To set off information more strongly than with commas. *Joe (the first actor) was ready.*
		3. In numbering or lettering a series. *Choices: (a) a game or (b) a song; two steps: (1) Open the door. (2) Step in.*
[ ]	Brackets	1. Alternate parentheses, stronger, less traditional and/or within parentheses. *Joe (whom he did [not] like) was home.*
:	Colon	1. To introduce a series. *He has three things: a pen, a book, and a backpack.*
		2. To show a subtitle. *The book: How to read it.*
		3. To separate clauses. *The rule is this: Keep it simple.*
		4. After a business letter greeting. *Dear Ms. Turner:*
		5. To separate hours and minutes or to show ratio. *10:15 A.M. 3:1 ratio*

Symbol	Name	Purpose
;	Semicolon	1. To separate sentence parts more strongly than a comma. *November was cold; January was freezing.* 2. To separate sentence parts that contain commas. *He was tired; therefore, he took a nap.*
-	Hyphen	1. In adjectives of almost compounded words. *air-cooled, brick-red* 2. Hyphenated phrase to make it a noun. *In the sweet by-and-by.*
—	En-Dash	1. To show period of time or distance between. *2000–2005, Chicago–Boston*
——	Em-Dash	1. To show the insertion of descriptive information. *Carla—the tallest student—held the flag.*
. . .	Ellipsis	1. To show words have been left out. *The boy . . . was not at home . . . but his mom answered the phone.* 2. To show a pause for suspense or to heighten mood. *The announcer called out, "The winner is . . . Chris."*

●	Bullet	1. To show items in a list or call attention to them. *Things to do on Saturday:*
		   • *Go swimming*
		   • *Visit Uncle Chuck*
		   • *Clean my room*
		
		2. Between syllables in some dictionaries. *run•ning*

/	Slash, Virgule, Stroke, Diagonal	1. To show lines of poetry. *Twinkle, twinkle little star / how I wonder . . .* 2. To set off numbers or symbols. */a/ first point, /b/ second point* 3. To indicate phonemes. */b/ is the first phoneme in "boy"* 4. To show common fractions. *3/4*

List 110 Proofreaders' Symbols

Also see the punctuation marks, List 109, and printers' symbols, List 111, in this chapter.

¶	Begin a new paragraph
No ¶	Do not begin a new paragraph
^	Insert (caret)
⊙	Insert a period
^,	Insert a comma
No ^,	Delete a comma
^;	Insert a semicolon
^:	Insert a colon
lc	Lower case
^"	Insert quotation marks
//	Make these items parallel
⌒	Cut this word or phrase (also /)
#	Leave a space
‿	Close up space
✕	Problem here; fix it
∿	Reverse these items
≡	Capitalize (triple underline)
stet	Restore (ignore change)
~~	Bold face (wavy underline)
____	Italics (straight underline)

List 111 Printers' Symbols

´	**accent mark** shows an accent on a syllable (may´ be)
&	**ampersand** means "and"
< >	**angle brackets** signify a key on the keyboard (<ENTER>)
*	**asterisk** refers to a footnote, also called a star or splat
\	**backslash** back stroke, reverse solidus
˘	**breve** indicates a short vowel
^	**circumflex** indicates vowel pronunciation (ôr)
©	**copyright mark**
†	**dagger** indicates a reference or a person who died, also called an "obelisk"
è	**diacritical mark** any mark indicating pronunciation such as a breve or accent
¨	**dieresis** placed over vowels to indicate pronunciation like the German umlaut (Lübeck)
"	**ditto mark** indicates repetition of above line
$	**dollar sign** used for numbers in U.S. dollars ($15)
‡	**double dagger** also indicates a reference or footnote
€	**Eurodollar sign** indicates numbers are in Eurodollars
¯	**macron** a horizontal line over a vowel indicating a long sound (gō)
¶	**paragraph mark** used to indicate a new paragraph, also called a pilcrow
#	**pound sign** number, hash, space sign, octothorp
®	**registered trademark**
§	**section mark**
H_2O	**subscript** any symbol written below the line
3^4	**superscript** any symbol written above the line
~	**swing dash** used in place of a part of a word previously spelled out (dia~)
~	**tilde** indicates Spanish phonome (cañon)

Chemical Secret Writing

Students love a little mystery, so teach them to write a secret message for their next encounter. It is simple; just write in clear potato juice on a paper. The writing will be invisible. To make it visible, heat the paper.

To get potato juice, squeeze pulp of a raw potato. You might have more trouble finding an old-fashioned dip-in-ink pen. Try an antique store, your grandfather's attic, or maybe use a tiny brush. Slash a quill (bird feather) with a pen knife.

Cryptography

A related fun activity is to write in code. A simple code is simply to assign a number to each letter such as:

A = 1	B = 2	C = 3	D = 4
E = 5	F = 6	G = 7	H = 8
I = 9	J = 10	K = 11	L = 12
M = 13	N = 14	O = 15	P = 16
Q = 17	R = 18	S = 19	T = 20
U = 21	V = 22	W = 23	X = 24
Y = 25	Z = 26		

Then your written message, when encrypted, would be just a string of numbers:

$$8 - 5 - 12 - 12 - 15 \quad 20 - 8 - 5 - 18 - 5$$

To be more hidden and make the code harder to crack, assign random numbers to letters. Or you can assign one letter to stand for another letter, for example A = T, B = S, and so on. Then only the person possessing the key (equivalence table) can crack the code.

Crypto- is the root meaning secret or hidden. *Cryptology* is the science of making and cracking codes. These words come from the *crypt,* which is the area under churches where people are buried. In ancient Rome when Christians were persecuted, they held secret meetings in crypts.

It is a world of words to the end of it,
In which nothing solid is its solid self.

— Wallace Stevens, "Description Without Place"

Chapter 6

FOREIGN WORDS
(Exonyms)

Exonyms are words from a foreign language that have become English words. These lists are not exhaustive, but they do show some of the diversity and richness of sources for English vocabulary.

List 113   African Words

banana

chimpanzee

cola

marimba

mumbo jumbo

raffia

safari

samba

yam

zombie

List 114   Arabic Words

admiral	alchemic
alcohol	alcove
alfalfa	algebra
almanac	amalgam
artichoke	carafe
coffee	cotton
cipher	elixir
kebab	magazine
monsoon	nadir
sofa	sherbet
tariff	zenith
zero	

List 115 Australian Aboriginal Words

boomerang
kangaroo
koala

List 116 British and American English Terms

British	American
Jolly decent!	Fine! Good!
inverted commas	quotation marks
form	school class
jersey	sweater
boot	car trunk
biscuit (sweet)	cookie
biscuit (savory)	cracker
bird	girl
bloke	guy
bobby	police officer
scones	biscuit
lorry	truck
loo	bathroom
estate agent	Realtor
chips	French fries
chemist	pharmacist
loft	attic
matron	head nurse
sister	nurse
the tube	subway
ring off	hang up (phone)
scent	perfume
provision shop	grocery store
new milk	fresh milk
acid drop	lemon drop
grill	broil
hire charge	rental
tram	street car
waste ground	empty lot
flat	apartment
haversack	backpack
draughts	checkers
off license	liquor store
waistcoat	vest

Foreign Words (Exonyms)

Celtic Words

banshee

bard

blarney

bog

craig

glen

pete

vassal

Chinese Words

china

chop suey

chow

chow mein

gung-ho

kowtow

mahjong

shantung

silk

soy

tea

tofu

typhoon

A good word is like a good tree whose root is firmly fixed, and who's top is in the sky

—The Koran, 14:24

List 119 Dutch Words

boor	buoy
bush	coleslaw
cookie	drill
etching	Santa Claus
pickle	sketch
skate	sled
skipper	sloop
sleigh	split
spoor	stoop
stove	tattoo
wagon	yacht
yawl	

List 120 French Words

annul	attorney
authority	avant-garde
bail	bizarre
bon voyage	bureau
carte blanche	café au lait
clergy	charity
coroner	cliché
elite	crime
esprit de corps	ensemble
faux pas	essay
government	gourmand
judge	grotesque
justice	jury
Mardi Gras	liberty
minister	mayor
pastor	objet d'art
public	plateau
reconnoiter	progress
résumé	quiche
ticket	rebel
traitor	religion
troop	svelt
verdict	tour de force
	treasurer
	trophy

Note: Some French words retain in English the very French spelling of –EAU endings; for example, plateau, bureau.

List 121　French Phrases

á la carte

avant-garde

bon voyage

café au lait

carte blanche

esprit de corps

faux pas

Mardi Gras

objet d'art

tour de force

List 122　German Words

angst	bivouac
delicatessen	diesel
ecology	Fahrenheit
flak	frankfurter
gestalt	Gestapo
gesundheit	hamburger
kaput	liverwurst
loaf	panzer
plunder	polka
pumpernickel	quartz
sauerkraut	schema
strudel	spiel
wanderlust	zwieback

List 123   Greek Words

academy
architect
arithmetic
athlete
cylinder
diet
drama
energy
gymnasium
homonym
logic
mathematics
monarchy
mystery
olive
philosophy
rhythm
school
tone

alphabet
aristocracy
astronomy
chaos
democracy
dialect
echo
grammar
hero
idiot
machine
method
music
ocean
organ
poem
stadium
technical

See Chapters 2, 3, and 10 for many more Greek words.

List 124   Indian Words (Native American)

chipmunk
hickory
moccasin
moose
opossum
persimmon
raccoon
skunk
squash
squaw
tepee
toboggan

Indian Words (East Indian)

bangle   bungalow
cashmere   cheetah
chintz   chit
curry   dinghy
dungaree   ginger
Juggernaut   jungle
jute   loot
pajamas   pundit
shampoo   shawl
teak   thug
veranda

Israeli Hebrew and American English Words

Israeli Hebrew	American English
Bar Mitzvah	confirmation of boys
Bat Mitzvah	confirmation of girls
Bomba	peanut-flavored snack
Challah	braided bread
Matzo (matzah)	cracker-like bread
Mazel Tov!	Congratulations! Best wishes!
Menorah	candelabra
Mitzvah	good deed
Pesach	Passover
Rosh Hashanah	New Year
Shabbat	Sabbath
Shalom	hello, goodbye, peace
Yom Kippur	Day of Atonement

Hebrew Words in Regular English

amen
balsam
behemoth
cabalistic
cherub
hosanna
jubilee
Sabbath
satanic
shibboleth

List 127 ## Italian Words

adagio	alfresco
attitude	balcony
bandit	bandit
banister	bologna
brigade	bronze
cannon	carnival
cavalry	cello
colonel	colonnade
dilettante	duel
fresco	ghetto
infantry	jean
libretto	macaroni
malaria	oratorio
parapet	pasta
pastel	piano
picturesque	pizza
relief	rotunda
sentinel	spaghetti
stiletto	stucco
trill	volcano
wig	

List 128 ## Japanese Words

bonsai
hibachi
judo
jujitsu
kamikaze
karate
origami
sayonara
sukiyaki
sushi
teriyaki
tycoon

Latin Words

Most Italian, Spanish, and French words come from Latin, hence the overlap. This list is simply some common words from Latin. There are thousands more (see Chapter 2, Roots; Chapter 3, Word Origins; and Chapter 10, Affixes and Roots). Also see Latin Phrases, List 139 in this chapter.

admire	alibi	animal
art	bland	bona fide
candidate	capitol	city
convert	culture	cum laude
data	dictator	dignity
education	fortune	fragile
genius	glory	grand
honor	judge	library
literature	luxury	marine
mental	moderate	nation
nature	noble	people
perfect	public	quality
rural	senate	solemn
stupid	tradition	tribe
via		

List 130 **Persian Words**

azure

cummerbund

divan

gypsum

jasmine

julep

scarlet

seersucker

List 131   Russian Words

commissar   cosmonaut
czar   dacha
intelligentsia   kremlin
mammoth   parka
pogrom   politburo
samovar   soviet
Sputnik   stable
steppe   troika
vodka

List 132   Spanish Words

adobe   alfalfa
alpaca   anchovy
avocado   banana
bravado   burro
cafeteria   canoe
canyon   chocolate
coyote   escapade
fiesta   hurricane
indigo   loco
maize   mesa
mosquito   palomino
patio   pinto
plaza   poncho
potato   quinine
ranch   rumba
sierra   tobacco
tomato   tornado

Other Languages

Lap Word	Philippine Word	Polynesian Word
tundra	boondocks	taboo

Portuguese Words	Turkish Words
commando	sherbet
pagoda	shish kebab
peon	yogurt
samba	

Morphemes are meaning units.
A whole word is a *morpheme.*
It is a *free* morpheme because it can stand alone.
A *bound* morpheme is a part of a word that can't stand alone.

For example, *run* is a free morpheme.
In the word *runs* the *s* is a bound morpheme because it has meaning but can't stand alone.
Most prefixes and suffixes are bound morphemes.

Prefix	Root	Suffix
un-	happi	-ness

English is truly a universal language. It is a first language in most of what was the British Empire, including the United States, Canada, Australia, and New Zealand. English is a strong second language in most of East and South Africa, India, the Fiji Islands, and places almost too numerous to mention. However, each of these places has its own dialect. A dialect is both pronunciation and the use of words. The difference between a different dialect and a different language is mutual intelligibility. Theoretically, the speaker of one language can understand, perhaps with effort, any other dialect of that language. Sometimes a dialect can be so changed that it really becomes a separate language. Pigeon English spoken in New Guinea is such a language. It is based on English vocabulary and grammar, but so different in pronunciation and word usage that it is unintelligible without study.

The Jamaican dialect is certainly a dialect of English, but it has so many words or modifications of English words that it is at first difficult to understand if you are not familiar with it. Jamaican English is a version of the Calypso English spoken in the Caribbean region. Here are some Jamaican words and their translation in the dialect called American English. Linguists tell us that everyone speaks with a dialect, but the popular notion is that a dialect is someone speaking a little differently from me.

a = is, am, to, of, to be: de bwoy a go to town

a go forein = go overseas, leave Jamaica

a wa du yu = what's wrong

aback = ago, sometime

all fruits ripe = everything is going well for you

baan = born

bad mine = to carry a grudge

bad mout = to wish bad

bad wud = bad words

badda badda = to bother constantly

badderation = problems

bakra = white supervisor

bankra = a covered picnic basket

beeny = small, tiny

booguman = a ghost, duppy

booguyaga = low class

boonoonunus = beautiful

bredda = brother, friend

bruk = broke

callaloo = Jamaican spinach

chaka chaka = cluttered

chi-chi bud = a Jamaican bird

chile = child, a young girl

chimmy = night pot, bedpan

clap down = to control

coco head = a dunce

coo dem = look at them

cotch = to support, to lean

croomoojin = deceitful

cubbitch = selfish, greedy

cum yah = come here

curry favor = favoritism

d'jew = dew, drizzle

dat = that

dawta = daughter

degge degge = only one

deh ya so = here

dreadlocks = a long matted or braided hair style

dukunu = sweet cornmeal dumplings

dun = finished

duppy = ghost

ease mi up = give me a break

eeh? = a response like yeah

eena dem wats = drunk

eggs up = a social climber

faas = inquisitive

fenky-fenky = finicky

free paper bun = holiday is over

galong = go along

guzu = witchcraft

higgler = small itinerant vendor

hurry come up = nouveau riche

irie = it's good

Jah = Rastafarian deity

jam = trouble

jinnal = a crafty person

juk = to prick

kimbo = hands on your hips

labrish = news, gossip

likka = liquor

mawga = emaciated

mek = make

mon = the most famous word in Jamaican language, as "No problem, mon!"

nize = noise

nuh = do not, don't

obeah = witchcraft

ole = old

oonu = you all

pasaro = friend

pickney = child

poppy show = show off

quashi = fool

rackstone = stone

raw-chaw = coarse, vulgar

reggae = a musical form indigenous to Jamaica

sah = sir

scuffler = thief

sinting = something

su-su = gossip

tek = take

tekkeer = so long

unnu = you (plural)

wah = what

Wah yuh a duh? = What are you doing?

wid = with

yah = here

yuh = you

zed = last letter of the alphabet

List 135 — Food with Place Names

Asian pear (Japan)
Boston baked beans (New England)
Brazil nut (Amazon jungle)
Brussels sprouts (Belgium)
Camembert cheese (Normandy, France)
Cheddar cheese (England)
Concord grapes (East Coast)
Cortland apple (Midwest)
Creole cream cheese (Louisiana)

Danish blue cheese (Denmark)
Darjeeling tea (India)
Devonshire cheese (England)
Dijon mustard (France)
Monterey Jack cheese (California)
Peking duck (China)
Puerto Rican cherry (West Indies)
Quiche Lorraine (France)
Tillamook cheese (Oregon)

List 136 — Foreign and Specialty Foods

baked Alaska—sponge cake topped with ice cream and meringue
Bavarian cream—German dessert of rich custard and gelatin
bouillabaisse—French fish stew
cajun popcorn—Louisiana shrimp deep fried
chorizo—Mexican pork sausage
chutney—East Indian condiment of fruit, sugar, vinegar, and spice
coquilles St. Jacques—French scallops in wine sauce
couscous—North African course ground wheat steamed or boiled and seasoned
dau miu—Chinese green pea shoots fried
gelato—Italian ice cream
gnocchi—Italian dumplings
haggis—Scottish animal organs and spice
hasenpfeffer—German rabbit stew
kulich—Russian Easter cake with candied fruit and saffron
menudo—Spanish tripe soup
mulligan stew—American hobo stew of meat, potatoes, and anything else
mulligatawny—East Indian soup of chicken stock and curry
nasi goreng—Indonesian fried rice with meat or fish
Oysters Rockefeller (New Orleans)—oysters baked with spinach, butter, bread crumbs
paella—Spanish saffron-flavored dish containing rice, meat, seafood, and vegetables
pemmican—American Indian cakes of dried meat and berries
pfeffernuesse—German spicy ball-shaped cookies
Reuben sandwich (New York)—corned beef, Swiss cheese, and sauerkraut on rye
roti—East Indian griddle baked bread
scalloppine—Italian thin veal floured and sautéed in wine sauce
shepherd's pie—English ground lamb topped with mashed potatoes
teriyaki—Japanese beef or chicken marinated in sweetened soy sauce
tiramisu—Italian dessert of sponge cake layered with coffee-flavored cream cheese
tsukemono—Japanese pickled vegetables
vichyssoise—French creamy potato and leek soup served cold
wonton—Chinese meat or vegetable dumplings

Major Languages

Language	Hub	Number of Speakers (in Millions)
Chinese, Mandarin	China	874
Hindi	India	366
English	United Kingdom	341
Spanish	Spain	322–358
Bengali	Bangladesh	207
Portuguese	Portugal	176
Russian	Russia	167
Japanese	Japan	125
German	Germany	100
Korean	Korea, south	78
French	France	77
Chinese, Wu	China	77
Javanese	Indonesia	75
Chinese, Yue	China	71
Telugu	India	69
Marathi	India	68
Vietnamese	Vietnam	68
Tamil	India	66
Italian	Italy	62
Turkish	Turkey	61
Urdu	Pakistan	60
Ukrainian	Ukraine	47
Gujarati	India	46
Arabic	Egypt	46

Other Chinese languages include Jinyu, Min Nan, Xiang, Hakka, Gan, and Min Bei

Note: A "Hub" is the country of origin, not necessarily the country where the most speakers reside.

Without knowing the force of words, it is impossible to know me.

—Confucius, 479 B.C.

List 138 Foreign Phrases

There are a number of foreign phrases that crop up in English conversation or writing. Although they are often several words, they must be understood as one vocabulary word or a single concept. Here are some common ones:

affair d'amour (Fr.)—a love affair
á la carte (Fr.)—each item on the menu has a separate price
á la mode (Fr.)—served with ice cream; also fashionable
alfresco (Fr.)—outdoors
alter ego (Lat.)—another side of oneself
antebellum (Lat.)—before the war, especially before the Civil War
bon vivant (Fr.)—a person who has refined tastes
bon voyage (Fr.)—have a nice trip
carte blanche (Fr.)—unlimited authority
caveat emptor (Lat.)—let the buyer beware
coup de grace (Fr.)—a merciful ending blow
cum laude (Lat.)—with honor or praise
en masse (Fr.)—in a large group
esprit de corps (Fr.)—group spirit
fait accompli (Fr.)—an established fact
faux pas (Fr.)—a social blunder
hors d'oeuvre (Fr.)—appetizer
in medias res (Lat.)—in or into the middle of a narrative or plot
in memoriam (Lat.)—in the memory of
laissez faire (Fr.)—noninterference, especially regarding trade
magnum opus (Lat.)—a masterpiece
modus operandi (Lat.)—method of operating (also M.O.)
nom de plume (Fr.)—a pen name; pseudonym
non sequitur (Lat.)—something that does not follow
nouveau riche (Fr.)—the newly rich
per annum (Lat.)—annually
per capita (Lat.)—per person
per diem (Lat.)—daily
persona non grata (Lat.)—an unacceptable person
piece de resistance (Fr.)—the main dish of a meal; the main thing or event
prima donna (Lat.)—a temperamental and conceited person
quid pro quo (Lat.)—something given or received for something else
rigor mortis (Lat.)—muscular stiffening that follows death
savoir-faire (Fr.)—ability to say and do the right thing
sholom aleichim (Heb.)—peace be with you
status quo (Lat.)—the existing condition
terra firma (Lat.)—solid ground
tour de force (Fr.)—a feat of great strength

Of course you can speak Latin. Here are some common Latin phrases that are almost English words. Also see the Latin words in List 17 of this chapter.

ad infinitum—and so on (forever)

bona fide—in good faith

caveat emptor—buyer beware

ex officio—by virtue or because of an office

ex post facto—after the fact

per annum—by the year

per capita—by the head, for each person

per diem—by the day

post mortem—after death

quid pro quo—something given or received for something else

sina qua non—essential

status quo—no change

Myths are about gods—somebody's religion. They are often allegories for psychological truths.

Legends are fantasy tales that often have some basis in historical fact.

Folktales are stories for entertainment, but they often have a moral or psychological truth.

Chapter 7

SPELLING, ABBREVIATIONS, AND PHONICS

Acronyms

Acronyms (acr-onym-s)(end + name + plural) are an interesting type of word in which each letter or a small group of letters makes up the basis and meaning of the word. For example, NATO is not pronounced N-A-T-O, but it is pronounced as if it were all one word "nato." However, NATO is an *acronym* in which each beginning letter stands for North Atlantic Treaty Organization. Here are a few other acronyms that you might be familiar with that use initial letters:

SWAT	Special Weapons and Team
NASA	National Aeronautics and Space Administration
NIMBY	Not in My Back Yard

Some acronyms use a bit more of the word than just the initial letter:

radar	RAdio Detecting and Ranging
Teflon	TEtraFLOroethylene resiN
FedEx	FEDeral EXpress

The military is a great user of acronyms; for example, COMSOPAC means the COMmander of the SOuth PACific.

It is important for vocabulary building to know what the acronym stands for, but acronyms have another interesting use and that is as a study technique. If you want to memorize a list of terms or ideas, you can put it into an acronym. For example, to memorize the colors in the spectrum and the order in which they occur, the way a prism or rainbow breaks up the white light spectrum, all you need to remember is ROY G BIV, which stands for: Red, Orange, Yellow, Green, Blue, Indigo, Violet.

Do you want to know the names of the Great Lakes? Think of HOMES: Huron, Ontario, Michigan, Erie, Superior.

Anatonyms

This is not a misspelling of antonym (words of opposite meaning) but an anatonym (anatomy + name) is using a body part as a verb such as:

foot the bill	face the music	eye a jewel
nose into something	belly up to the bar	knuckle under
head up the road	toe the line	skin a knee
hand me a spoon	finger a suspect	

Note that body parts used as adjectives are not anatonyms such as a "leggy" girl or to be "knee" deep in alligators.

List 141   Initializations

Initializations are much like acronyms except they are pronounced by each individual letter; for example, USA is pronounced U-S-A. They are widely used because of Zipf's Principle, which states that frequently used terms are shortened and, in this instance, shortened to just initials. Some initializations tend to occur in groups or related areas such as:

Business—**COD, UPS, IBM**

Crime—**DOA, DA, MO, PD**

Diseases—**AIDS, HIV, MS, CP**

Government—**IRS, CIA, USN**

Instruments—**VCR, EKG, TV**

Nations and States—**US, UK, NY, CA**

Organizations—**PTA, IRA, UN**

Positions—**CEO, VP, MD, CPA, DJ**

Radio and TV—**NBC, CBS, BBC, CNN, PBS**

Slang—**IOU, TGIF, BYOB, NIMBY, VIP**

Social—**RSVP, SWAK, WASP**

Tests—**SAT, GRE, IQ, CAT**

Universities—**MIT, NYU, USC, UCLA, BYU**

In fact, almost any term or title that is used frequently is initialized. To understand many, you need to know the local context. Many states have a DMV, which is Department of Motor Vehicles; other states might call the equivalent department the MVD. Some schools use BMOC for Big Man On Campus, while in other schools the term is not used. But if you don't know what RSVP means, you can get into a pack of human relations trouble.

A word to the wise is enough.

—Miguel de Cervantes, *Don Quixote*

Spelling, Abbreviations, and Phonics

Abbreviations are a shortened form of writing a word; for example, *Feb.* for February. They usually have several letters from the word. In this they differ from initializations and acronyms, which usually have just the first letter; for example, *USA.* But just to make matters confusing, initializations sometimes use several letters from the beginning of the word; for example, FedEx.

Abbreviations are usually followed by a period; for example, *adj.* for adjective. Initializations usually do not have a period.

What is the difference between an acronym and an initialization? The answer is pronounceability. Both use letters to refer to a group of words, but an acronym is pronounceable; for example, AIDS is a pronounceable word standing for Acquired Immune Deficiency Syndrome, whereas USA is an initialization spoken by pronouncing each letter separately. An abbreviation is a small group of letters from a pronounceable word and ends with a period.

Acronyms	Initializations	Abbreviations
AWOL	CIA	Mr.
GIGO	HMO	St.
WASP	SAT	Feb.
NATO	MRI	ex.
snafu	IQ	gal.
	SOS	adj.

See Chapter 8, Lists 167, 175, 176, 177, for abbreviations of all the U.S. and Mexican states and Canadian provinces.

Review:

acronym (acro = end, nym = name)
initialization (init = beginning, ization = noun form)
abbreviation (ab = to, brev = short)

Also see List 11.

I don't think any (one) word can explain a man's life.

—Orson Wells, *Citizen Kane*

List 143 The Most Common Abbreviations

These abbreviations are in a rough frequency order, hence, this is also a suggested teaching order. Note that different capitalization or use of a period can change the meaning. Context is very important in getting the meaning also.

Raw Abbreviation	Common Form and Meaning
Mr.	Mister; title for male adult
Mrs.	Mistress; title for married female
Miss	Mistress; title for unmarried female
Dr.	title for a doctor, drive
Fig. or fig.	figure or illustration
TV or tv	television
US or U.S.	United States
B.C.	Before Christ (date), British Columbia (Canada)
C	centigrade, Celsius, music note, cent, calorie, carbon
Ms.	title for any woman
M.S.	master of science degree
OK or ok	slang for all correct, Oklahoma
A.D.	Anno Domini (date after Christ)
ad	advertisement
F	Fahrenheit, female, French, franc, February, Friday
M	meter, mile, minute, month, male, married
etc.	et cetera, and so forth
DC or D.C.	District of Columbia, Doctor of Chiropractic
p.	page, past, penny, print, phosphorus
St.	Street, Saint, Strait
km	kilometer
A.M. or a.m.	before noon (ante meridian), amplitude modulation
com	commercial
Com.	Commander, Commodore
P.M. or p.m.	after noon (post meridian), Prime Minister
No., N., no.	number, north
DNA	deoxyribonucleic acid (in chromosomes)
e.g.	for example (exempli gratia)
DDT	an insecticide (prohibited in U.S.)
J	journal, (cards) jack
MC	master of ceremonies, Member of Congress
v	verb, volt, victory, versus, Roman numeral 5
Jr.	junior, journal
mm	millimeter
HO	head office
ho	house, also a greeting
IQ	intelligence quotient
i.e.	that is (id est)
IE	Indo-European

(continued)

Raw Abbreviation	Common Form and Meaning
N or n	north, Navy, nitrogen, November
K or k	kilobyte, slang: thousand, kilogram
UN	United Nations
ft.	feet
Ft.	fort
GNP	gross national product
USSR	Union of Soviet Socialist Republics
kg	kilogram, kegs
S	South, September, Saturday, Signor, shilling
al.	other persons (alia)
AL	Alabama, American League
g	gram
G	German, gulf, general intelligence
l	liter
L	British pound, lira, lake, long (clothing)
mi.	miles
MI	Michigan, military intelligence
Ph.	philosophy (Ph.D.)
pH	acidity scale
Co.	company, county
CO	Colorado, commanding officer
D	Democrat, December, day, doctor (Ph.D.)
d	pence
FBI	Federal Bureau of Investigation
H	hour, high, hydrogen, hits, husband, heroin
R	Republican, right, rupee, radius, river, road, royal
Mt.	mountain
MT	Montana, Mountain Time, megaton
Inc.	incorporated, included
Sec. or sec	second, secretary, section
W	West, Wednesday, watt, white, widowed, width
in.	inch
IN	Indiana
at.	attorney, atomic
AT	Atlantic Time
E	east, Easter, English, earl, earth, electronic as in (e-mail)
USA	United States of America
mph	miles per hour
t.	teaspoon, time, ton
T	tablespoon, Tuesday, territory
NASA	National Aeronautics and Space Administration

List 144   Clipped Words

Clipped words are words that are used a lot and tend to be shortened. Sometimes shortened words are close to slang (informal register), but sometimes they become quite proper words (formal register).

Most students study "math" (mathematics), go to the "gym" (gymnasium), eat a "burger" (hamburger), and sleep in a "dorm" (dormitory). If a student wanted to get dressed up, he might put on a "tie" (necktie) or if it was a really formal occasion he might wear a "tux" (tuxedo) and take a "cab" (cabriolet) or a "limo" (limousine) to the "prom" (promenade).

Here are a few other clipped words:

fridge—refrigerator
gas—gasoline
margarine—oleomargarine
mart—market, supermarket
memo—memorandum
miss—mistress
plane—airplane
zoo—zoological garden

Now see if you can expand some clipped words into their full words or vice versa.

List 145   Lengthening Words

We all know about shortening words. We say *grad* for *graduate* or *sub* for *submarine,* but how about doing the reverse? Our vocabulary might be improved if we knew that *pants* was short for *pantaloons* or *cello* was short for *violincello.* Here are a few others:

Short Form	Longer Form
bus	omnibus
cab	cabriolet
canter	Canterbury gallop
chemist	alchemist
fan	fanatic
fortnight	fourteen nights
iron	flatiron
knickers	knickerbockers
mum	chrysanthemum
perk	perquisite
piano	pianoforte
prom	promenade
wig	periwig

Geminates–Double Letters

Letter doubling is called *geminating,* which comes from the Latin *Geminorum,* literally the mythologial twins Castor and Pollux. You might also think of the Gemini (two-person space-craft) space program of the early 1960s or the third sign of the zodiac in astrology (represented as the twins).

Teachers often find it helpful to give a little explanation when they see a student making spelling errors. A common type of spelling error is failure to double a letter. The following spelling patterns might be helpful when used at the "teachable moment" in a classroom explanation. (See Chapter 9, Method 6.)

Spelling Pattern 1: Syllabification

Many double letters are explained by syllabification. If a syllable ends in a consonant and the next syllable begins with the same consonant, a double letter occurs. This often has to do with phonics; if the syllable ends in a consonant, the vowel is short. For example:

BB	hobby = hob by	**NN**	penny = pen ny
CC	occur = oc cur	**PP**	supper = sup per
DD	bladder = blad der	**RR**	hurry = hur ry
FF	office = of fice	**SS**	missal = mis sal
GG	luggage = lug gage	**TT**	little = lit tle
LL	follow = fol low	**ZZ**	blizzard = bliz zard

Spelling Pattern 2: Compound Words and Prefixes

A variation of Pattern 1, Syllabification, is the doubling of letters in compound words or when adding prefixes. The general rule in spelling compound words or adding prefixes is that both keep the full spelling of both. For example:

Compound Words

KK	bookkeeper = book + keeper
SS	misspell = mis + spell
TT	cattail = cat + tail

Prefixes

EE	reelect = re + elect
MM	commit = com + mit
NN	unnatural = un + natural

Spelling Pattern 3: Vowel Digraphs

Two vowel digraphs, OO and EE, are a source of many double-letter spellings. For example:

EE	see, three (long E sound)
OO	moon, room (long OO sound)
OO	look, cook (short OO sound)

Spelling Pattern 4: Prefix A

Some prefixes change their ending to be the same as the beginning consonant of the root. (Thus causing a double letter.)

AC	accident, accord	**AP**	applause, appeal
AF	affluent, affix	**AR**	arrest, arrive
AG	aggrandize, aggregate	**AS**	asset, associate
AL	allege, alliance	**AT**	attach, attire
AN	annex, annual		

Unfortunately, this prefix A pattern does not always work. For example, it does not work when the prefix A means "on" as in the words:

aboard	ashore
afoot	atop

Nor does it work when the prefix AB means "from" as in the words:

abhor	abolish
abnormal	abstain

Nor does it work when the prefix A means "not" as in the words:

apathy	atrophy
atheist	atypical

Nor does it work when the prefix AN means "not" as in the words:

anarchy	anesthesia
anemia	anorexia

Nor does it work when the prefix AD means "to or toward"—some words remain AD:

admit	adventure
adopt	adverse

Spelling Pattern 5: Final Consonants F, L, S, and Z

The letters F, L, S, and Z are often doubled at the end of a word. For example:

FF	cliff, off, staff
LL	ball, mill, toll, dull
SS	class, fuss, kiss
ZZ	jazz, buzz, fuzz

Spelling Pattern 6: Suffixes

Suffixes are a bit confusing, but here is a basic doubling rule:

> "You double the final consonant when the word ends in a single consonant preceded by a single vowel and the suffix begins with a vowel."

There is a nice mnemonic, "1+1+1," which means one vowel (1) followed by one consonant (+1) and you add (double) one consonant (+1). Here are some examples that follow the basic doubling rule (1+1+1):

bat—batting
big—bigger
get—getting
plan—planning
run—running
ship—shipping

Note that you *do not double* these final consonants:

find—finding *(because the root ends in two consonants)*
rain—rained *(because the vowel has two letters)*
run—runs *(because the suffix begins with a consonant)*
saw—sawing *(because AW is a vowel digraph)*
say—saying *(because AY is a vowel digraph)*

Spelling Pattern 7: Prefix Sub-

The prefix *sub-,* meaning "under," usually is spelled sub- as in "subscribe"; however, sometimes the "b" is changed to the beginning consonant to make a double letter in the word, for example:

CC	success (cess = go) (to go from under)
FF	suffer (fer = bear)
GG	suggest (gest = carry)
MM	summary (ary = noun)
PP	support (port = carry)
RR	surround (round = round)

Spelling Pattern 8: Prefix Com-

Although much less common, the prefix *com-,* meaning "with," sometimes doubles the root beginning consonant, for example:

LL	collateral (lateral = side)
MM	comment (men = mind)
NN	connect (nect = tie)
RR	correlate (cor = relation)

A number of English words contain silent letters. Often this is just fine if you wish to trace the word's origin, but they sure cause a lot of trouble for spellers.

Silent A	soared
Silent B	climb, thumb, bomb (MB final consonant digraph), subtle, debt, doubt
Silent C	muscle
Silent G	gnaw, gnat (GN digraph), sign, malign, paradigm
Silent H	ghost, honest, chord, heir, vehicle; /h/ /wh/ (many WH words have either a silent H or HW pronunciation, such as *what*, *who*)
Silent GH	caught, tight, fight, thought, night
Silent K	knight, knife, knead (KN digraph)
Silent L	could, would, half
Silent N	solemn, column, autumn (MN digraph)
Silent P	raspberry, pneumonia
Silent T	listen, fasten, castle
Silent W	sword, wreath, wrong, write, answer (W before R)
Silent E	robe, side (Final E Rule makes vowel long) battle, possible (Final LE digraph) toe, Joe (OE digraph) fasten, listen (Final EN digraph) come, above (the final E in other vowel words)

Spelling bees are done informally in many schools, but there is a formal structure (contest) sponsored by the Scripps Howard Newspapers every year with local winners going to Washington, D.C., for the National Spelling Bee. Here are some words used in those contests. If you are interested in entering any child or getting a practice booklet of words, contact your local Scripps Howard Newspaper or write: Scripps Howard National Spelling Bee, 1100 Central Trust Tower, Cincinnati, OH 45202. Entrants must not have graduated from the 8th grade.

These words are obviously for very gifted spellers. For more traditional spelling lists, you might use the *Instant Words* in List 161 or select words from the many other lists in this book.

First-Round Words

abate	aggravate	barbed
bracket	cellblock	dank
downright	favoring	garment
heavyset	injure	killjoy
lodging	minefield	orally
pierce	quarterback	sackcloth
separate	tawny	vacant

Intermediate Words

abactor	aplastic	belaud
bunion	cholesterol	controversy
deflationary	drippage	evolvable
forename	grandeur	horsehair
intestine	jabberwocky	lexical
mainprise	myopia	oncology
paraph	plauditory	protractor
reassert	ruinous	sealskin
septic	sturgeon	thyroid

Final-Round Words

aardwolf	apiculus	bellwort
bungee	chogset	contrabass
deflocculate	drisheen	evulsion
foreordain	grandeeship	honestone
intrait	lebbek	maricolous
movimento	opeidoscope	pergelisol
potpourri	radzimir	rosorial
serfism	solvolysis	stupulose
thaumatology	turriferous	vorago

Winning Words

abbacy	acquiesced	asceticism
brethren	cambist	condominium
croissant	deification	elucubrate
hydrophyte	incisor	luge
maculature	milieu	narcolepsy
onerous	propitiatory	propylaeum
psoriasis	purim	sarcophagus
shalloon	transept	vouchsafe

Most people have enough trouble trying to spell even ordinary words; then along comes some clever advertising executive who shows us how to spell many things wrong. But it is interesting that advertising respells actually have some rules, or at least classifications. Linguists even have a term for intentional misspellings; they call them disglossia. Here are some of them:

Types of Respells	Examples
1. Shortening	**flo, blok**
2. Schwa deletion	**chickn, flavr**
3. Use of homophones	**hart** for **heart, lox** for **locks**
4. Omitting "gh"	**do** for **dough, delit** for **delight**
5. Old English spelling	**Olde, Shoppe, Publick**
6. Use of letter names	**EZ** for **easy, NU** for **new**
7. Inventive respelling	**cum** for **come, Tylenol**
8. Use of numbers	**Factory 2 You, The Best 1, Flowers 4 Her**
9. Letter doubling	**Exxon, Ladd, Xxtra, Flyy, Arrid**
10. Infrequent letter use (k, q, x, z)	**Klean, Sudz Laundry, Noz Drops, Xtra care**

Examples of Respells

Uneeda biscuit	You need a
Publick House	Old English
Cheez-it	Cheese It
Bake-n-serve	Bake and serve
Snoop Doggy Dogg	Dog
Ice-T	ice tea
Sit-N-Bull	Chief Sitting Bull
Az-Nu enamel	As new
Kopper Kettle Klub	Cooper Kettle Club
EZ Walker	Easy Walker
Ride Rite	Ride right

Advertising Suffixes   **Examples**

(add to almost any word)

-orama or -arama	**foodarama, scoutorama**
-wise	**pricewise, timewise**
-athon	**saleathon, walkathon**
-ize or –ise	**sanatize, rubberize**
-proof	**childproof, rainproof**
-ola	**granola, Crayola, payola**

Here is a list of vowel phonemes (sounds) in English. Some dictionaries might have a few more minor distinctions, but this is about the amount of phonics taught in most schools. They are presented in an order of commonness (frequency of occurrence), as well as a suggested teaching order (teach the most common first).

Main Graphemes	Phoneme Example	Grapheme Example	Common Alternate Graphemes and Example
I	Short /i/	*in*	I – E *give*, A – E *village*, Y *system*
A	Short /a/	*at*	A – E *dance*
E	Short /e/	*end*	EA *head*, E – E *fence*
ER	Schwa R /ər/	*her*	OR *labor*, UR *turn*, AR *dollar*, IR *girl*
O	Long /ō/	*open*	O – E *home*, OA *oat*, OW *own*
E	Long /ē/	*me*	Y *funny*, EE *keep*, EA *eat*
U	Short /u/	*other*	U *up*, A *ago*, I *animal*, E *effect*, OU *double*, O *son*, E – E *violence*
O	Short /o/	*not*	
A	Long /ā/	*agent*	A – E *ate*, AI *rain*, AY *day*, A *danger*
U	Long /ū/	*unit*	U – E *tune*, OO *moon*, EW *new*
I	Long /ī/	*ice*	I *item*, Y *my*
A	Broad /ä/	*are*	
O	Broad /ô/	*for*	AL *all*, AU *auto*, O *off*, AW *awful*
OU	/ou/	*out*	OW *owl*
OO	Short /o͝o/	*pull*	OO *look*
OI	/oi/	*oil*	OY *toy*
AR	/ê/ or /â/	*vary*	ARE *care*, AIR *fair*

---

[*]We apologize if this phonics vowel list is too condensed, but it contains most of the pertinent phonics information for teaching reading. If you want to see phonics laid out more leisurely and with many examples, see *The Reading Teacher's Book of Lists,* fourth edition (Fry et al., 2002) and/or *Phonic Patterns* (Fry, 1999c).

Here is a list of consonant graphemes (letters and digraphs). Like the vowel phoneme list, it is presented in a frequency order, which is also a suggested teaching order.

Grapheme	Example	Irregularities
R	rat	/r/ spelled WR *write*
T	ten	/t/ spelled ED *hooked*
N	not	/n/ spelled EN *dozen,* KN *knife*
S	sat	S=/s/ *sat,* S=/z/ *his*
L	lap	/l/ spelled LE *able*
C	cat	no phoneme, C=/k/, C=/s/
D	dog	
P	pet	
M	man	
B	boy	
F	fat	/f/ spelled PH *phone*
V	van	
G	gap	
H	him	
K	key	/k/ most commonly spelled C *cat,* CK
W	wet	
TH	thin	voiceless/th/ *thin,* voiced/TH/ *this*
SH	she	/sh/ most commonly spelled TI *action,* CI
NG	sing	/ng/ spelled N *think*
CH	chat	/ch/ spelled T *picture*
X	box	no phoneme, X represents /ks/ *box*
Z	zoo	/z/ most commonly spelled S *his*
J	job	/j/ most commonly spelled G *gem*
QU	quiz	no phoneme, QU represents /kw/ *quit*
WH	what	WH= /hw/ or /w/ *when*
Y	yes	Y is most commonly a vowel as in *very*

*We apologize if this phonics consonant list is too condensed, but it contains most of the pertinent phonics information for teaching reading. If you want to see phonics laid out more leisurely and with many examples, see *The Reading Teacher's Book of Lists,* fourth edition (Fry et al., 2002) and/or *Phonic Patterns* (Fry, 1999c).

Phonics—Phonograms

Phonograms are a part of a word that contains the vowel and following consonant sound. They are often used in teaching phonics because substituting the initial consonant sound is a time-honored, interesting, and effective teaching technique. Breaking a single-syllable word into the *onset* (initial consonant) and *rime* (phonogram) is a more modern technique used in some contexts.

Phonogram	Example Words
-ay	jay, say, pay, day, play
-ill	hill, Bill, will, fill, spill
-ip	ship, dip, tip, skip, trip
-at	cat, fat, bat, rat, sat
-am	ham, jam, dam, ram, Sam
-ag	bag, rag, tag, wag, sag
-ack	back, sack, Jack, black, track
-ank	bank, sank, tank, blank, drank
-ick	sick, Dick, pick, quick, chick
-ell	bell, sell, fell, tell, yell
-ot	pot, not, hot, dot, got
-ing	ring, sing, king, wing, thing
-ap	cap, map, tap, clap, trap
-unk	sunk, junk, bunk, flunk, skunk
-ail	pail, jail, nail, sail, tail
-ain	rain, pain, main, chain, plain
-eed	feed, seed, weed, need, freed
-y	my, by, dry, try, fly
-out	pout, trout, scout, shout, spout
-ug	rug, bug, hug, dug, tug
-op	mop, cop, pop, top, hop
-in	pin, tin, win, chin, thin
-an	pan, man, ran, tan, Dan
-est	best, nest, pest, rest, test
-ink	pink, sink, rink, link, drink
-ow	low, slow, grow, show, snow
-ew	new, few, chew, grew, blew
-ore	more, sore, tore, store, score
-ed	bed, red, fed, led, Ted
-ab	cab, dab, jab, lab, crab
-ob	cob, job, rob, Bob, knob
-ock	sock, rock, lock, dock, block
-ake	cake, lake, make, take, brake
-ine	line, nine, pine, fine, shine
-ight	knight, light, right, night, fight
-im	swim, him, Kim, rim, brim
-uck	duck, luck, suck, truck, buck
-um	gum, bum, hum, drum, plum

Here is a list of commonly misspelled words to watch out for or to use to make a tricky spelling lesson.

Wrong	Right	Wrong	Right
absolutly	absolutely	gaurdian	guardian
abundent	abundant	graditude	gratitude
acceptence	acceptance	ignorence	ignorance
accomodate	accommodate	imortal	immortal
accordence	accordance	inocent	innocent
acknowlege	acknowledge	interupt	interrupt
addministration	administration	labratory	laboratory
advertisment	advertisement	memry	memory
ammendment	amendment	magnificient	magnificent
antisipate	anticipate	merchandize	merchandise
anual	annual	morgage	mortgage
appitite	appetite	murmer	murmur
aquire	acquire	neice	niece
artifical	artificial	occured	occurred
beniefit	benefit	offical	official
boundry	boundary	pamflet	pamphlet
bullitin	bulletin	parliment	parliament
campain	campaign	pecular	peculiar
Christain	Christian	posibility	possibility
civilazation	civilization	posibly	possibly
commencment	commencement	positivly	positively
commision	commission	presense	presence
comunication	communication	recieving	receiving
concience	conscience	rememberance	remembrance
condem	condemn	representitive	representative
courtious	courteous	resturant	restaurant
curcumstance	circumstance	similiar	similar
curiousity	curiosity	sincerly	sincerely
curtesy	courtesy	subsitute	substitute
decend	descend	succeded	succeeded
equiped	equipped	sufficint	sufficient
exibition	exhibition	temperary	temporary
extention	extension	transfered	transferred
Febuary	February	unecessary	unnecessary

Allophone = slight variations in the pronunciation of a phoneme caused by the phoneme's environment (adjacent sounds) and speaker's dialect.

Phoenician Alphabet = The Phoenicians started our whole writing system around 1000 B.C. It was modified by the Romans so we call our alphabet the Roman alphabet.

Phoneme = The minimal speech sound that changes meaning. Ex. "cat-can." Most consonant letters have one phoneme. Ex. T = /t/ as in "top." Most vowel letters have several phonemes. Ex. A = /ā/ as in "may" and /ă/ as in "cat."

Phonemic Analysis = Linguistic research identifying speech sounds. Also done by speech therapists.

Phonemic Awareness = The awareness that spoken words are composed of phonemes (different sounds). Also called phonological awareness. Some feel it should be taught in kindergarten or to any beginning or remedial reader.

Phonetic Alphabet = A special alphabet for writing down phonemes (phonetic transcription) in any language such as the IPA, International Phonetic Alphabet. Used in research. Some dictionaries or research projects may have their own phonetic alphabet or system of respellings.

Phonetic Spelling = The respelling of words to more simply show how the word is spoken. Ex. season = see sun. Dictionaries have their own pronunciation systems.

Phonetic Transcription = A linguist's way of writing down phonemes usually using the IPA, International Phonetic Alphabet. Also called phonemic transcription. Very distantly related to invented spelling.

Phonetics = The linguistic study of speech sounds. Some teachers say "phonetics" when they mean "phonics." "Phonemics" is an even more technical linguistic term. All are part of phonology.

Phonic Analysis = A reading teaching practice that attempts to apply phonics to reading by attacking unknown words using phoneme-grapheme and phonic generalizations (sounding out words).

Phonic Generalization = A statement or rule that identifies the conditions in which a letter or group of letters make a specific sound. Ex. Final E Rule.

Phonics = A way of teaching reading that stresses letter-sound relationships (phoneme-grapheme correspondence).

Suprasegmental Phoneme = A change in sound other than a phoneme that changes meaning. Ex. word emphasis in a sentence, juncture, and/or pause. Note the meaning change: *I* did not say no. I did not *say* no. I did not say *no*.

List 155 Anagrams

An *anagram* is a word or a phrase made by rearranging the letters in another word or phrase; for example, "angel" is an anagram for "glean" or vice versa (ana = against, gram = letter or write). They are useful to interest students in words and their spelling and units. Anagrams also are part of many games such as Scrabble and worksheets found in classroom lessons on spelling and vocabulary building.

Shorten Words

rail – air
bear – ear
rate – rat

Rearrange Letters

united – untied
swine – wines
care – race
rail – lair
bear – bare
rate – tear

Hidden Parts

April – rip
black – balk
spelling – pen gills

"When I use a word," Humpty Dumpty said in a rather scornful tone, "It means just what I chose it to mean—neither more nor less."
"The question is," said Alice, "whether you can make words mean so many things."

—Lewis Carroll, *Through the Looking Glass*

Homographs

Homographs are words that have the same spelling but different meanings. Most homographs have the same pronunciation (homo = same, graph = write). An example of a homograph is *hawk,* as in "the *hawk* is flying" and "to *hawk* wares at a market." The thing that makes a homograph rather than just a word with multiple meanings is that a *homograph* has a different origin; about the only practical way to find this out is to look up the word in a dictionary. A homograph has two or more entries (words and their definitions appear separately).

In this list, all of these words are *homophones;* they are pronounced the same. If they were pronounced differently, they would be *heteronyms* (see List 158 in this chapter).

arms (body parts) — **arms** (weapons)

bail (money for release) — **bail** (handle of a pail) — **bail** (throw water out)

chuck (throw or toss) — **chuck** (cut of beef)

date (day, month, and year) — **date** (sweet dark fruit)

egg (oval or round body laid by a bird) — **egg** (encourage)

fan (device to stir up the air) — **fan** (admirer)

game (pastime) — **game** (lame) — **game** (hunted animals)

hide (conceal; keep out of sight) — **hide** (animal skin)

jam (fruit preserve) — **jam** (press or squeeze) — **jam** (impromptu musical performance)

kind (friendly; helpful) — **kind** (same class)

last (at the end) — **last** (continue; endure)

mule (cross between donkey and horse) — **mule** (type of slipper)

net (open-weave fabric) — **net** (remaining after deductions)

pen (instrument for writing) — **pen** (enclosed yard)

rank (row or line) — **rank** (having a bad odor)

sage (wise person) — **sage** (herb)

tap (strike lightly) — **tap** (faucet)

vault (storehouse for valuables) — **vault** (jump over)

wake (stop sleeping) — **wake** (trail left behind a ship)

yen (strong desire) — **yen** (unit of money in Japan)

Second Meaning Versus Homographs

Many words have several different meanings (polysemy). Here are a few words that have different meanings:

major	**First meaning:** large or important ("major corporations")
major	**Second meaning:** rank of officer in the army ("Major Smith was in charge of trucks.")
story	**First meaning:** a tale or description of some happening ("The boys saw a story on TV.")
story	**Second meaning:** a set of rooms on one level of a building ("They live in a two-story house.")

Here are some more double-meaning words. These are called homographs because, besides having multiple meanings, they have different origins (dictionaries list each one):

bay (alcove between columns)	**bay** (aromatic leaf used in cooking)	
bay (howl)	**bay** (part of a sea)	**bay** (reddish brown)
fawn (try to get favor by slavish acts)	**fawn** (young deer)	
hatch (bring forth young from an egg)	**hatch** (opening in a ship's deck)	
scale (balance)	**scale** (outer layer of fish and snakes)	**scale** (series of steps)
staple (metal fastener for paper)	**staple** (principal element)	
strain (group with an inherited quality)	**strain** (pull tight)	
temple (building for worship)	**temple** (side of forehead)	
tick (pillow covering)	**tick** (small insect)	**tick** (sound of a clock)

Also see Method 16.

Spelling, Abbreviations, and Phonics

A *heteronym* is a special kind of homograph. Like a homograph, a heteronym has the same spelling and different meanings, but *heteronyms have different pronunciations*. For example: a *bass* fish and a *bass* voice.

bass (low male voice)	**bass** (kind of fish)
close (shut)	**close** (near)
commune (talk intimately)	**commune** (group of people living together)
content (all things inside)	**content** (satisfied)
converse (talk)	**converse** (opposite)
desert (dry barren region)	**desert** (go away from)
does (plural of *doe*)	**does** (present tense of *to do*)
dove (pigeon)	**dove** (did dive)
entrance (going in)	**entrance** (delight; charm)
incense (substance with a sweet smell when burned)	**incense** (make very angry)
intimate (very familiar)	**intimate** (suggest)
invalid (disabled person)	**invalid** (not valid)
lead (show the way)	**lead** (metallic element)
live (exist)	**live** (having life)
minute (sixty seconds)	**minute** (very small)
object (a thing)	**object** (to protest)
record (music disk)	**record** (write down)
refuse (say no)	**refuse** (waste; trash)
sow (scatter seeds)	**sow** (female pig)
tear (drop of liquid from the eye)	**tear** (pull apart)

A *heteronym* is a word that is spelled the same as another word but has a different pronunciation and meaning. For example, the word *address* is pronounced with the stress on the first syllable when it is a noun—"the *address* of my school," and the stress is on the second syllable when it is a verb—"to *address* the audience." Actually this shifts the schwa (unaccented vowel).

It is tough and not always accurate to make generalizations, but there is another class of heterophones in which there is a larger change of *phoneme* and a change in meaning; for example, *bow* as in "the *bow* of the ship" and "*bow* and arrow."

And as is usual with generalizations, there are always some words that do not fit either generalization; for example, *read* as in "*read* to me" and "he *read* a book."

Stress Shift (Schwa)/Meaning Change	Phoneme Change/Meaning Change
address	bow
annex	bass
convict	close
escort	dose
object	invalid
protest	lead
release	row
uplift	wind

Adjective/Verb

deliberate

duplicate

Phoenix—mythical bird representing death and rebirth

After 500 years, the phoenix's nest burst into flames so that a new phoenix could rise from the ashes.

One Word or Two? The Compound Problem

When in doubt, for more common terms, make them into one word (a compound word). For example: *airplane* and *airline* are more common than *air force* or *air express*. Likewise *backpack* is more common than *back street*.

Hyphenated words are much less common, and they tend to be adjectives (modifying a noun). For example: *air-cooled* engine or *brick-red* paint.

But hyphenated words are also used to turn a common saying into a noun, for example: "in the sweet *by-and-by*" or "without even a *by-your-leave*."

Here are a few more compound versus two-word terms; remember that there are many common compound words using these initial combining forms.

Compound Word	Two Words	Hyphenated Words
ballfield	ball bearing	ball-like
bellboy	bell jar	bell-bottom
corncob	corn bread	corn-fed
debate	de facto	de-emphasize
grandmother	grand master	grand-slammed
greyhound	gray paint (also note spelling difference)	
indoor	in excess	
jobseeker	job lot	job-hopping
lowdown	low rent	low-grade
roommate	room clerk	room-sized
roundtable	round steak	round-trip
setback	set forth	set-in
soundstage	sound effects	sound-and-light show
ticketholder	ticket office	

I have reported on what I saw and heard, but only part of it. For most of it, I have no words.

—Edward R. Murrow, Broadcast on Buchenwald Camp

Instant Words

The Instant Words are important because:

1. You can't read a sentence or a paragraph without knowing at least the most common.

2. You can't write a sentence or a paragraph without knowing at least the most common.

3. They are ranked in a frequency order, the most common first. This gives a teaching order based on need. The most common word in the English language is *the,* the next most common is *of,* and so on. The first 100 Instant Words are 50 percent of all written materials and the first 300 Instant Words are 65 percent of all written materials.

4. They are well-researched. They are based on a five-million-word count, which has been modified to give the most common form of the word.

5. They are well-used in thousands of regular elementary classrooms, in remedial reading and inner city situations, and in ESL (English as a second language) classes.

Research Base

Many educators are concerned about the research base of the curriculum they are teaching because of their professional training and because some government-funded grants require it. Here is the research base for the Instant Words.

The first version of the Instant Words was published by Fry in 1957, based on early reading and writing word frequency counts by Thorndike (1944) and others, including a Japanese World War II code crackers' list. But the present Instant Words are based on a five-million-word count done by Carroll et al. (1971) and modified by Sakiey (1977) and Fry (1998, 2000).

The 1971 word count of 5,088,721 words, known as the Carroll List or the American Heritage List, was based on a wide variety of school texts and popular magazines. They counted every variant form of a word as a separate word. Hence the words "run, runs, running, run," and so on each received a different frequency count and a different rank. Sakiey and Fry collapsed each of those variant word forms into one word, the most common form. Hence the counts from each of the variant forms of "run" were added together and the most common form, "run," was reranked using that total count. The Instant Words then had a far different ranking from the Carroll count.

Use

The use of the Instant Words has been validated by many years of use in many classrooms. They were first used in the Reading Clinic of Loyola University in Los Angeles and later at Rutgers University in New Jersey, where Fry taught graduate courses in reading. They subsequently have appeared in numerous college textbooks on reading teaching methods and have been incorporated in the curriculum of many school districts for both reading instruction and spelling instruction. The first 1,000 Instant Words are currently being published in *The Reading Teacher's Book of Lists,* which has sold over 300,000 copies, and all 3,000 Instant Words are in the spelling book and other curriculum materials by Teacher Created Materials.

Standards

Some standards were established for the amount of Instant Words that should be known in the primary grades based on data from a large California school that had a fairly high percentage of students with limited English. Here are the Instant Words that should be known (read) by the end of the first three grades:

Grade	Standard: Number of Words Known	Percent of Students Reaching the Standard
Kindergarten	50	45
1st Grade	150	76
2nd Grade	300	77

The Instant Words were only part of the language arts curriculum. The Instant Words were taught by flashcard, word walls, games, and writing lessons. Students also read many books and were frequently tested (three times a year) on the number of Instant Words that they could read orally. No meaningful standard that is objective and numerical can be reached by all students, but having approximately three out of four students reaching the standard in grades 1 and 2 is a reasonable goal.

First Hundred

Words 1-25	Words 26-50	Words 51-75	Words 76-100
the	or	will	number
of	one	up	no
and	had	other	way
a	by	about	could
to	word	out	people
in	but	many	my
is	not	then	than
you	what	them	first
that	all	these	water
it	were	so	been
he	we	some	call
was	when	her	who
for	your	would	oil
on	can	make	its
are	said	like	now
as	there	him	find
with	use	into	long
his	an	time	down
they	each	has	day
I	which	look	did
at	she	two	get
be	do	more	come
this	how	write	made
have	their	go	may
from	if	see	part

Common suffixes: -s, -ing, -ed, -er, -ly, -est

Second Hundred

Words 101-125	Words 126-150	Words 151-175	Words 176-100
over	say	set	try
new	great	put	kind
sound	where	end	hand
take	help	does	picture
only	through	another	again
little	much	well	change
work	before	large	off
know	line	must	play
place	right	big	spell
year	too	even	air
live	mean	such	away
me	old	because	animal
back	any	turn	house
give	same	here	point
most	tell	why	page
very	boy	ask	letter
after	follow	went	mother
thing	came	men	answer
our	want	read	found
just	show	need	study
name	also	land	still
good	around	different	learn
sentence	farm	home	should
man	three	us	America
think	small	move	world

Common suffixes: -s, -ing, -ed, -er, -ly, -est

Third Hundred

Words 201-225	Words 226-250	Words 251-275	Words 276-300
high	saw	important	miss
every	left	until	idea
near	don't	children	enough
add	few	side	eat
food	while	feet	facet
between	along	car	watch
own	might	mile	far
below	close	night	Indian
country	something	walk	really
plant	seem	white	almost
last	next	sea	let
school	hard	began	above
father	open	grow	girl
keep	example	took	sometimes
tree	begin	river	mountain
never	life	four	cut
start	always	carry	young
city	those	state	talk
earth	both	once	soon
eye	paper	book	list
light	together	hear	song
thought	got	stop	being
head	group	without	leave
under	often	second	family
story	run	later	it's

Common suffixes: -s, -ing, -ed, -er, -ly, -est

Fourth Hundred

Words 301-325	Words 326-350	Words 351-375	Words 376-400
body	order	listen	farm
music	red	wind	pulled
color	door	rock	draw
stand	sure	space	voice
sun	become	covered	seen
question	top	fast	cold
fish	ship	several	cried
area	across	hold	plan
mark	today	himself	notice
dog	during	toward	south
horse	short	five	sing
birds	better	step	war
problem	best	morning	ground
complete	however	passed	fall
room	low	vowel	king
knew	hours	true	town
since	black	hundred	I'll
ever	products	against	unit
piece	happened	pattern	figure
told	whole	numeral	certain
usually	measure	table	field
didn't	remember	north	travel
friends	early	slowly	wood
easy	waves	money	fire
heard	reached	map	upon

Fifth Hundred

Words 401-425	Words 426-450	Words 451-475	Words 476-500
done	decided	plane	filled
English	contain	system	heat
road	course	behind	full
halt	surface	ran	hot
ten	produce	round	check
fly	building	boat	am
gave	ocean	game	object
box	class	force	rule
finally	note	brought	among
wait	nothing	understand	noun
correct	rest	warm	power
oh	carefully	common	cannot
quickly	scientists	bring	able
person	inside	explain	six
became	wheels	dry	size
shown	stay	though	dark
minutes	green	language	ball
strong	known	shape	material
verb	island	deep	special
stars	week	thousands	heavy
front	less	yes	fine
feel	machine	clear	pair
fact	base	equation	circle
inches	ago	yet	include
street	stood	government	built

Sixth Hundred

Words 501-525	Words 526-550	Words 551-575	Words 576-600
can't	pickled	legs	beside
matter	simple	sat	gone
square	cells	main	sky
syllables	paint	winter	glass
perhaps	mind	wide	million
bill	love	written	west
felt	cause	length	lay
suddenly	rain	reason	weather
test	exercise	kept	root
direction	eggs	interest	instruments
center	train	arms	meet
farmers	blue	brother	third
ready	wish	race	months
anything	drop	present	paragraph
divided	developed	beautiful	raised
general	window	store	represent
energy	difference	job	soft
subject	distance	edge	whether
Europe	heart	past	clothes
moon	sit	sign	flowers
region	sum	record	shall
return	summer	finished	teacher
believe	wall	discovered	held
dance	forest	wild	describe
members	probably	happy	drive

Seventh Hundred

Words 601-625	Words 626-650	Words 651-675	Words 676-700
cross	already	hair	rolled
speak	instead	age	bear
solve	phrase	amount	wonder
appear	soil	scale	smiled
metal	bed	pounds	angle
son	copy	although	fraction
either	free	per	Africa
ice	hope	broken	killed
sleep	spring	moment	melody
village	case	tiny	bottom
factors	laughed	possible	trip
result	nation	gold	hole
jumped	quite	milk	poor
snow	type	quiet	let's
ride	themselves	natural	fight
care	temperature	lot	surprise
floor	bright	stone	French
hill	lead	act	died
pushed	everyone	build	beat
baby	method	middle	exactly
buy	section	speed	remain
century	lake	count	dress
outside	consonant	cat	iron
everything	within	someone	couldn't
tall	dictionary	sail	fingers

Eighth Hundred

Words 701-725	Words 726-750	Words 751-775	Words 776-800
row	president	yourself	caught
least	brown	control	fell
catch	trouble	practice	team
climbed	cool	report	God
wrote	cloud	straight	captain
shouted	lost	rise	direct
continued	sent	statement	ring
itself	symbols	stick	serve
else	wear	party	child
plains	bad	seeds	desert
gas	save	suppose	increase
England	experiment	woman	history
burning	engine	coast	cost
design	alone	bank	maybe
joined	drawing	period	business
foot	east	wire	separate
law	pay	choose	break
ears	single	clean	uncle
grass	touch	visit	hunting
you're	information	bit	flow
grew	express	whose	lady
skin	mouth	received	students
valley	yard	garden	human
cents	equal	please	art
key	decimal	strange	feeling

Ninth Hundred

Words 801-825	Words 826-850	Words 851-875	Words 876-900
supply	guess	thick	major
corner	silent	blood	observe
electric	trade	lie	tube
insects	rather	spot	necessary
crops	compare	bell	weight
tone	crowd	fun	meat
hit	poem	loud	lifted
sand	enjoy	consider	process
doctor	elements	suggested	army
provide	indicate	thin	hat
thus	except	position	property
won't	expect	entered	particular
cook	flat	fruit	swim
bones	seven	tied	terms
tail	interesting	rich	current
board	sense	dollars	park
modern	string	send	sell
compound	blow	sight	shoulder
mine	famous	chief	industry
wasn't	value	Japanese	wash
fit	wings	stream	block
addition	movement	planets	spread
belong	pole	rhythm	cattle
safe	exciting	eight	wife
soldiers	branches	science	sharp

Tenth Hundred

Words 901-925	Words 926-950	Words 951-975	Words 976-1,000
company	sister	gun	total
radio	oxygen	similar	deal
we'll	plural	death	determine
action	various	score	evening
capital	agreed	forward	nor
factories	opposite	stretched	rope
settled	wrong	experience	cotton
yellow	chart	rose	apple
isn't	prepared	allow	details
southern	pretty	fear	entire
truck	solution	workers	corn
fair	fresh	Washington	substances
printed	shop	Greek	smell
wouldn't	suffix	women	tools
ahead	especially	bought	conditions
chance	shoes	led	cows
born	actually	march	track
level	nose	northern	arrived
triangle	afraid	create	located
molecules	dead	British	sir
France	sugar	difficult	seat
repeated	adjective	match	division
column	fig	win	effect
western	office	doesn't	underline
church	huge	steel	view

Spelling Demons

Six out of ten eighth graders can't spell these words (Greene, 1954). And many college students would miss quite a few. So teach them. See Methods 22, 23, and 24 in Chapter 9 for teaching suggestions.

accommodate	accustomed	achievement
acknowledgement	acquaint	acquire
adequate	affidavit	altar
analysis	anticipate	anxiety
appetite	approximately	artificial
bankruptcy	benefit	bough
boys' (pl. poss.)	bulletin	bureau
campaign	cancellation	characteristic
circuit	collateral	colonel
committed	committee	competition
compliment	conceive	condemn
conscience	conscious	consequence
continuous	controversy	convenience
counsel	courteous	crisis
criticism	curiosity	cylinder
debtor	definite	definitely
descend	despair	discipline
distinguish	doctrine	dormitory
efficiency	efficient	eligible
eliminate	embroidery	encouraging
epistle	equipped	exceptionally
excessive	executive	exhibition
existence	extraordinary	facilities
fascinating	financial	flu
foliage	fortunately	fraternity
guarantee	hygiene	icicles
immediately	immense	incidentally
inconvenience	indefinitely	inevitable
initial	initiation	installation
intellectual	intelligence	intimate
laboratory	license	lieutenant
manufacturer	mathematics	minimum
mortgage	murmur	necessarily
occasionally	occurred	offense
opportunities	ordinarily	originally
pamphlet	pamphlets	parliament
partial	peculiar	perceive
peril	petition	philosophy
physician	pilgrims	politician
possess	practically	precisely
principle	prior	privilege
psychology	pursuit	receipt
recommend	recommended	reign
remembrance	representative	requisition
restaurant	schedule	separately
shepherd	skis	solemn
sorority	specific	statistics
statues	sufficient	sufficiently
supplement	suspicion	temporarily
thorough	thoroughly	tournament
tragedy	transferred	unanimous
undoubtedly	unnecessary	utilize
vacancies	vague	veil
wretched	wrought	

Spelling, Abbreviations, and Phonics

There are a number of special spelling rules for adding suffixes that change the form of a word (tense of a verb, part of speech) or the meaning (root word + suffix). Most of them are aids to pronouncing the new word; that is, they help make the transition of sounds within the word smoother. Focus on one rule at a time and use lots of examples. (See List 164, Plurals, in this chapter for additional information on spelling rules for forming plurals.)

One spelling rule is that the suffix spelling never changes (except for plural "s" to "es"), but the root can change ("make" to "making").

Basic rule for adding suffixes to change the verb form, compare adjectives, change a word to an adverb, or make a word plural: Just add the suffix.

want + s = wants	want + ing = wanting	want + ed = wanted
talk + s = talks	talk + ing = talking	talk + ed = talked
tall + er = taller	smart + er = smarter	slow + ly = slowly
tall + est = tallest	smart + est = smartest	quick + ly = quickly
chair + s = chairs	book + s = books	bill + s = bills

If a word ends in "e":

- If a word ends in "e," drop the final "e" if the suffix begins with a vowel.
  rose to *rosy*   *dine* to *dining*   *name* to *named*   *note* to *notable*
- If a word ends in "e," keep the final "e" if the suffix begins with a consonant.
  safe to *safely*   *care* to *careful*   *tire* to *tireless*   *strange* to *strangeness*
- If a word ends in "e," keep the final "e" if it is preceded by a vowel.
  see to *seeing*

If a word ends in "y":

- If a word ends in "y," change the "y" to "i" if the "y" is preceded by a consonant.
  carry to *carried*
- Sometimes change "y" to "ie."
  cry to *cries*   *lady* to *ladies*
- If a word ends in "y," keep the "y" if it is preceded by a vowel.
  joy to *joyful*
- If a word ends in "y," keep the "y" if the suffix begins with "i."
  marry to *marrying*

If a word ends in "c":

- If a word ends in "c," add a "k" before a suffix beginning with an "e," "i," or "y."
  picnic to *picnicking*   *panic* to *panicky*

If a word ends in a single consonant:

- If a one-syllable word ends in a consonant (or the final syllable is accented), double the final consonant.

  brag to *bragged* (1 + 1 + 1 Rule)

- If the word ends in two consonants, do not double the final one.

  hard to *harder* (Negative 1 + 1 + 1 Rule)

- If a word ends in a single vowel letter, double the final consonant.

  run to *running*

- If a word has a two-letter vowel, do not double the consonant.

  rain to *rained* (Also 1 + 1 + 1 Rule)

- If a word ends in a single consonant and the suffix begins with a vowel, double the consonant.

  bag to *bagged*

- If a word ends in "le" and the suffix is "ly," drop the final "le" before adding the suffix.

  able to *ably*

- But if the word ends in "l," leave the "l" before adding "ly."
  cool to *coolly*

Suit the word to the action and the action to the word.

—Shakespeare, *Hamlet*

Mastery of these rules will help students in any grade. The irregular spellings must be memorized. Try a fast-paced spelling bee for practice.

1. **The plural form of most nouns is made by adding -s to the end of a word.**

   chair to *chairs*   *floor* to *floors*

   president to *presidents* *desk* to *desks*

   face to *faces*   *drill* to *drills*

2. **If the word ends in -s, -ss, -sh, -ch, -x, or -z, the plural is formed by adding -es.**

   boss to *bosses*   *dish* to *dishes*   *gas* to *gases*

   bench to *benches*   *fox* to *foxes*

   waltz to *waltzes*   *tax* to *taxes*

3. **If the word ends in a -y preceded by a consonant, the plural is formed by changing the -y to -i and adding -es.**

   city to *cities*   *country* to *countries*

   variety to *varieties* *candy* to *candies*

   family to *families*   *cherry* to *cherries*

4. **If the word ends in a -y preceded by a vowel, the plural is formed by adding -s.**

   valley to *valleys*   *turkey* to *turkeys*

   key to *keys*   *play* to *plays*

   journey to *journeys*   *boy* to *boys*

5. **The plurals of most nouns ending with -f or -fe are formed by adding -s.**

   gulf to *gulfs*   *belief* to *beliefs*

   cuff to *cuffs*   *roof* to *roofs*

   cliff to *cliffs*   *hoof* to *hoofs* (*hooves* also correct)

6. **Some words that end in -f or -fe are formed by changing the -f or -fe to -ves.**

   knife to *knives*   *wife* to *wives*

   leaf to *leaves*   *elf* to *elves*

   thief to *thieves*   *life* to *lives*

   loaf to *loaves*   *wolf* to *wolves*

   half to *halves*   *self* to *selves*

   calf to *calves*   *dwarf* to *dwarves*

7. **If the word ends in an -o preceded by a consonant, form the plural by adding -es.**

   hero to *heroes*   *potato* to *potatoes*

   tomato to *tomatoes*   *echo* to *echoes*

   zero to *zeroes*   *cargo* to *cargoes*

8. **If the word ends in an -o preceded by a vowel, form the plural by adding -s.**

   video to *videos*   *radio* to *radios*

   studio to *studios*   *patio* to *patios*

9. **To form the plural of a compound word, make the base noun plural.**

   brother-in-law to *brothers-in-law*   *bucket seat* to *bucket seats*

   sandbox to *sandboxes*   *passerby* to *passersby*

   attorney general to *attorneys general*

10. **Some words have irregular plural forms.**

    child to *children*   *ox* to *oxen*

    man to *men*   *basis* to *bases*

    crisis to *crises*   *index* to *indices*

    axis to *axes*   *oasis* to *oases*

    die to *dice*   *foot* to *feet*

    mouse to *mice*   *radius* to *radii*

    tooth to *teeth*   *goose* to *geese*

    woman to *women*   *medium* to *media*

    stimulus to *stimuli*   *focus* to *foci*

    criterion to *criteria*   *datum* to *data*

    parenthesis to *parentheses*

11. **Some words are used for both singular and plural meanings, and never use an -s or -es suffix. These are called invariable nouns.**

cod	moose	barley
traffic	salmon	series
specimen	deer	bass
mackerel	dozen	hay
dirt	music	trout
corps	rye	fish
sheep	wheat	gross
Swiss	British	aircraft

12. **Some nouns look singular but are always plural.**

police	people	vermin
folk	livestock	cattle

Spelling, Abbreviations, and Phonics

<u>A Method of Teaching Spelling for Teachers</u>

1. Use the Test-Study Method. For example, you might give a spelling test of twenty words.

2. Have the students correct their own papers. Make sure they properly spell all the words they spelled incorrectly.

3. Have the students carefully study the words that they missed, paying careful attention to just the incorrect or missing letters, perhaps by circling the incorrect letter(s) and writing the word correctly from memory several times.

4. Give a second spelling test a few days later.

5. Reward students for doing well and/or showing improvement with much praise, public recognition, good grades, and so on.

<u>Spelling Study Method for Students</u>

1. **Look** at the whole word carefully.

2. **Say** the word aloud to yourself.

3. **Spell** (say) each letter to yourself.

4. **Write** the word from memory. (Cover word and write it.)

5. **Check** your written word against the correct spelling.

6. **Circle** errors (wrong or missing letters) and repeat Steps 4 and 5.

Also see Chapter 9, Methods.

Most spelling experts agree that good pronunciation helps learning to spell. Exaggerate enunciation when giving the spelling words. Some teachers introduce the words by pronouncing them syllable by syllable. You may have noticed that National Spelling Bee champions often do that.

- **Point out trouble parts** of words like silent letters or unusual or non-phonetic parts of words.
- **Point out regular rules** and regular phonic principles in words.
- **Discuss meaning** and use of each word. Use the word in a sentence when giving the spelling test.
- **Vowels cause more trouble** than consonants. Stress vowel sounds and the way they are spelled.
- **Give students a lot of praise** for good spelling, particularly if they are showing improvement. Look at their spelling progress charts regularly.
- **Don't let spelling get in the way of good story writing.** Let students use invented spelling on first drafts. Later they can proofread and correct.
- **Have a little fun.** Play some spelling games like Scrabble or have a spelling bee. Laugh at some mistakes, both theirs and yours. Remember that the only people who don't make spelling errors are people who don't write anything.
- For most writers, **a relatively few words account for a large percentage of their spelling errors**. This weakness can be helped by keeping a personal list of words often misspelled.
- Many students are helped by emphasizing a **visual approach**. Have them stop and look very carefully at corrected spellings.
- A remedial method used by many classroom and special education teachers is the **kinesthetic approach**. In this method, a student traces a large version of the word with a finger while saying the word, syllable by syllable. Next, the student writes the word without looking at the sample. This is also used by some primary teachers.
- **Reference works** help every writer. Nearly every computer word-processing program has a spelling checker; students have long been told to "look it up in the dictionary"; and most secretaries and writers have a "word book," which is simply a big list of words (without definitions so it is faster to find the word than in the dictionary).
- There are also **simple "word books"** for students. For example, Fry has written the *Word Book for Beginning Writers* for those children or adults with first- through third-grade ability, which has a 1,000-word list. Also available is the *Beginning Writers Manual* for those with third- through eighth-grade writing ability.
- Don't forget to give some occasional lessons on **dictionary use**. Good school dictionaries usually have helpful suggestions in their introduction. Knowing phonics will definitely help you in teaching any dictionary pronunciation system.
- **Memory devices** (mnemonics) sometimes help students to remember difficult parts of words. For example, "Is there one 'n' or two 'n's in 'annual'?" A memory device is that Ann's name is at the beginning. Another memory device is that Al is in the navy, so "naval" has "al" at the end. "Navel" means something in the middle of the belly. Note that "arc" ends in "c," which is like the part of a circle; the other "ark" is a boat for biblical animals.

Also see Chapter 9, Methods.

Chapter 8

MEASUREMENT AND GEOGRAPHY

The Metric System

The metric system of measurements is used in Europe, Latin America, and many other countries. Unfortunately, the United States started to adopt it in the 1970s, then later dropped it. However, you will note that most of the terms are Latin-based, and those roots are seen in many other vocabulary words. For very large and very small measurement amounts, see Super Numbers, Lists 169 and 170, in this chapter.

Learning the metric system makes interesting and thought-provoking science or mathematics lessons.

Length (Linear)

10 millimeter (mm) = 1 centimeter (cm)
10 centimeters = 1 decimeter (dm) or 100 millimeters
10 decimeters = 1 meter (m) or 1,000 millimeters
10 meters = 1 dekameter (dam)
10 dekameters = 1 hectometer (hm) or 100 meters
10 hectometers = 1 kilometer (km) or 1,000 meters

Area (Square)

100 square millimeters = 1 square centimeter (cm^2)
10,000 square centimeters = 1 square meter (m^2) or 1,000,000 square millimeters
100 square meters = 1 are (a) (square decameter)
100 ares = 1 hectare (ha) or 10,000 square meters
100 hectares = 1 square kilometer (km^2) or 1,000,000 square meters

Volume (Liquid)

10 milliliters (mL) = 1 centiliter (cL)
10 centiliters = 1 deciliter (dL) or 100 milliliters
10 deciliters = 1 liter (L) or 1,000 milliliters
10 liters = 1 dekaliter (daL)
10 dekaliters = 1 hectoliter (hL) or 100 liters
10 hectoliters = 1 kiloliter (kL) or 1,000 liters

Volume (Cubic Measure)

1,000 cubic millimeters (mm^3) = 1 cubic centimeter (cm^3)
1,000 cubic centimeters = 1 cubic decimeters (dm^3) or 1,000,000 cubic millimeters
1,000 cubic decimeters = 1 cubic meter (m^3) or 1 stere or 1,000,000 cubic centimeters or 1,000,000,000 cubic millimeters

Weight (Mass)

10 milligrams (mg) = 1 centigram (cg)
10 centigrams = 1 decigram (dg) or 100 milligrams
10 decigrams = 1 gram (g) or 1,000 milligrams
10 grams = 1 dekagram (dag)
10 dekagrams = 1 hectogram (hg) or 100 grams
10 hectograms = 1 kilogram (kg) or 1,000 grams
1,000 kilograms = 1 metric ton (t)

U.S. Weights and Measures

Unfortunately, the United States uses an ancient system of measurement, but educated people need to know it and those in some occupations use it regularly.

Linear
12 inches = 1 foot
3 feet = 1 yard
5½ yards = 1 rod
40 rods = 1 furlong
8 furlongs = 1 mile

Liquid
4 gills = 1 pint
2 pints = 1 quart
4 quarts = 1 gallon
31½ gals. = 1 barrel
2 barrels = 1 hogshead

Metric Equivalents
1 inch = 2.54000 centimeters
1 foot = 0.3048 meter
1 yard = 0.9144 meter
1 mile = 1.6093 kilometers

1 centimeter = 0.3937 inch
1 decimeter = 3.9370 inches
1 meter = 39.3701 inches
1 kilometer = 0.6214 mile

1 quart = 1.1012 liters
1 quart = 0.9464 liter
1 gallon = 3.7854 liters

1 liter = 0.9081 dry quart
1 liter = 1.0567 liquid quarts

Square
144 sq. inches = 1 sq. foot
9 sq. feet = 1 sq. yard
30¼ sq. yards. = 1 sq. rod
640 acres = 1 sq. mile

Circular
60 sec. = 1 minute
60 min. = 1 degree
180 degrees = 1 semicircle
360 degrees = 1 circle

Metric Equivalents
1 sq. inch = 6.452 sq. centimeters
1 sq. foot = 929.030 sq. centimeters
1 sq. mile = 2.590 sq. kilometers

1 sq. centimeter = 0.155 sq. inch
1 sq. meter = 1.196 sq. yards
1 sq. kilometer = 0.386 sq. mile

U.S. Weights and Measures *(continued)*

Cubic

1,728 cu. inches = 1 cu. foot

27 cu. feet = 1 cu. yard

128 cu. feet = 1 cord (wood)

Dry

2 pints = 1 quart

8 quarts = 1 peck

4 pecks = 1 bushel

Metric Equivalents

1 cu. inch = 16.3871 cu. centimeters = 0.0164 liter

1 cu. foot = 0.0283 cu. meter = 28.3169 cu. feet

1 cu. meter = 35.3147 cu. feet

1 ounce = 28.3495 grams

1 pound = 0.4536 kilogram

1 gram = 0.0353 ounce

1 kilogram = 2.2046 lbs.

1 ton (2,000 lbs.) = 907.1848 kilograms

Longitude and Time

1 second of longitude = $\frac{1}{15}$ seconds of time

1 minute of longitude = 4 seconds of time

1 degree of longitude = 4 minutes of time

15 degrees of longitude = 1 hour

360 degrees of longitude = 24 hours

To understand the relationship between longitude and time, just remember that the earth rotates 360 degrees in 24 hours and a "time zone" is approximately 15 degrees of longitude wide.

Temperature Conversion Formulas

F° (Fahrenheit) = 32 + $\frac{9}{5}$ (C°)

C° (Celsius) = $\frac{5}{9}$ (F° − 32)

Super Numbers

Modern science and modern economics have found a need for very large numbers. They sometimes use names for the numbers, but they also use an exponential number (the superscript number after the 10). The exponent is the number of 0's following the 1 and is read "ten to the ninth" (10^9), "ten to the twelfth" (10^{12}), and so on.

Watch out if you are reading a newspaper in France or Germany because what the U.S. calls a billion (10^9), they call a millard and what the U.S. calls a trillion (10^{12}), they call a billion.

Positive Numbers

Prefix	Symbol	U.S. Name	Example	European Name
deca-	da	ten, 10	decameter	dix (French)
kilo-	k	thousand, 10^3	kilometer	thousand
mega-	M	million, 10^6	megameter	million
giga-	B	billion, 10^9	gigameter	millard
tera-	T	trillion, 10^{12}	terameter	billion
peta-	P	quadrillion, 10^{15}	petameter	1,000 billion
exa-	E	quintillion, 10^{18}	exameter	trillion
sex- or zetta	Z	sextillion, 10^{21}	zettameter	1,000 trillion
yotta	Y	septillion, 10^{24}	yottameter	

Fractions

What goes up can also go down. Here are the tiniest numbers you will ever need. Incidentally, you read these as "ten to the minus ninth" (10^{-9}), and so on.

Prefix	Symbol	Meaning	Example
deci-	d	tenth, 10^{-1}	decimeter
centi-	c	hundredth, 10^{-2}	centimeter
milli-	m	thousandth, 10^{-3}	millimeter
micro-	u	millionth, 10^{-6}	micrometer
nano-	n	billionth, 10^{-9}	nanometer (10^{-10} = angstrom)
pico-	p	trillionth, 10^{-12}	picometer
femto-	f	quadrillionth, 10^{-15}	femtometer (fermi)
atto-	a	quintillionth, 10^{-18}	attometer
zepto-	z	sextillionth, 10^{-21}	zeptometer
yocto-	y	septillionth, 10^{-24}	yoctometer

For more numbers, see List 25.

Using Super Numbers

Who would ever use super numbers? The answer is maybe you when you are buying a computer, an astronomer when mapping the sky, a physicist collecting data from an atom smasher.

Here are some super numbers used in computer science. Just to remind you, a computer thinks and remembers *bits,* which are 0 or 1 (just 2 numbers). But to be more useful, computer memory uses *bytes,* which are combinations of 8 bits that represent a letter or a conventional (base 10) number.

1 **Kilobyte**	10^3	Old home computer memory
1 **Megabyte** (millions)	10^6	Floppy disc
1 **Gigabyte** (billions)	10^9	Hard drive storage
1 **Terabyte**	10^{12}	All the words in Library of Congress = 40 Terabytes; Sloan map of every visible object in the sky = 40 Terabytes
1 **Petabyte**	10^{15}	Syntopic map of every visible object in the sky = 10 Petabytes; CERN particle accelerator data output = 100 Petabytes

Data vs. Information

Clause Shannon, Bell Labs, said anything not noise (static) was information (1940s). He figured out how he could send bits over the phone. Modern information theory separates data and information. Information is data made meaningful.

Data of sound bits may have information of speech or music. Data of millions of chemical combinations may have useful drug information. Data of 100 petabytes of particle data may show new atom parts (information).

Search for Life in the Universe

SETI@home (Search for Extraterrestrial Intelligence) got help in analyzing 35 gigabytes of data from the Arecibo, Puente Rico, radio astronomy telescope from over two million volunteer home computer operators, Sun Microsystems, and Fuji Film tapes. So far, it is all data; no intelligence coming in from outer space.

Using many computers to analyze data is called "distributed computing."

List 171   Old Measurement

In days of yore, Abraham Lincoln measured years in **scores** and Jules Vern measured submarine distance in **leagues**. Here are some other old measuring units, with some still in use.

score	20 (four score = 80)
bushel	a dry measure of volume equal to about 35 liters or 2,150 cubic inches
peck	one-fourth of a bushel
league	20 miles
furlong	220 yards or one-eighth of a mile (used in horse racing)
fathom	6 feet (used in measuring water depth)
quire	24 sheets of paper (used in bookkeeping)
ream	500 sheets of paper (normally 20 quires)
dozen	12 units (used in selling eggs or flowers)
gross	12 dozen (used in wholesale)
carat	200 milligrams (used for diamond weight). Also spelled *karat*.

List 172   Some Scientific Measures

Astronomers, engineers, and navigators use special measuring units. Here are a few of them:

Astronomical unit	93,000 miles or the average distance from the earth to the sun (used in measuring the distance of planets).
Light year	The distance light travels in one year or 5,880,000,000,000 miles. That's 5.88 trillion (used in measuring the distance to stars).
Speed of sound	1,088 feet per second or about 740 miles per hour in air. In water the speed of sound is about 1,056 feet per second and in granite it is about 12,960 feet per second.
Mach	A unit of 1 speed of sound. An airplane going at 1.5 mach is going one and a half times the speed of sound.
Hertz	Cycles per second; measures electromagnetic wave frequencies like radio waves. AM radio dials are in kilohertz (thousand waves) and FM radio dials are in megahertz (million waves).
Nautical Mile	About 1.15 statute mile or 1.85 kilometers. It is also 1 minute (1/60th of a degree) of latitude (used in navigation of ships and planes).
Knot	A unit of speed of 1 nautical mile per hour.

Polygons

Polygons are any closed figure with three or more straight sides (and angles). Here are samples of some you may be familiar with.

Square	Quadrangle	Trapezium
4 equal-length sides 4 right angles	any 4-sided figure, such as a square, trapezoid, or rectangle any quadrangle is also a quadrilateral	4 sides none are parallel

Trapezoid	Parallelogram	Rectangle

2 sides parallel 2 sides not parallel	4-sided figure opposite sides parallel	any 4 right-angled figure hence 4 parallel sides

Oblong	Diagonal	Transversal

longer than wide	a line connecting 2 corners	one line intersecting 2 or more lines

Triangle	Right Triangle	Equilateral Triangle
3 sides	a triangle with 1 90° angle	each angle is 60°, hence must have equal-length sides

Geometric Figures *(continued)*

Pentagon

any 5-sided, 5-angled figure

Hexagon

any 6-sided, 6-angled figure

Heptagon

any 7-sided, 7-angled figure

Octagon

any 8-sided, 8-angled figure

Decagon

any 10-sided, 10-angled figure

Regular figure means equal sides; *irregular* figure means unequal sides.

Circles

Circle

all radii equal length

Concentric Circles

having the same center

Semicircle

one half circle

Oval

irregular circle (unequal diameters); may be egg shaped

Ellipse

oval shape with both ends alike

Diameter

a line passing through the center of a circle

Radius

a line from the center to the circle

Cord

a straight line connecting any two points of a circle

Measurement and Geography

Arc

a segment of a circle

Quadrant

1/4 or 90º of a circle

Octant

1/8 or 45º of a circle

Angles

Right Angle

exactly 90º

Acute Angle

under 90º

Obtuse Angle

over 90º, less than 180º

A straight line (no angle) is 180º.

Complementary Angle

either of 2 angles that
sum to 90º

Oblique Angle

any angle not a
right angle

Altitude

height from the base (b) to
the highest angle (a)

Degrees of Arc (Angle)

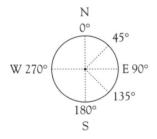

Symmetrical

equal shape on the
opposite sides
of a line

Asymmetrical

unequal shape on the
opposite sides of a line

Geometric Figures *(continued)*

Solid Figures (Three-Dimensional)

Straight Lines

Cube

6 square faces (hence, right angles equal-length sides)

Hexahedron

a solid figure with 6 faces (ex., any box with right angles on faces)

Pyramid

any polygon base and triangular sides that must meet in a point

Cylinder

a tube shape, two equal parallel circles for ends connected by a curved surface

Curves

Cone

circular base

Parabola

curve formed by a plane slicing a cone

Parabolic Curve

reflected light from the focus point is parallel

Lenses

Concave

Convex

Some Terms

Pentagon is a noun.
Pentagonal is an adjective.
Euclidean Geometry (Euclid about 300 B.C.) is basically plane and solid figures.
Analytic Geometry (Descartes, 1637) uses more complex curves.
Differential Geometry is based on calculus.
Circumference is the distance around a circle, square, cube, or any figure.

Nations of the World with Capitals

Geography is a much-neglected subject in many schools. Locating these countries on a globe, map, or atlas will keep a bright student busy for many hours. Knowing capital cities of major countries crops up on some tests.

Nation	Capital City	Currency
Afghanistan	Kabul	afghani
Albania	Tirana	lek
Algeria	Algiers	dinar
Andorra	Andorra la Vella	*(Fr.)* franc; *(Sp.)* peseta
Angola	Luanda	kwanza
Antigua and Barbuda	St. John's	dollar
Argentina	Buenos Aires	peso
Armenia	Yerevan	dram
Australia	Canberra	dollar
Austria	Vienna	schilling
Azerbaijan	Baku	manat
Bahamas	Nassau	dollar
Bahrain	Manama	dinar
Bangladesh	Dhaka	taka
Barbados	Bridgetown	dollar
Belarus	Minsk	ruble
Belgium	Brussels	franc
Belize	Belmopan	dollar
Benin	Porto Novo	franc
Bhutan	Thimphu	ngultrum
Bolivia	La Paz; Sucre	boliviano
Bosnia and Herzegovina	Sarajevo	dinar
Botswana	Gaborone	pula
Brazil	Brasilia	real
Brunei	Bandar Seri Begawan	dollar
Bulgaria	Sofia	lev
Burkina Faso	Ouagadougou	franc
Burundi	Bujumbura	franc
Cambodia	Phnom Penh	riel
Cameroon	Yaounde	franc
Canada	Ottawa	dollar
Cape Verde	Praia	escudo
Central African Republic	Bengui	franc
Chad	N'Djamena	franc
Chili	Santiago	peso
China	Beijing	yuan
Colombia	Bogota	peso
Comoros	Moroni	franc
Congo, Democratic Republic of the	Kinshasa	zaire
Congo, Republic of the	Brazzaville	franc
Costa Rica	San Jose	colon
Croatia	Zagreb	kuna
Cuba	Havana	peso
Cyprus	Nicosia	pound

Nations of the World with Capitals *(continued)*

Nation	Capital City	Currency
Czech Republic	Prague	koruna
Denmark	Copenhagen	krone
Djibouti	Djibouti	franc
Dominica	Roseau	dollar
Dominican Republic	Santo Domingo	peso
Ecuador	Quito	sucre
Egypt	Cairo	pound
El Salvador	San Salvador	colon
Equatorial Guinea	Malabo	franc
Eritrea	Asmara	birr
Estonia	Tallinn	kroon
Ethiopia	Addis Ababa	birr
Fiji	Suva	dollar
Finland	Helsinki	markka
France	Paris	franc
Gabon	Libreville	franc
Gambia	Banjul	dalasi
Georgia	Tbilisi	lari
Germany	Berlin	deutsche mark
Ghana	Accra	cedi
Greece	Athens	drachma
Grenada	St. George's	dollar
Guatemala	Guatemala City	quetzal
Guinea	Conakry	franc
Guinea-Bissau	Bissau	peso
Guyana	Georgetown	dollar
Haiti	Port-au-Prince	gourde
Honduras	Tegucigalpa	lempira
Hungary	Budapest	forint
Iceland	Reykjavik	krona
India	New Delhi	rupee
Indonesia	Jarkata	rupiah
Iran	Tehran	rial
Iraq	Baghdad	dinar
Ireland	Dublin	pound
Israel	Jerusalem	shekel
Italy	Rome	lira
Ivory Coast	Yamoussoukro	franc
Jamaica	Kingston	dollar
Japan	Tokyo	yen
Jordan	Amman	dinar
Kazakhstan	Akmola	tenge
Kenya	Nairobi	shilling
Kiribati	Tarawa	*(Austral.)* dollar
Korea, North	Pyongyang	won
Korea, South	Seoul	won

Nations of the World with Capitals *(continued)*

Nation	Capital City	Currency
Kuwait	Kuwait	dinar
Kyrgyzstan	Bishkek	som
Laos	Vientiane	kip
Latvia	Riga	lats
Lebanon	Beirut	pound
Lesotho	Maseru	loti
Liberia	Monrovia	dollar
Libya	Tripoli	dinar
Liechtenstein	Vaduz	*(Swiss)* franc
Lithuania	Vilnius	litas
Luxembourg	Luxembourg	franc
Macedonia	Skopje	denar
Madagascar	Antananarivo	franc
Malawi	Lilongwe	kwacha
Malaysia	Kuala Lumpur	ringgit
Maldives	Male	rufiyaa
Mali	Bamako	franc
Malta	Valletta	lira
Marshall Islands	Dalap-Uliga-Darrit	dollar
Mauritania	Nouakchott	ouguiya
Mauritius	Port Louis	rupee
Mexico	Mexico City	peso
Micronesia	Palikir	dollar
Moldova	Chisinau	leu
Monaco	Monaco	*(Fr.)* franc
Mongolia	Ulan Bator	tugrik
Morocco	Rabat	dirham
Mozambique	Maputo	metical
Myanmar	Yangon	kyat
Namibia	Windhoek	dollar
Nauru	—	*(Austral.)* dollar
Nepal	Katmandu	rupee
Netherlands	Amsterdam	guilder
New Zealand	Wellington	dollar
Nicaragua	Managua	cordoba
Niger	Niamey	franc
Nigeria	Abuja	naira
Norway	Oslo	krone
Oman	Muscat	rial
Pakistan	Islamabad	rupee
Palau	Koror	dollar
Panama	Panama City	balboa
Papua New Guinea	Port Moresby	kina
Paraguay	Asuncion	guarani
Peru	Lima	sol
Philippines	Manila	peso

Nations of the World with Capitals *(continued)*

Nation	Capital City	Currency
Poland	Warsaw	zloty
Portugal	Lisbon	escudo
Qatar	Doha	riyal
Romania	Bucharest	leu
Russia	Moscow	ruble
Rwanda	Kigali	franc
San Marino	San Marino	*(It.)* lira
Sao Tome and Principe	Sao Tome	dobra
Saudi Arabia	Riyadh	riyal
Senegal	Dakar	franc
Seychelles	Victoria	rupee
Sierra Leone	Freetown	leone
Singapore	Singapore	dollar
Slovakia	Bratislava	koruna
Slovenia	Ljubljana	tolar
Solomon Islands	Honiara	dollar
Somalia	Mogadishu	shilling
South Africa	Pretoria	rand
Spain	Madrid	peseta
Sri Lanka	Colombo	rupee
St. Kitts and Nevis	Basseterre	dollar
St. Lucia	Castries	dollar
St. Vincent and the Grenadines	Kingstown	dollar
Sudan	Khartoum	pound
Suriname	Paramaribo	guilder
Swaziland	Mbabane	lilangeni
Sweden	Stockholm	krona
Switzerland	Bern	franc
Syria	Damascus	pound
Taiwan	Taipei	dollar
Tajikistan	Dushanbe	ruble
Tanzania	Dodoma	shilling
Thailand	Bangkok	bath
Togo	Lome	franc
Tonga	Nukualofa	pa'anga
Trinidad and Tobago	Port-of-Spain	dollar
Tunisia	Tunis	dinar
Turkey	Ankara	lira
Turkemenistan	Ashgahat	manat
Tuvalu	Fongafale	*(Austral.)* dollar
Uganda	Kampala	shilling
Ukraine	Kiev	hryvnia
United Arab Emirates	Abu Dhabi	dirham
United Kingdom	London	pound
United States	Washington, D.C.	dollar
Uruguay	Montevideo	peso

Nations of the World
with Capitals *(continued)*

Nation	Capital City	Currency
Uzbekistan	Tashkent	som
Vanuatu	Vila	vatu
Vatican City	—	*(It.)* lira
Venezuela	Caracas	Bolivar
Vietnam	Hanoi	dong
Western Samoa	Apia	tala
Yemen	Sana	rial
Yugoslavia	Belgrade	dinar
Zambia	Lusaka	kwacha
Zimbabwe	Harare	dollar

Oh, give me a home where the buffalo roam
Where the deer and the antelope play
Where seldom is heard a discouraging word
And the skies are not cloudy all day

—Anonymous Cowboy, "Home on the Range"

The United States

U.S. Postal Service Abbreviation	Capital City	Old Style Abbreviation
AL (Alabama)	Montgomery	Ala.
AK (Alaska)	Juneau	Alaska
AZ (Arizona)	Phoenix	Ariz.
AR (Arkansas)	Little Rock	Ark.
CA (California)	Sacramento	Calif.
CO (Colorado)	Denver	Colo.
CT (Connecticut)	Hartford	Conn.
DE (Delaware)	Dover	Del.
DC (Washington, D.C.)	Washington	D.C.
FL (Florida)	Tallahassee	Fla.
GA (Georgia)	Atlanta	Ga.
HI (Hawaii)	Honolulu	Hawaii
ID (Idaho)	Boise	Idaho
IL (Illinois)	Springfield	Ill.
IN (Indiana)	Indianapolis	Ind.
IA (Iowa)	Des Moines	Iowa
KS (Kansas)	Topeka	Kans.
KY (Kentucky)	Frankfort	Ky.
LA (Louisiana)	Baton Rouge	La.
ME (Maine)	Augusta	Maine
MD (Maryland)	Annapolis	Md.
MA (Massachusetts)	Boston	Mass.
MI (Michigan)	Lansing	Mich.
MN (Minnesota)	St. Paul	Minn.
MS (Mississippi)	Jackson	Miss.
MO (Missouri)	Jefferson City	Mo.
MT (Montana)	Helena	Mont.
NE (Nebraska)	Lincoln	Nebr.
NV (Nevada)	Carson City	Nev.
NH (New Hampshire)	Concord	N.H.
NJ (New Jersey)	Trenton	N.J.
NM (New Mexico)	Santa Fe	N.Mex.
NY (New York)	Albany	N.Y.
NC (North Carolina)	Raleigh	N.C.
ND (North Dakota)	Bismarck	N.Dak.
OH (Ohio)	Columbus	Ohio
OK (Oklahoma)	Oklahoma City	Okla.
OR (Oregon)	Salem	Ore.
PA (Pennsylvania)	Harrisburg	Penn.
PR (Puerto Rico)	San Juan	P.R.
RI (Rhode Island)	Providence	R.I.
SC (South Carolina)	Columbia	S.C.
SD (South Dakota)	Pierre	S.Dak.
TN (Tennessee)	Nashville	Tenn.
TX (Texas)	Austin	Tex.
UT (Utah)	Salt Lake City	Utah
VT (Vermont)	Montpelier	Vt.
VI (Virgin Islands)	Charlotte Amalie	V.I.
VA (Virginia)	Richmond	Va.
WA (Washington)	Olympia	Wash.
WV (West Virginia)	Charleston	W.Va.
WI (Wisconsin)	Madison	Wis.
WY (Wyoming)	Cheyenne	Wyo.

U.S. Cities by Population

Rank*	City	Population (Thousands)	Land Area (Sq. Miles)	Density (Average Population per Sq. Mile)
1	New York, NY	7,323	309	23,700
2	Los Angeles, CA	3,485	469	7,400
3	Chicago, IL	2,784	227	12,300
4	Houston, TX	1,631	540	3,000
5	Philadelphia, PA	1,586	135	11,700
6	San Diego, CA	1,111	324	3,400
7	Detroit, MI	1,028	139	7,400
8	Dallas, TX	1,007	432	2,900
9	Phoenix, AZ	983	420	2,300
10	San Antonio, TX	936	333	2,800
11	San Jose, CA	782	171	4,600
12	Baltimore, MD	736	81	9,100
13	Indianapolis, IN	731	362	2,000
14	San Francisco, CA	724	47	15,500
15	Jacksonville, FL	635	759	800
16	Columbus, OH	633	191	3,300
17	Milwaukee, WI	628	96	6,500
18	Memphis, TN	610	256	2,400
19	Washington, DC	607	61	9,900
20	Boston, MA	574	48	11,900

*Ranked by estimated 2002 population.

Provinces of Canada

Province or Territory	Capital	Postal Code
Alberta	Edmonton	AB
British Columbia	Victoria	BC
Manitoba	Winnipeg	MB
New Brunswick	Fredericton	NB
Newfoundland/Labrador	St. John's	NF
Northwest Territories	Yellowknife	NT
Nova Scotia	Halifax	NS
Ontario	Toronto	ON
Prince Edward Island	Charlottetown	PE
Quebec	Quebec	QC*
Saskatchewan	Regina	SK
Yukon Territory	Whitehorse	YT

*PQ is also acceptable.

States of Mexico

State	Capital	Postal Code
Aguascalientes	Aguascalientes	AGS
Baja California	Mexicali	BCN
Baja California Sur	La Paz	BCS
Campeche	Campeche	CAM
Chiapas	Tuxtla Gutierrez	CHIS
Chihuahua	Chihuahua	CHIH
Coahuila	Saltillo	COAH
Colima	Colima	COL
Distrito Federal (Federal District)	Mexico City	DFJ
Durango	Victoria de Durango	DGO
Guanajuato	Guanajuato	GTO
Guerrero	Chilpancingo	GRO
Hidalgo	Pachuca de Soto	HGO
Jalisco	Guadalajara	JAL
Mexico	Toluca de Lerdo	MEX
Michoacan	Morelia	MICH
Morelos	Cuernavaca	MOR
Nayarit	Tepic	NAY
Nuevo Leon	Monterrey	NL
Oaxaca	Oaxaca de Juarez	OAX
Puebla	Puebla de Zaragoza	PUE
Queretaro	Queretaro	QRO
Quintana Roo	Chetumal	QROO
San Luis Potosi	San Luis Potosf	SLP
Sinaloa	Culiacan Rosales	SIN
Sonora	Hermosillo	SON
Tabasco	Villahermosa	TAB
Tamaulipas	Ciudad Victoria	TAMPS
Tlaxcala	Tlaxcala	TLAX
Veracruz	Jalapa Enriquez	VER
Yucatan	Merida	YUC
Zacatecas	Zacatecas	ZAC

Largest Countries by Population

Rank	Country	Population*
1	China	1,284
2	India	1,045
3	United States	280
4	Indonesia	232
5	Brazil	176
6	Pakistan	147
7	Russia	144
8	Bangladesh	133
9	Nigeria	129
10	Japan	126
11	Mexico	103
12	Philippines	84
13	Germany	83
14	Vietnam	81
15	Egypt	70
16	Ethiopia	67
17	Turkey	67
18	Iran	66
19	Thailand	62
20	United Kingdom	59

*Approximate population in millions in 2002 by U.S. census estimate.

---

*A word is dead/When it's said,/Some say.
I say it just/Begins to live/That day.*

—Emily Dickinson, No. 1212

Continents

Africa
Antarctica (South Pole)
Asia
Australia
Europe
North America
South America

Bodies of Water

Andaman Sea
Arctic Ocean
Atlantic Ocean
Baltic Sea
Bering Sea
Black Sea
Caribbean Sea
East China Sea
Gulf of California
Gulf of Mexico
Hudson Bay

Indian Ocean
Mediterranean Sea
North Sea
Pacific Ocean
Persian Gulf
Red Sea
Sea of Japan
Sea of Okhotsk
South China Sea
Yellow Sea

Geographic Concerns

biodiversity—classifying species
biosphere—all living things
climate—rainfall, temperature, and related items
cultures—languages, customs
economy—money, products
energy—amount, kinds, distribution
food—amount, diversity, distribution
minerals—from the earth, includes oil
oceanography—study of oceans
population—amount and distribution of humans
tectonics—movement of the earth's crust

Maps

Atlas—a bound collection of maps
Gazetteer—geographical dictionary, index of places
Globe—a spherical representation of the earth
Physical maps—mountains, rivers, lakes, and land forms
Political maps—location of nations, states, cities
Satellite maps—photos of earth from space

List 181 Learning Place Names

Learning the vocabulary of place names is not so much a matter of roots and affixes or meaning; it is more a matter of place and function. Learning function is most properly called *geography,* but you can start learning of location by having your students locate the places, countries, and cities on a blank map. Don't try to learn about the whole world in a day. Take five or ten countries and place them on a blank map, then put a dot where the capital is. Use a map, globe, or atlas for a reference.

For states and provinces, place the postal code abbreviations in each state or province on the blank map and put a dot at the approximate location of the capital. Postal state abbreviations and state capital names are in List 175 of this chapter. Canada and Mexico lists are Lists 177 and 178 in this chapter. For locations you need maps or an atlas.

You can also use associative learning by placing the country name on one side of a flashcard and the capital name on the other. Have the student try to look at the country and name the capital and vice versa. See Chapter 9 for flashcard use.

Oh, this might be challenging and hard, but who said learning is always easy? It doesn't hurt to learn discipline too. It is well to have some reward and recognition for your successful scholars.

You can use the same techniques to teach the names of the counties, cities, and features of your own state. Some blank maps follow.

The World

The United States

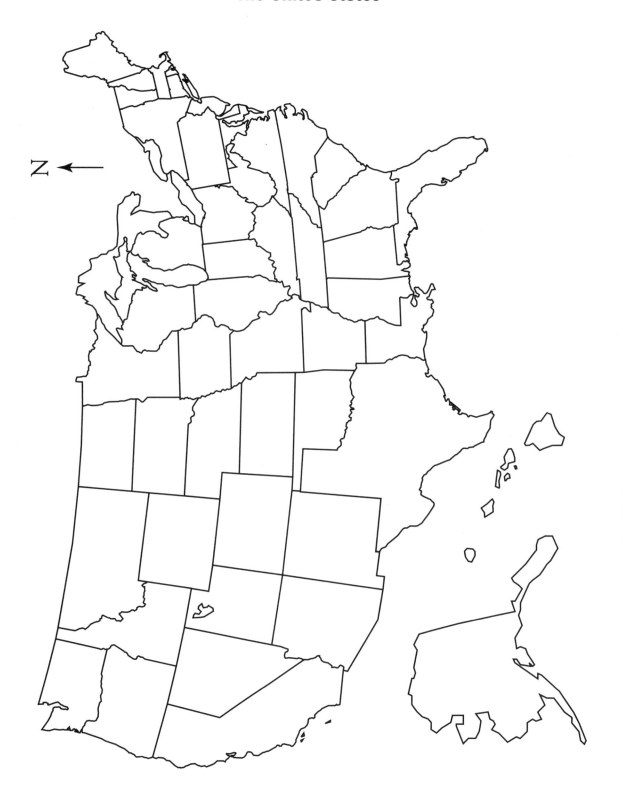

Canada

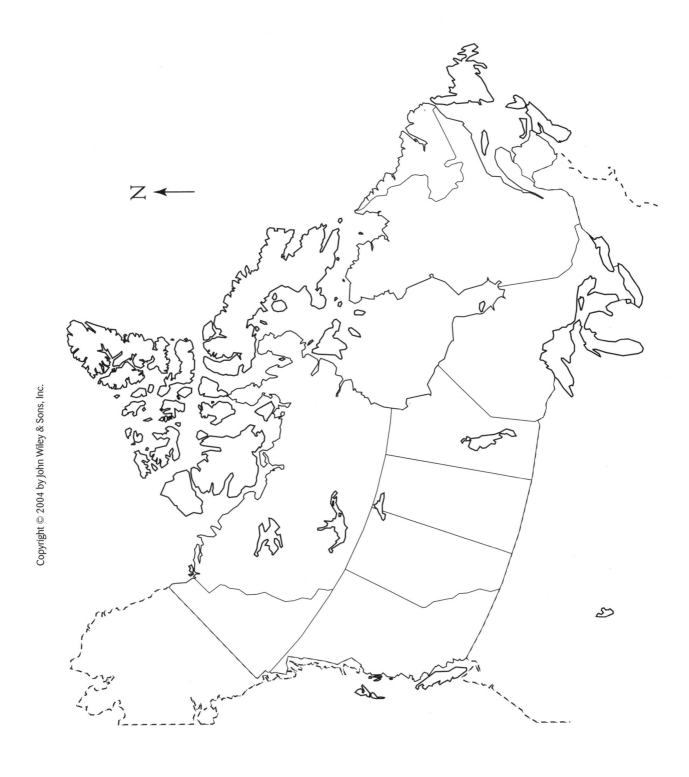

Mexico

Chapter 9

METHODS

Method 1	**Read**
Method 2	**Pay Attention to New Words**
Method 3	**Direct Instruction**
Method 4	**Time**
Method 5	**Integrate Vocabulary Instruction with Every Subject**
Method 6	**The Teachable Moment**
Method 7	**Systematic Self-Instruction**
Method 8	**Teacher Enthusiasm and Fun**
Method 9	**Use**
Method 10	**Glossing**
Method 11	**Testing**
Method 12	**Reward**
Method 13	**Writing**
Method 14	**Group Work**
Method 15	**Flashcards**
Method 16	**Depth of Knowledge**
Method 17	**Polysemy—Multiple Meanings**
Method 18	**Ways to Define a Word**
Method 19	**Vocabulary on the Internet**
Method 20	**Graphic Organizers**
Method 21	**Vocabulary Workbooks**
Method 22	**Visualization**
Method 23	**Simple, Old-Fashioned Vocabulary Lesson**
Method 24	**Word-a-Day**

Method 1 **Read**

People who read a lot have better vocabularies. Hence an obvious method of improving your vocabulary is simply to read a lot. Read a variety—fun stuff like Harry Potter, series books like Nancy Drew, detective stories, romance novels—but also read some more solid things like good literature, autobiographies, politics, popular medicine, or science. They all use vocabulary words, some of which are new to you. Reading a variety of newspaper articles and magazines will also improve vocabulary.

Method 2 **Pay Attention to New Words**

I once taught a vocabulary-building course to a group of aircraft foremen who were in training for higher ranks. After several weeks, one of them came to me and informed me that *Time* magazine started using the words that I was teaching them in class. Others noticed that the *Los Angeles Times* was using some of my words too.

Now what was happening? Did *Time* have a spy in my class? No, as often happens in a good vocabulary course, the students were becoming aware of words that they never noticed before. Previously, they were just skipping over words they didn't know. They were using context, the words surrounding the unknown word, to get the gist of the story.

Hence, one obvious method of improving your vocabulary is to pay attention to new words in anything you read.

Teachers sometimes have students *keep a notebook,* or at least a scrap of paper, and write down new or unknown words. These words can then be looked up later in a dictionary or brought to class for discussion. Even if students don't do that, just the act of *copying the word* will help them to pay attention to it.

Underlining is a milder version of the same thing. You shouldn't do it in borrowed books, but in your own book, underling new words is a good thing.

A still milder version is *mental underlining,* which means just hesitating while reading to pay attention to the word, to notice its roots or how it is used in that sentence. It is pretty hard to get students, or yourself, to look up new words while you are interested in the story or in a hurry to finish the reading soon. Mental underlining is a simple method and considerably better than nothing.

Nothing is just skipping over unknown words. Sure, you do it when you must, but if you want to improve your vocabulary, like my foremen, or your students who want higher scores on a standardized test or to get better grades in a course, then you'd best do something more.

Method 3   Direct Instruction

The major part of our education system is based on classes. A teacher gathers some students and gives them some information and some techniques or exercises for learning the material. One of the most important things a teacher does is to call *attention* to the materials to be learned. Attention is a fundamental part of the laws of learning. The old laws of learning were concepts that psychologists felt were necessary for learning. Psychologists have now become more humble and wiser and don't admit that there is any set of laws for learning anymore, but rather that there are a lot of different ways of learning something, some of which might work better with one student than with another. But it is pretty clear that paying attention to something is still an important method of learning.

So a teacher is partly an *attention pointer*. She or he is also an important *content selector*, determining what and how much of the content is to be taught. This book has a lot of content for a vocabulary class, but the teacher must do the selecting. This chapter on methods provides some teaching ideas; experienced teachers know many more. Selecting content and teaching method is part of what makes teaching creative.

And while we are on the subject of teaching, let me suggest one important idea: "What any good teacher does is to move *every* student ahead a notch." What she or he does not do is to get every student up to some level or standard, but rather a good teacher makes sure that each student improves. The good ones get better, and the poor ones get better. If you do this, the class average or standard will take care of itself. True, some students will always learn more than other students, but at least the teacher will not be engaged in the undemocratic practice of concentrating on one group and ignoring the other group.

Textbook companies also produce vocabulary improvement texts for classes at different levels. These can be a real help for both teacher and student.

Method 4   Time

It takes time to learn anything. Students don't learn to read and write in a day; it takes years.

To improve a student's vocabulary takes time. Spend some time every day teaching vocabulary in a formal or specific way, even if it is only a word-a-day, as is often advocated. Better yet would be to teach a cluster of words such as words having a similar root (*error, erratic, errant*) or a similar topic (*happiness*).

And review the new words you have taught at a previous time—maybe at the end of the day or the end of the week, or both.

It takes a lifetime to improve your vocabulary; there is no end. I can assure you that I have learned plenty of new words just putting this book together. If you are not learning new words, you are mentally dead and so is your reading and conversation. Tell this to your students.

Schools, teachers, and students must be committed to teaching and learning vocabulary over the long term.

Method 5 Integrate Vocabulary Instruction with Every Subject

There is not a subject, from surfing to astronomy, that does not have a specific vocabulary. In order to develop in that subject, you need to learn the vocabulary of that subject. Surfers can quickly discover a novice simply by the new surfer's vocabulary, and so can astronomers spot novice astronomers.

So when you are teaching mathematics, put some stress on mathematical vocabulary, and the same for literature, physics, cooking, and basketball. Nowdays students who have no intention of becoming mathematicians need some math words simply to score well on standardized tests. But more important than that, they need some mathematical vocabulary just to intelligently read the newspaper or books that are a cut above the lowest. Surprisingly enough, to really comprehend and have fun reading science fiction often requires quite a bit of mathematical knowledge. So you can never tell when good vocabulary knowledge will come in handy in situations, such as getting into trouble with the law or talking to your doctor.

Even students who have something less than an academic inclination might be interested in automobiles and somewhat surprised to learn that *carburetor* and *ignition* are Latin-based words (carbo- is a combining form for carbon and ignito = set on fire). If you can find anything a student is interested in, it has a vocabulary. And that vocabulary is related to more vocabulary words.

Method 6 The Teachable Moment

Some of the best instruction occurs incidentally. An incident occurs when a student is stuck on spelling a new word, or a new word crops up in an unexpected place. Good teachers take advantage of the situation and stick in a bit of instruction. "Oh look, that root is dict-, which means 'say' like we see in *dictation* and *dictator*."

To help the teacher along in such incidental teaching, we have lists of prefixes, roots, and suffixes in Chapter 10, Affixes and Roots.

Method 7 Systematic Self-Instruction

Students sometimes are motivated to engage in vocabulary self-instruction. Frequently, the motivation is caused by upcoming examinations like the SATs, College Board, or some other formal examination. But for whatever reason, self-motivated students can learn a lot from self-help books on vocabulary. Every bookstore and library has self-help vocabulary books, ranging from the classic Norman Lewis books like *30 Days to a Better Vocabulary* for general interest to the newest Barron's books aimed straight at major tests.

It has long been known that executives have better vocabularies than lower paid workers, so one of the many ways of getting a key to the executive washroom is to have a better vocabulary. A number of organizations sell vocabulary improvement courses via the Internet, by mail installments, or in self-study book form. Do they work? Yes, sometimes spectacularly and sometimes in the better-than-nothing category.

Needless to say, much of the success in any self-study is dependent on the student's motivation and self-discipline.

It is also a well-known study technique to quickly learn some of the vocabulary in any new course you are taking. Clever students look ahead and cram some vocabulary even before it comes up so they are better prepared to learn. Learning the roots of commonly used words in biology, psychology, or philosophy can give you a real step ahead on putting meaning to the new words of that subject.

Method 8 Teacher Enthusiasm and Fun

If the teacher is enthusiastic about finding a new word and learning a bit about it, the student might just catch a bit of that enthusiasm.

Vocabulary teaching can't be all "bore and chore."

- Play a few games. There are some free hangman games and hidden word puzzles on the Internet for your computer.
- How about a spelling bee type game-lesson where students must define words instead of spelling them?
- Let students call each other *oligophrenic* instead of stupid.
- You should use new or "big" words when talking to students.
- Don't "talk down" to students; make them "listen up" to you.
  Students are not lazy; they are *recalcitrant*.
  It's not sort of green; it is *chartreuse*.
  Don't leave the door partly open; leave it *ajar*.
- Jokes are fun and can teach multiple meanings (polysemy).
  "Why did the teacher wear sunglasses?"
  "Because her pupils were too bright."

Also see List 21, Palindromes, for more fun.

Method 9   **Use**

You make a word your own by using it. It is one thing to memorize a word so that you might recognize it in a printed text or in a multiple-choice question, but quite another if you can use the new word in conversation or in a written essay. So encourage use of new words.

Encourage the use of new words even if the use is not correct or if the pronunciation is not correct. You can improve meaning, spelling, and pronunciation later. The important thing is the attempt at use.

Don't laugh or be sarcastic at wrong use; pat the student on the back for the attempt. Give a prize for the student who uses new words the most frequently or in the best instances.

One type of classroom activity is to take a word, discuss it a little, then ask five students to orally use it in a sentence. The students all vote on the best sentence and use. Next take another word and five other students.

It is not a bad idea to have a quiz on new words regularly; it lets the student and the teacher know if progress is being made.

Old English—The forms of English spoken from the earliest evidence of the language until about 1100.

Middle English—The period from about 1100 to about 1500. Middle English can be viewed as a transition from the form of English spoken in the first half of the Middle Ages to the form spoken at the end of the Middle Ages and the beginning of printing.

Modern English—The forms of English spoken after Middle English—that is, from about 1500 until now.

Method 10 **Glossing**

How about a nice old teaching method. Here is one straight from the Middle Ages and still excellent for today. To have a glossing lesson, here is all you have to do:

1. Read aloud a passage from a textbook or literature.
2. Stop and explain a difficult word or concept.
3. Read on.

Great idea! It works in every subject, for every age student. It teaches both vocabulary and reading comprehension. It teaches the subject matter of the passage. It teaches some reading fluency as the students hear a passage read correctly with intonation (super-segmental phonemes).

It gives the teacher a chance to be creative with selection of passage and where to stop and explain.

Like every other type of lesson, don't overuse it.

It works better if the teacher really knows the subject of the passage and the level of his or her students.

It can lead to good student discussions.

Like other lessons, it often helps if the teacher has done a little preparation for the explanations, but in case of emergencies when there has been no time to prepare, this method can be used "cold."

Gloss is an interesting verb; the dictionary says it means "a series of verbal explanations of a text." They can also be written, in which case they might be called marginal notes or footnotes. At the end of a text a *glossary* is a series of brief explanations for terms used in the text. To *gloss* over something means to hurriedly pass over it, perhaps with a comment but not really reading it or getting into the subject.

The Greek root *gloss-* means "tongue" in the sense that tongue is a metaphor for "language," as in "he speaks many tongues" or worse "with forked tongue." There is a religious ceremony in which people speak in tongues, called *glossolalia*. Linguists even have a word for intentional misspellings ("nu" car). They call it *disglossia*.

Method 11 Testing

Testing is not all bad. It is just overused and abused. Curriculum-based, teacher-made vocabulary tests can be a great teaching tool.

Test not for the purpose of flunking students, grading students, or humiliating students. Test students to help them learn, to give them feedback on improvement, to give them a goal. Look at all the study of vocabulary that the SAT creates.

Testing should not add to the teacher's chores. If you give a vocabulary quiz every Friday, let the students correct their own tests. After all, if tests are supposed to give feedback to the students, here is a very direct way.

Look over the students' tests too so you can get some feedback on your teaching effectiveness: Are too many new words being introduced? Is the teaching method effective? Are the words too difficult? Don't just guess; look at the test results.

Let the students take the test home and discuss the words with a parent or sibling.

Do an end-of-semester review and quiz.

Method 12 Reward

Sometimes you might want to reward good students with a little praise, a take-home certificate, or publishing a name on the bulletin board. A reward need not be money or a prize; praise, recognition, or privilege work fine too.

Don't just reward the naturally best students continually. Reward students who have made the most progress. Weaker students who learn two new words one week and four new words the next week have made 100 percent progress—I'll bet your best students didn't make that much progress.

Be generous with your recognition. Don't just reward the best student; reward the ten best students. The more praise that is handed out, the better for everybody. Let the principal, supervisor, teacher's aide, or parent volunteer help you with the praising; students like a little outside support.

Method 13 Writing

Just as reading helps vocabulary improvement, so does writing. Everybody has several sizes of vocabulary. Your listening vocabulary is largest, your reading vocabulary is next largest, after that comes your speaking vocabulary, and last of all is your writing vocabulary. It is the one that needs the most improvement.

So teachers should encourage writing in many ways such as:

- Writing in their own journals
- Writing short stories
- Writing business and friendly letters
- Writing essays
- Writing news articles
- Writing nonfiction, descriptions, science experiments, directions, and so forth

But more than writing in different genres and styles, teach growing writers to write with better vocabularies. Cross out tired adjectives like "nice" and "good." Cross out tired figures of speech like "it rained cats and dogs." Drive students into the thesaurus. Encourage them to use some words you have taught in a vocabulary lesson.

Writing, like most other skills, improves with practice. And so does using a better vocabulary when you write.

Occasionally, you might have a student who develops a pedantic writing style, using big words and complicated sentences just to show off. These poor individuals must learn that the first purpose of writing is to communicate, a second is to entertain, and a third is not to bore the heck out of the reader. Teach them that using just the right word in the right place meets all three criteria. But for neophytes, stretching and trying out the use of new words is laudatory.

Method 14 Group Work

Students learn from one another. Give them the opportunity. Let them criticize each other's writing and suggest improvements. Let them play games using vocabulary words. Let them test out using new words in a sentence.

Maybe one group or one student could challenge another group or student to a vocabulary duel or a homophone duel. One group calls out a homophone and the other group must say the meaning and spell the homophone pair word.

Some students will say and do things in a small group that they would never do in a whole class.

Monitor your vocabulary groups to see that there is not too much down time or fooling around, and if you find it, gently encourage them back on task.

Method 15 Flashcards

For students who want to get serious about learning new words, take an idea from foreign language learners and use flashcards.

To make flashcards is easy: (1) write the word on one side of the card and (2) write the definition on the other side.

It will help if the student makes his or her own flashcards, because just writing the word and copying the definition will cause some learning.

To study with a pack of flashcards is simple:

1. Look at the word and try to **recall** the definition.

2. Turn the card over and see if your definition was correct for immediate **feedback**.

3. If you get the *correct* or a satisfactory definition, **sort** the card into one pile.

4. If you could not remember the definition or the definition was too skimpy or otherwise unsatisfactory, *sort* the card into the "**To Study**" pile.

5. Go back and **study** the "To Study" pile.

6. **Review** or do the whole process again at a later date.

7. **Add new vocabulary** word flashcards. Build a large pile of cards.

8. *Reverse* or study the cards backwards. That means look at the definition and try to recall the word.

The definition side of the card can be simple with just a brief definition or more complex, giving the root, the noun form, or second meaning.

Making and studying flashcards takes a little time, but it is a first-class study method that can be used in many subjects.

Try using this flashcard study method with homophones, root = meaning, math terms, or measurement abbreviations.

Atlantis—a mythical Greek island beyond the Strait of Gibraltar. It sank into the sea after an earthquake, but the name lives on as the Atlantic Ocean.

The Vocabulary Teacher's Book of Lists

Method 16 Depth of Knowledge

What does it mean to "know" a word? Ah, this is a very difficult question. If you really want to know how complicated it is, you can start with the Bauman et al. (2003) article. Also, you can look at Method 18 in this chapter, Ways to Define a Word.

But to start with a simple answer, there are two types of *receptive* vocabulary (reading and listening) and two types of *expressive* vocabulary (speaking and writing). Some would argue that if you really know a word, you could use it in all four instances. But this is not true. All of us can read and listen to more words than we use in our writing and speaking.

There is another problem of what it means to know a word that we can see in Method 18. Do you know a word if you can give a simple dictionary definition? Do you know a word if you can give a synonym or antonym for it? Do you know a word if you understand the feeling associated with it? The answer is "yes" to each question. But the overall answer is that we know any word in various depths, associations, and contexts.

So all of our lives, we are not only adding words to our vocabularies but we are adding depth to the words we already "know." Teachers need to tell this to students and then use any method they can to increase depth.

Teachers need to add depth by incidental comment, personal reference, formal definitions, and roots or other origin information. Everything helps. Be not discouraged if your student only gets to the level of "I've seen this word before" or to the next level of knowing the simplest definition. Depth will come with more education, more reading, more life.

For example, see List 12.

Convivial means sociable, friendly, and jovial. No wonder, because con = with and vivi = life. Hence, a convivial person is "full of life."

Vital statistics are counts about life and death. And something vital is as important as life itself.

Polysemy—Multiple Meanings

Now polysemy might be a new word for you, but you already know what it means—it means words that have more than one meaning (poly = many, sema = sign). There is a little irony in polysemy because of the generalization that "the more common the word, the more meanings it has." For example, a common word like *let* has a number of meanings such as:

> Let up on him (*ease*)
> Let me do it (*permit*)
> Let's go (*hurry*)
> Don't let on (*tell*)
> Let go of (*release*)
> Let the apartment (*rent, lease*)

At the other end of the continuum, a rare word like *arachnophobia* has only one meaning, "fear of spiders."

Somewhere in the middle might be the word *penetration,* which, broadly defined is "the act of penetrating," but it has some slightly different meanings such as (1) "obtaining market share" or (2) "a military attack" or (3) "the depth of field of a telescope."

Learning a new meaning for a word is like learning a new word. It might be a little easier because often there is some relationship between the second meaning and the first meaning.

Homographs are two or more words that are spelled the same but have different origins as well as different meanings, usually totally unrelated meanings. For example, *pen* means (1) a writing instrument and (2) an enclosure for animals.

The origin of pen (1) is *feather* and the origin of pen (2) is *enclosure*. Like all true homographs, they have separate entries in the dictionary.

But whether a word is a homograph like *pen* or just a word with several meanings like *penetration,* multiple meanings enrich word depth and should be taught. And call the topic by its right name—*polysemy*.

The difference between the almost right word and the right word is really a large matter—it's the difference between the lightening bug and lightning.

—Mark Twain, Letter to George Bainton

Method 18 Ways to Define a Word

Following is a list of traditional and nontraditional ways to define a word. You may want to try some of these the next time you give your students a word definition assignment.

Formal Definition
word = A word is a sound or group of sounds that has meaning and is an independent unit of speech. A printed word is a group of symbols with a space on either side. A word is a free morpheme (meaning a unit that can stand alone).

Definition by Example
phoneme = An example of a phoneme is the /p/ sound in "pin."

Definition by Description
rectangle = A rectangle is a geometric shape that has four straight line sides and four right angles.

Definition by Metaphor
moon = The moon looks *like a lighted disk* in the sky (simile). *Note:* similes use "like" or "as."

moon = The moon *is a lighted ball* in the sky (metaphor).

Definition by Contrast
occupation = You might call it just a *job,* but I call it an *occupation.*

Definition by Synonym
consent = We want your *consent* that you *agree* to everything.

Definition by Antonym
dead = He wasn't *dead*; he was very much *alive.*

Definition by Apposition
(a meaning put in parentheses or set off by commas)
plaintiff = The plaintiff (*person bringing suit*) spoke to the judge first.

mango = The mango, the fruit that tastes something like a blend of peach and pineapple, is his favorite dessert.

Definition by Origin
telescope = The word *telescope* comes from the root *tele,* which means "far," and the root *scope,* which means "view."

Denotation and Connotation

The *denotation* meaning is the dictionary definition and is similar to most of the definition types listed here. The *connotation* meaning involves the feeling that surrounds the word. Note the differences in these sets of words:

> prison—house of correction
> bum—unemployed person
> moron—mentally handicapped
> fat—overweight, heavy

Morpheme Assistance to Definition

Morphemes are meaning units. Often a word will have several meaning units; for example, *un-happi-ness* has three morphemes. By just knowing some morphemes, we know something about a word. Look at these examples:

> xxx **s** = it's probably a plural noun or third-person singular of a verb
> xxx **ed** = it's probably a past tense verb
> xxx **er** = it's probably a noun for a person or a comparative adjective
> **un** xxx = it is not something

If we know the root, we know something about the meaning. For example, if we know that dic = say, then we come across a new word, *dictation*. We can now guess that probably *dictation* has something to do with "saying."

■ Method 19 ■ Vocabulary on the Internet

The Internet can be a great help and a great time waster, so be your own judge. The Google search engine has over 3,000,000 entries under *Vocabulary*. Here are a few of them. Some sites have excellent information such as word lists and word games; some sites have free and for-sale (subscription) materials; and some sites are straight-out selling books, courses, and other services. (Be aware that sites constantly change!)

www.vocabulary.com
Vocabulary University site has many games and drills; middle school and high school college prep

www.voycabulary.com
You select any page on the web through voycabulary (note spelling "voy-") and it will look up any word in any of 250 dictionaries for you.

www.a4esi.org
Aimed at ESL but good for any student mid-elementary level up

www.edu4kids.com
Vocabulary quizzes with feedback; middle school level

www.wsmith@wordsmith.org
Interesting changing themes

www.m-w.com
Merriam-Webster on-line; looks up meaning in their dictionaries, word of the day, games, and more; fourteen-day free trial, then costs money

www.freevocabulary.com
Five thousand collegiate words with short definitions for study for SAT, GRE, TOEFL, and other tests

www.manythings.org
Anagrams for ESL and others (rearranging the letters in a word to form a new word)

www.superkids.com
Vocabulary section includes hangman games, word-a-day, make your own hidden word puzzles; elementary school level; also advertises software for sale

www.quizhub.com
Free quizzes of vocabulary in subject areas; grades 6–12

www.edhelper.com
Some free vocabulary worksheets, then you pay

www.earthlink.net
Big site, word links, and many advanced vocabulary sites and references

www.educationalpress.org
Converts word lists into flashcards, bingo cards, matching drills, word search puzzles, and more

Method 20 Graphic Organizers

Graphic organizers are a way of making some definitions visually related. They can provide an interesting way for a teacher to discuss a word using the chalkboard or an overhead, and they can provide interesting exercises for the students. Give the student a word or two and have them work on building a graphic organizer.

Semantic Map

This organizer builds vocabulary. A word for study is placed in the center of the page, and four categories are made around it. The categories expand on the nature of the word and relate it back to personal knowledge and experience of the students.

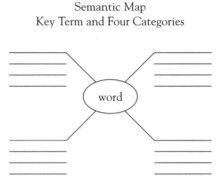

Semantic Map
Key Term and Four Categories

Here is a four-step teaching method for using a semantic map.

1. Select a key or central word from a reading selection about which you can assume that the students have some familiarity.
2. Have the students free associate on the core word and generate a list of related words.
3. Organize the words into categories (and perhaps label them).
4. Discuss alternate ways of categorizing the words, adding new words, and forming new categories.

Categories to be associated with the study word might include:

- Definitions (several)
- Antonyms
- Synonyms
- Related by concept (subject)
- Related by root
- Metaphors

The following graphic organizers can be used to contrast two or more different words.

Semantic Feature Analysis

This grid can be used to show which features or classes have things in common (using a plus sign) or not in common (using a minus sign).

Semantic Feature Analysis
(Matrix)

Fill squares with + or −.

Features

Term (class or example)	animal	mammal	fur					
dog	+	+	+					
cat	+	+	+					
snake	+	−	−					

Structured Overview

This is another type of map, similar to the first simple semantic map, that shows clusters of ideas, terms, or features. The figure shows the general class on top, members of the class in the boxes, and properties of members of the class on the lines.

Structured Overview

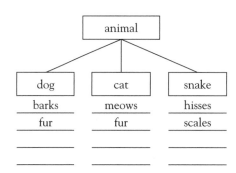

Venn Diagram

This is often used in mathematics, but can easily be used with words and ideas to show features in common between two different concepts.

Venn Diagram

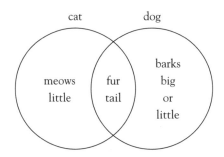

Method 21 Vocabulary Workbooks

A number of major publishers put out student workbooks (also called worksheets) aimed at improving students' vocabulary. These are used in regular language arts classes, remedial and ESL classes, and in special programs such as summer school.

Here are two sample pages from a workbook I worked on entitled *Vocabulary Drills— Middle Level.*

You probably know that *transport* means "to carry something from one place to another." The word part *trans-* means "across" or "beyond," and the root *port* means "to carry." A porter is a person who carries things for other people. The root *port* also means "harbor" or "gate." The place in which ships anchor may be called either a harbor or port. The places where airplanes land and are kept is, of course, called an air*port*. Likewise, space vehicles are kept in space*ports,* and automobiles in car*ports*.

It is from ports of various kinds that goods are *exported* and *imported*—sent out and taken in. The prefix *ex-* means "out of" or "from," and the prefix *im-* means "in."

Transfer has a meaning that is similar to the meaning of *transport*. The root *fer* means "to carry" or "to bear." Both *transport* and *transfer* refer to moving things, but transport refers to the action of actually carrying something somewhere, while transfer refers to the changing of location without mention of the actual carrying.

Word Part	Meaning	English Word
trans-	across; beyond	transport, transfer
port	to carry; harbor; gate	transport, porter, port
ex-	out of; from	export
im-	in	import
fer	to carry; to bear	transfer

Finding Meanings

Write each word or word part beside its meaning.

trans-   **port**   **ex-**   **im-**   **transfer**

1. carrying something from one place to another_____

2. out of; from_____

3. in _____

4. harbor _____

5. across; beyond_____

True or False

Write T if a statement is true or F if it is false.

_____ 1. A landing and taking off place for a helicopter is called a heliport.

_____ 2. A policewoman who is sent from one precinct to another across town has been given a transfer.

_____ 3. An import is something that cannot be brought in from another place.

_____ 4. When a person sells a house, he turns over the deed to the new owner. In other words, the two people transport the deed.

_____ 5. When the United States takes in coffee beans from South America, the United States imports those beans.

Choose an Answer

Put an **X** in the box beside the correct answer.

1. A radio message that is sent across the ocean from England to America could be called

   ☐ a. transatlantic.
   ☐ b. transported.
   ☐ c. exported.

2. A building that explodes sends particles hurtling out, so a building that collapses in on itself, sending particles inward, is said to

   ☐ a. deplode.
   ☐ b. implode.
   ☐ c. unplode.

3. Since *port* means "to carry" and *-able* means "capable of," it stands to reason that *portable* means "capable of

   ☐ a. standing still."
   ☐ b. being carried."
   ☐ c. generating power."

4. If we know re- means "back" or "again," then newspaper people who observe events, write about those events, and send what they've written back to their papers are called

   ☐ a. readers.
   ☐ b. recorders.
   ☐ c. reporters.

5. Coffee is a Colombian

   ☐ a. transfer.
   ☐ b. transport.
   ☐ c. export.

Being able to associate a word (written or spoken) with a graphic image, such as a picture, a map, or a graph, is an important part of vocabulary learning. Teachers have long used pictures, maps, graphs, and realia in their instruction, and these are very important. The Internet increasingly contains pictures for a multitude of topics. Associating words with other words is a big part of vocabulary instruction, but whenever you can make a word graphically visual, you should do so. Dictionaries often use illustrations for words and they are really helpful. Here are two words illustrated in *Webster's New World Basic Dictionary.*

sloth

snorkel

A verbal description might be good, but "A picture is worth a thousand words," as Confucius is reputed to have said.

There are a number of picture dictionaries suitable for beginning readers or English language learners.

There are even whole dictionaries that define by illustration and textbooks or how-to-do-it books that rely heavily on illustrations. Your librarian can help you find some of these types of books, such as *The Facts on File Visual Dictionary* or *Royce's Sailing Illustrated.* Have a few heavily illustrated books lying around the classroom. Some of your students will learn a lot of vocabulary from them.

Method 23 Simple, Old-Fashioned Vocabulary Lesson

Confused by too many methods? Try this with List 152 in Chapter 2, Roots, or any of the other lists in that chapter.

1. Select a root and some example words.

2. Write them on the chalkboard as you discuss them.

3. Refer to word meanings and uses.

4. Ask the students for meanings and uses.

For more instruction, do one or more of the following:

1. Have the students copy the words.

2. Have the students write or say the words in a sentence.

3. Use the words in a spelling lesson (see Chapter 7, Spelling, Abbreviations, and Phonics).

4. Review the words (see Method 4, in this chapter, on Time).

5. Later, have a quiz on the words (see Method 11, in this chapter, on Testing).

> *In composing, as a general rule, run your pen through every other word you have written; you have no idea what vigor it will give your style.*
>
> —Sydney Smith, *Lady Holland's Memoir*

Many teacher methods books suggest that every day the teacher should teach a new word. That is okay, but you will never live long enough to use most of that book. There are only about 180 teaching days in the school year.

So how about teaching a word family a day or several times a week? Chapter 2 has many interesting root families and even a group of Easy Root Lessons (List 52).

You can add to your vocabulary words several interesting homophone pairs from Chapter 11.

Teaching vocabulary for reading, writing, speaking, and listening is one of the most important things a teacher can do.

Here are some word clusters for your chalkboard, word wall, poster, class discussion, student notebooks, or spelling lessons.

SAT words	Synonyms for Carry	Phobias
aberration	move	acrophobia
abridge	transfer	aquaphobia
accessible	remove	claustrophobia
antidote	transmit	kleptophobia
appease	transport	thermophobia

Numbers	Ruling	Words
quad	plutocracy	synonyms
penta	aristocracy	eponyms
quint	democracy	exonyms
hex	monarchy	antonyms
sex	theocracy	homonyms

Indian Tribes	Musical Instruments	Animals
Cherokee	piccolo	heifer
Navajo	bassoon	doe
Sioux	guitar	stallion
Chippewa	mandolin	gander
Choctaw	oboe	fledgling

For homophone teaching methods, see List 197.
For spelling teaching methods, see List 165.

Chapter 10

AFFIXES AND ROOTS

Introduction

Introduction

Everybody knows what an affix is. It is a general term to include both prefixes and suffixes. Here is a simple example: take the word *unhappiness*. Quite obviously *un-* is the prefix, *happy* is the root, and *-ness* is the suffix.

The Problem

But let's take a word like *agoraphobia*. Is *agra* the "prefix" and *phobia* the "suffix"? Or is one a "root" and the other an "affix"? Or are they both roots? We could partially solve the problem by calling them both "combining forms." Dictionaries are not much help either, as they give some canned common definition like "a prefix is fixed before a root."

We might get a little help from the linguistic concept of *morphemes*. A morpheme is a meaning unit. A *free* morpheme can stand alone, for example, every word is a free morpheme; and a *bound* morpheme must have a root or word to attach. So back to our examples. Obviously, *un-* and *-ness* are bound morphemes. But is *phobia* a bound morpheme? It can stand alone, for example, when we talk about a person having *phobias*. But can *agra* stand alone?

All this discussion leads to a very real problem in the master list, where we have assigned combining forms into the categories of prefixes, roots, and suffixes. This is done partially on the basis of simple definition, partially on authority of others, and partially on the subjective judgment of the author. So do not be surprised if you find a combining form one place or another or maybe even two places. I have even thought of abandoning the whole idea of affixes and calling them all morphemes—and maybe I should have—but I bowed to convention and confusion. However, I would at least like to make you aware of the problem.

Prefixes

Prefixes really do affect meaning, and that emphasizes the "Is it a prefix or a root?" problem. To help teachers decide what prefixes to teach, we have several lists of prefixes based on their commonness or frequency of occurrence—Lists 182, 183, and 184 in this chapter.

Also, the prefixes *ad-* and *sub-* have a nasty habit of changing their final consonant to be like the beginning consonant of the root. See Lists 185 and 186 in this chapter.

Suffixes

Prefixes are rather nice in that they nearly always contribute substantially to the meaning of the word. Suffixes, on the other hand, while often contributing to the meaning of the word, frequently form a grammatical function of assigning the part of speech to the root. Take the root *like,* which is normally a verb, as in "I *like* you." By adding *-ness* we can make it into a noun, as in "I don't see the *likeness,*" or we can make it the past tense of a verb by adding *-ed* as in "he *liked* her yesterday." In both cases of the suffixes *-ed* and *-ness,* not much different meaning is added to the root *like,* but they are certainly necessary for grammar rules.

Hence, in addition to a suffix meaning list, we have added (or selected) a list of suffixes that change words into different parts of speech. See List 193, Suffix Grammar List, and List 187, Suffix Review, in this chapter. However, the suffixes meaning list, List 192 in this chapter, our largest suffix list, can be used as a reference list, like a dictionary, to look up suffix meanings. It overlaps the suffix grammar and suffix review lists and the most common suffixes found in List 188.

Roots

We have a whole chapter on Roots (see Chapter 2) and more in other places like Chapter 3 on word origins, but our largest list of roots appears in this chapter because, in breaking up words, you need the three main elements: prefixes, roots, and suffixes. Hence, if you want to teach a new word by breaking it apart, this chapter will be a lot of help.

List 182   The Most Common Prefix (un-)

The most common prefix in English is *un-* meaning "not." We see it in hundreds of English words, or more correctly, it is used in over ten thousand English words. It is so common that just about anybody who speaks even a little English knows what it means and how to use it. Lewis Carroll did not have any trouble communicating the meaning of an *unbirthday* to children when Alice was in Wonderland.

The meaning of "not" is clear in adjectives like *unfair*; adverbs like *unfairly*; or nouns like *unfairness*.

However, in verbs, it sometimes takes on a slightly different meaning of "reversal," as in such verbs as *unbend* or *unfasten*.

In general, knowing that *un-* means "not" will help you unlock the meaning in a lot of words.

Watch out! The prefix *uni-* is different; it means "one" as in *unilateral* (uni-lateral) (one + sided) or *unilingual* (uni-lingual) (one + tongue).

Review:

unfair	**unbend**	**unilateral**
unfairly	**unfasten**	**unilingual**
unfairness		

List 183   The Second Most Common Prefix (re-)

The second most common prefix by a landslide is *re-* meaning "back" or "again." It occurs in over 3,400 English words. Between *react* and *rezone* you already know hundreds of words. So if you want to increase your vocabulary quickly and effortlessly, just put *re-* or an *un-* in front of any word you know (well, not quite).

When the root has an obvious meaning, as in *rezone,* then the meaning of the word is obvious. But many words beginning with *re-* use Latin or Greek roots, so here is where you need to learn a little more.

A *rebate* (re-bate) (back + beat) is a return part of a payment or you could say that the original price is beaten down. When a storm *abates*, its intensity is lowered (a-bates) (not + beat), it is not beating so hard.

Or we could say that the storm is *receding* (re-ced-ing) (back + go + verb). The storm is leaving or going back where it came from.

The opposite of *re-* is *pro-,* which means "forward, coming forth, or in favor of." Hence, *proceed* means to go forward as in a *procession*.

When *pro-* is used with the meaning "in favor of" in front of a proper noun (capitalized word), it is in a hyphenated word, as in *pro-American* or *pro-British;* otherwise, in a compound word, there is no hyphen, such as in the word *proslavery* or *proeducation*.

Review:

react	**receding**	**proslavery**
rezone	**proceed**	**proeducation**
rebate	**procession**	

Prefixes are morphemes (meaning units) that come at the first part of a word (pre = before) and they are a bound morpheme, which means that they cannot stand alone and must have a root. Just to remind you, a free morpheme is basically a word and can stand alone. It is difficult to determine what is a prefix and what is a root, and it is often just a matter of subjective judgment. However, there are some guidelines: as we said, a prefix is usually at the front of a word and requires a root.

A word must have a root, but a word does not necessarily need a prefix.

A root is often buried deep in a word and may even be behind another root.

However, it is possible to have two prefixes in a word; for example, *unreformed*.

The same prefix can appear in many words. Here is a list of the most common prefixes. If you like, this is also a suggested teaching order for beginners.

Prefix frequency is much like word frequency (see the Instant Words, List 161, in Chapter 7). A small number of prefixes make up a large percentage of the total uses of prefixes (number of words in which they occur). Of the most common prefixes, the first ten make up about 79 percent of the uses and these twenty (with variant spellings) make up over 90 percent of the uses.

Prefix	Meaning	Example
un-	not	unhappy
re-	again	rewrite
in-, im-, ir-, il-	not	inaccurate, impossible, irregular, illegal
dis-	not	disagree
en-, em-	in	enclose, embed
non-	not	nonfiction
in-, im-	in or into	inhale, immerse
over-	too much	overpriced
mis-	bad	misbehave
sub-	under, below	subzero
pre-	before	precaution
inter-	among, between	international
fore-	in front, before	foresee
de-	not, opposite	deform
trans-	across	transport
super-	over	superimpose
semi-	half	semicircle
anti-	against	antiwar
mid-	middle	midsummer
under-	too little	undernourished

Note: The prefix "a" is very common but it has many forms. See the next list.

The prefix a- is very tricky and very common so it will help you to know a bit about it.

The prefix a-, meaning "to or toward," usually occurs in a strange and wonderful spelling pattern. It picks up the first letter of the root and adds it to the prefix, forming a double letter as in *affix* (af-fix) (to + fix). Take a look at these examples.

ab-	*abbreviate*
ac-	*accident, accord*
af-	*affluent, affix*
ag-	*aggrandize, aggregate*
al-	*allege, alliance*
am-	*ammeter, ammunition*
an-	*annex, annual*
ap-	*applause, appeal*
ar-	*arrest, arrive*
as-	*asset, associate*
at-	*attach, attire*

The prefix ad- also means "to or toward," as in *adventure* (to + venture or go forth). Here are a few more examples:

admit	*adopt*	*adventure*	*adverse*

And just to make matters worse, the prefix a- also sometimes means *on,* as in *afoot, ashore,* or *aboard.*

Problems with Prefix a-

Well, just after we learn that the prefix a- means "to or toward," we find that it has quite a different meaning because the prefix a- also means "not," as in *atheist* (a-the-ist) (not + god + person). Here are a few more words with a- meaning not:

apathy	*atrophy*	*atypical*

Note that there is no doubling of the root consonant.

The prefix an- also means "not," as in *anarchy* (an-arch-y) (not + rule + ing). Here are a few more words with the an- prefix:

anarchy	*anemia*	*anesthesia*	*anorexia*

Note that the prefix an- meaning "not" (no consonant doubling) is unfortunately confused with the prefix an- meaning "to" in *annex* (with consonant doubling).

Review:

an- = not	**ad- = to**	**a- = on**	**a- = not**
anarchy	adventure	afoot	atypical
anemia	adverse	ashore	apathy
anorexia	adopt	aboard	atrophy
anesthesia	admit	affix	

Spelling of Prefixes sub- and com-

The prefix *sub-* (meaning under) is a very common prefix. When it occurs as the prefix for a free morpheme (a word that can stand alone), such as *subzero* or *subatomic*, there are over nine hundred words in the dictionary.

When the prefix *sub-* is in front of a root that is a bound morpheme (can't stand alone), it is not as common and for spelling it does have some of the characteristics of the prefix *a-*, namely it picks up the initial letter of the root and substitutes it for the *b,* thus giving the word a double letter; for example, *success* (suc = under, cess = go). You might note that this only works when the root begins with a consonant and it does not work all the time; for example, *submerge* (sub + merge = dip or immerse).

Here are some of the instances where the prefix *sub-* meaning "under" picks up the first letter of the root.

Consonant Doubled	Example	Root
CC	**success**	cess = go (to go from under)
FF	**suffer**	fer = bear
GG	**suggest**	gest = carry
MM	**summary**	ary = noun
PP	**support**	port = carry
RR	**surround**	round = round

Some words in which just the *sub-* root is used unchanged:

submit	mit = send
subsist	sist = stand
submarine	mar = sea
substitute	stit = stand
subsidize	sid = sit

Although much less common, the prefix *com-* also sometimes doubles the root beginning.

LL	**collateral**	lateral = side
MM	**comment**	men = mind
NN	**connect**	nect = tie
RR	**correlate**	cor + relation

Let's take apart *adjudicate,* which means to have a judge say how to settle a dispute.

> ad = to
> ju = judge
> dic = say
> ate = a suffix, which makes it a verb

Now let's change the suffix.

In *adjudication,* the suffix -ion makes it a noun. Note that the test for a noun is that you can put the article "a" or "the" in front of it; hence, you can say "the adjudication" but you cannot say "the adjudicate" because "adjudicate" is a verb.

The suffix -or makes it a noun, but also means a person; hence, a judge is an *adjudicator.* And of course the -s makes nouns plural, so two judges are *adjudicators.*

But the -s also indicates third-person singular; for example, "I *adjudicate,*" but "he *adjudicates.*"

The judge can lawfully sit on *judicial days,* but not *holidays* (holy + days); the -al suffix makes the word an adjective. You can't just say "sit on judicial" because adjectives need a noun like "day" to follow.

The suffix -tion also changes its spelling a bit as in:

-ion	champion, ambition, suspicion
-sion	tension, session, pension
-ation	generation, liberation, libation, tribulation

Many suffixes are light on meaning; for example, the -tion means "state or quality of" but its real importance is grammar—changing the part of speech from verb to noun. For more information, see List 193 in this chapter, Suffix Grammar List.

Print communication demands in most businesses have increased. At the same time, demographic and economic trends are forcing employers to hire employees with lower skill levels.

—Larry Mikulecky

Suffixes are *morphemes* (meaning units) that come at the end of a word (suf = under), and most are a *bound* morpheme, which means that they cannot stand alone and must have a root. Just to remind you, a free morpheme is basically a word that can stand alone. It is difficult to determine what is a suffix and what is a root, and it is often just a matter of subjective judgment. However, there are some guidelines: As we said, a suffix is usually at the end of a word and requires a root.

A word must have a root, but a word does not necessarily need a suffix.

It is possible to have two suffixes in a word; for example, *actors* (-or + -s).

The same suffix can appear in many words. Here is a list of the most common suffixes. If you like, this is also a suggested teaching order for beginners.

Suffix frequency is much like word frequency (see the Instant Words, Chapter 7, List 161). A small number of suffixes make up a large percentage of the total uses of suffixes (number of words in which they occur). Of the most common suffixes, the first ten make up about 85 percent of the uses and these twenty (with variant spelling) make up over 90 percent of the uses.

Suffix	Meaning or Grammar	Example
-s, -es	plural	cats, boxes
	verb third-person	runs
-ed	past tense	walked
	state or quality of	married
-ing	action	singing
	material	stuffing
-ly	forms adverb	fatherly
	resembling	slowly
-er, -or (agentive)	one who (person)	teacher, sailor
-er	comparative adj. or adv.	stronger, faster
-ion, -tion, -ation, -ition	state or quality of	suspicion, caution
	forms noun	desperation, ignition
-ible, -able	is able	combustible, comfortable
-al, -ial	relating to	maternal, filial
-y	forms adj. or diminutive	chewy, Billy
-ness	state or quality of	happiness
-ity, -ty	state or quality of	necessity, loyalty
-ment	forms noun from verb	enjoyment
	product or thing	pavement
-ic	relating to, forms adj.	historic
-ous, -ious	full of, forms adj. and adv.	joyous, religious
-en	made of, forms adj.	wooden
	past completed action	taken
-ive, -ative, -itive	inclined to, forms adj.	negative, talkative, positive
-ful	full of	fearful
-less	without	thoughtless
-est	most	smartest

Suffixes for It's a Person

A number of suffixes indicate that the word designates a person. Frequently it changes a verb into a noun. Or to say it another way, it identifies the person with the action he or she performs. For example, a *teacher* teaches, an *actor* acts, and a *servant* serves.

Suffix	Example
-an	American, veteran
-ant	servant, assistant
-ar	beggar, liar
-arch	monarch, patriarch
-ard	drunkard, coward
-arian	librarian, humanitarian
-crat	autocrat, bureaucrat
-ent	resident, superintendent
-er	teacher, painter
-eer	engineer, puppeteer
-enne (f)	comedienne, equestrienne
-ess (f)	princess, waitress
-eur	chauffeur, connoisseur
-holic	alcoholic, chocoholic
-ician	physician, beautician
-ier	cashier, financier
-ina (f)	ballerina, czarina
-ine (f)	heroine, Josephine
-ist	biologist, capitalist
-ite	socialite, Luddite
-man	cameraman, doorman
-or	actor, doctor
-ster	gangster, gamester
-trix (f)	aviatrix, executrix
-yer	lawyer, sawyer

Master List of Prefixes

We have added some cross-references so that if you look up a prefix in this master list you will see a cross-reference (see 2:24), which means that for "bi-," for example, there is more information in Chapter 2: List 24.

A

Prefix	Meaning	Examples
a-	not	apathy, atheist, atypical
a-	on	aboard, afoot, ashore
a-	from, away from	avert, aback, aghast
ab-	from	abacus, abnormal, abolish, abstain

abacus

abs-	from, away from	absent, abstention
ac-	to (consonant doubling)	accent, accept, accident
aceto-	vinegar	acetometer, acetic acid
ad-	to	adapt, addict, adhere
af-	to (consonant doubling)	affect, affiliate, affirm
after-	after	afternoon, afterward, aftershock
ag-	to (consonant doubling)	agglomeration, aggrandize, aggravate
al-	to (consonant doubling)	allege, alliance, allotment
am-	to	amble, amputation, amnesia
ambi-	both, around	ambidextrous, ambiguous, ambivalent
amphi-	both, around	amphibian, amphitheater, amphora
an-	not (used before a vowel)	anarchy, anesthesia, anorexia
an-	to (consonant doubling)	annex, annihilate, annotate
an-	without, lacking	anonymous, anaerobic
ana-	against, up	analogy, anatomy, analysis
ante-	before	antebellum, antecedent, antedate
anti-	against	antiwar, antisocial, antislavery (see 2:30)
ap-	to (consonant doubling)	applause, appeal, appertain
ar-	to (consonant doubling)	arrest, arrive, arrange
as-	to	ascend, ascertain, aspire
at-	to (consonant doubling)	attach, attire, attend, attract
auto-	self	autobiography, automatic, autograph

B

Prefix	Meaning	Examples
be-	make	befriend, bewitch, beguile
bene-	good	benefit, benefactor, benediction (see 2:34)
bi-	two	bicycle, bifocal, bilingual (see 2:24)
bin-	two	binocular, binaural, binary
by-	near, side	bypass, bystander, byway

C

Prefix	Meaning	Examples
cata-	down, against	catastrophe, catapult, catalogue
cent-	hundred, hundredth	cent, century (see 2:27)
centi-	hundred, hundredth	centigrade, centimeter (see 2:27)
circu-	around	circulate, circumference, circus
co-	with, together	cooperate, co-author, coordinate
col-	with, together	collaborate, collateral, colleague
com-	with, together	combine, commune, compare
con-	with, together	concede, concur, concert (see 2:30)
contra-	against, opposite	contrary, contradict, contrast
cor-	with, together	correspond, correct, correlate
counter-	against, opposite	counteract, countermand

D

Prefix	Meaning	Examples
de-	down, away	deduct, descend, decrease
de-	not, opposite	deform, deplete, deforestation
de-	remove, reverse	decode, deactivate, debunk
de-	very thoroughly	derelict, denude
de-	off, away	desist
dec-	ten	decennial, December
deca-	ten	decade, decathlon, decameter (see 2:27)
deci-	tenth	decimeter, decimate, decibel (see 2:27)
demi-	half	demigod, demitasse, demimonde (see 2:25)
di-	two, double	dilemma, dioxide, dichotomy
dia-	through, across	diameter, dialogue, diagonal
dif-	reversal	differential, diffidence

rear axle

differential

rear axle

Prefix	Meaning	Examples
dis-	not, opposite	disappear, disagree, disarm (see 2:30)
dis-	off, away	dismiss, disability
du-, duo-	two	duo, duet, dual (see 3:63)
dys-	bad	dysfunctional, dysentery, dystrophy

E

Prefix	Meaning	Examples
e-	out, away, forth	eclipse, eject, evict

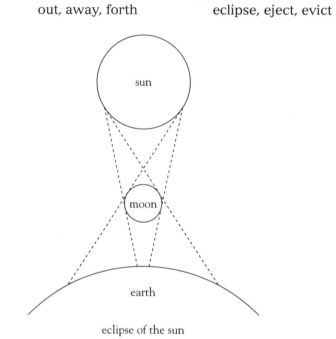

eclipse of the sun

ec-	out	eccentric, eclectic, eclipse
ef-	out, out of	efface
em-	in	embalm, embed, embezzle
en-	in	enchant, enclose, encounter
endo-	inside, within	endomorph, endoscopic, endoskeleton
ennea-	nine	enneagon, enneahedron, ennead
enter-	among, between	enterprise, entertain
eph-	outside	ephemeral
epi-	after	epilogue, epitaph, epidermis
epi-	upon	epicenter, epidemic
equi-	equal	equator, equation, equilibrium (see 2:41)
eu-	good	eulogy, euphoria, euphemism
ex-	former	ex-president, ex-student, ex-athlete
ex-	out	exceed, exhaust, exit
exa-	quintillion	exameter
extra-	outside	extracurricular, extraordinary, extravagant
extro-	outside	extrovert, extrorse

F

Prefix	Meaning	Examples
femto-	quadrillionth	femtometer
for-	prohibit	forbid, forget, forgo
fore-	in front	forecast, foresee, forebode

G

Prefix	Meaning	Examples
giga-	billion	gigawatt, gigahertz, gigabyte

H

Prefix	Meaning	Examples
hect-	hundred	hectogram, hectometer, hectare
hemi-	half	hemisphere, hemiplegia, hemicycle (see 2:25)
hept-	seven	heptagon, heptameter, heptarchy (see 2:27)
hetero-	different	heteronym, heterogeneous, hetero-sexual
hex-	six	hexagon, hexameter, hexagram (see 2:27)
homo-	same	homogeneous, homogenize, homo-sexual
hyper-	excessive	hyperactive, hypersensitive, hyper-bole (see 2:41)
hypo-	under	hypochondria, hypodermic, hypothesis (see 2:41)

I

Prefix	Meaning	Examples
il-	not	illegal, illegible, illiterate
il-	in, into	illuminate, illustrate
im-	into	immerse, immigrate, implant
im-	not	impossible, immobilize, innate
in-	into	incision, include, index, inhale

index finger

Affixes and Roots

Prefix	Meaning	Examples
in-	not	inaccurate, inactive, inadvertent
inter-	among, between	international, intermission, intervene
intra-	within	intramural, intrastate, intravenous
intro-	inside	introduce, introspect, introjection
ir-	not	irregular, irreconcilable, irrevocable
is-	equal	isometric, isosceles, isotope

K

Prefix	Meaning	Examples
kilo-	thousand	kilometer, kilogram, kilowatt (see 2:27)

M

Prefix	Meaning	Examples
macro-	large, long	macroeconomics, macron, macrobiotic
magni-	great, large	magnify, magnificent, magnitude
mal-	bad	maladjusted, malfunction, malice (see 2:34)
male-	bad	maleficent, malevolent, malediction
mega-	large, million	megaphone, megalith, megacycle
meta-	change	metamorphosis, metaphor, metastasis
micro-	small, short	microphone, microscope, microwave
mid-	middle	midnight, midway, midsummer
milli-, mili-	thousand	million, milligram, millimeter (see 2:25)
mis-	bad	mistrust, misbehave, miscarriage
mis-	wrong	mispronounce, miscount, mismatch (see 2:48)
mon-	one	monk, monarch
mono-	one	monocular, monorail, monogamy (see 2:24, 2:27)
multi-	many, much	multiply, multicolored, multi-millionaire
myria-	ten thousand	myriameter

N

Prefix	Meaning	Examples
nano-	billionth	nanometer, nanosecond
ne-	not	nefarious, never
net-	not	negative, neglect, negotiate
neo-	new	neoclassical, neonatal, neon
non-	not	nonsense, nonfiction, nonresistant
non-	nine	nonagenarian
nove-	nine	November, novena (see 2:27)

O

Prefix	Meaning	Examples
ob-	to, on, against	obelisk, obtain, object, obfuscate

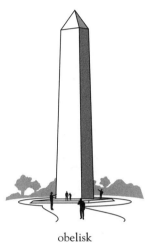

obelisk

Prefix	Meaning	Examples
oct-	eight	October, octagon, octopus (see 2:27)
off-	from	offset, offshoot, offshore
olig-	few	oligarchy, oligopoly, oligophagous (see 2:27)
omni-	all	omnibus, omnificent, omnipotent
on-	on	oncoming, ongoing, onshore
op-	opposite, against	oppose, opposition
out-	surpassing	outbid, outclass, outlive, outrun
over-	too much	overdue, overpriced, overbearing

P

Prefix	Meaning	Examples
pan-	all	panorama, panacea, pandemonium
par-	by	paramour, paraphrase
para-	almost	paramedic, paralegal, parasail (see 2:27)
para-	beside	paradigm, paragraph, parallel
pene-	almost	peneplain, peninsula, penultimate
pent-	five	pentagon, pentathalon, Penticostal (see 2:26)
per-	through, utterly	perennial, permeate, permit
peri-	around	perimeter, periscope, periphery
peta-	quadrillion	petameter
pico-	trillionth	picometer
poly-	many	polysyllabic, polyester, polygamy (see 2:27)
post-	after	postpone, postdate, postscript
pre-	before	prefix, precaution, prenatal
prime-	first	primer (see 2:27)

Prefix	Meaning	Examples
pro-	favor, for	pro-war, Pro-American, pro-education
pro-	forward	proceed, produce, progress, profess
prot-	first, chief	protagonist, proton, prototype (see 2:27)
pseudo-	false	pseudonym, pseudo-classical
pur-	in favor of	purport, purpose, pursue

Q

Prefix	Meaning	Examples
quadr-	four	quadrangle, quadrant, quadriplegic (see 2:26)

quadrant

quint-	five	quintuplet, quintet, quintessential (see 2:26)

R

Prefix	Meaning	Examples
re-	again	redo, rewrite, reappear
re-	back	recall, repay, retract
retro-	back	retroactive, retrogress, retro-rocket

S

Prefix	Meaning	Examples
se-	apart	seclude, sequester
self-	self	selfish, self-denial, self-respect
semi-	half	semiannual, semicircle, semiconscious (see 2:25)
sept-	seven	September, septet, septuagenarian
sex-	six	sextant, sextet, sextuple (see 2:26)
*sub-	under, below	submarine, subzero, submerge
super-	over	superimpose, superintendent
super-	more, better, higher	superhighway, superheated, superscript
sur-	above, over	surtax, surplus
syl-	together	syllable, syllogism
sym-	together	symbiosis, symbol, symmetry
syn-	with, together	synchronize, syndrome, synergy (same meaning as com-)

Note: The prefix sub- tends to drop the b and pick up the first letter of the root in some words; for example: *suffix, success, suggest, sudden, support, surrender.* This accounts for the spelling using double letters.

Master List of Prefixes *(continued)*

T

Prefix	Meaning	Examples
tele-	distant	telephone, television, telepathy
tera-	trillion	terameter
tetra-	four	tetrahedron, tetrameter (see 2:27)
through-	through	throughput, thoroughbred, thoroughfare
trans-	across	transport, transfer, translate
tri-	three	triangle, tricycle, trillion (see 2:24)

U

Prefix	Meaning	Examples
ultra-	beyond	ultramodern, ultraconservative, ultranationalist
un-	not, opposite	unhappy, unable, uncomfortable
under-	below, less than	underpaid, undercover, underground
uni-	one	unicorn, uniform, unite

unicorn

W

Prefix	Meaning	Examples
with-	back, away	withdraw, withhold, within

We have added some cross-references so if you look up a root in this master list, such as "allo," you will see a cross-reference (see 2:44), which means that there is more information on "allo" in Chapter 2: List 44.

A

Root	Meaning	Examples
ace	sour, sharp	acerbity, acetic, acetone
aci	sour, sharp	acidity, acid, acidify
acri	sour, bitter	acrid, acrimony, acrimonious
acous	hear	acoustics, acoustical, acoustically
acro	height, end	acropolis, acrobat, acrophobia, acronym
act	do, drive	action, actor, react, transact, enact
acu	sharp	acute, acupuncture, acumen, acuity
aero	air	aerobics, aerodynamics, aeronautics
aesthet	sense, perception	aesthetics, aesthetically, aesthete
ag	move, do	agent, agency, agenda
agi	drive, do	agile, agitate, agitation, agitator
agogue	leader	demagogue, pedagogue
agon	struggle	agony, antagonize, protagonist, agonize
agri	farming	agribusiness, agrichemical, agronomy
agro	field, crop	agriculture, agrobiology, agroeconomics
aholic	addicted	workaholic, alcoholic, chocaholic
al	feed, grow	alimentary, coalition, alimony, alumni
alb	white	album, albumen, albino, albatross
ali	another	alias, alibi, alien, alienate, inalienable
alle	other	allegory, parallel, allergy
allo	other	alloy, allotrope, allocation (see 2:44)
alt	high	altitude, altimeter, alto, altocumulus
alter	other	alter, alternate, alternative, altercation
ama(o)	love, friend	amateur, amatory, enamor (see 3:68)
amb	walk, go	amble, preamble, ambidexterity
ambul	walk, go	ambulance, circumambulate
ami	friend	amiable, amity, amigo, amie, amicus
amo	love	amorous, amour, paramour, amoretto
ampl	large, wide	ample, amplification, amplitude, amply
ang	bend	angle, triangle, rectangle, angular
ang	choke	anger, angina, anguish
angel	messenger	angel, evangelize, angelus
angl	angle	angle, triangle, quadrangle
anim	life, spirit	animate, animosity, animal, inanimate
ann(i, u)	year	annual, anniversary, annuity
ante	before	antebellum, antecedent, antedate
anthr(o)	man	anthropology, philanthropist
anti	against	antiwar, antisocial, anticlimax (see 2:30)
antiqu	ancient	antique, antiquary, antiquity

Root	Meaning	Examples
apo	away, off, apart	apostrophe, apology, apoplexy
apt	fit	apt, aptitude, adapt
aqu(a, i)	water	aquarium, aquatic, aquamarine, aquifer
arb	judge	arbiter, arbitrarily, arbitrate
arbor	tree	arbor, arborist, arboretum, arborescent
arc	vow, arch	arc, arch, arcade, archery
arch	ruler, leader	monarch, archbishop, matriarch (see 2:29)
archa(e)	primitive, original	archaic, archetype, archaeology
archi	primitive, original	archive, archival, architecture
ard	burn	ardent, ardor, arduous
aristo	best born	aristocrat, aristocracy, aristocratically
arm	weapon	armory, armaments, armada, armistice
ars	burn	arson, arsonist
art	skill	artful, artifice, artificial, artistically
arthr	relating to joints	arthritis, arthropod
artic	joint	article, articulate, inarticulate
asp	rough	aspirate, asperity, exasperate
ast(r)	star	astronaut, astronomy, disaster, asterisk
astut	crafty	astute, astutely, astuteness
athl	contest	athlete, athletically, decathlon
atmos	vapor	atmosphere, atmospherically
atroc	cruel	atrocity, atrocious, atrociousness
auc	add to, increase	auction, auctioneer
aud(i)	hear	audience, auditorium, audible, audition
aug	increase	augment, August, augmentation
augu	omen	augur, inaugural, reinaugurate
auri	ear	auricle, auricular, aurist, auriscope
aus	hear, listen	ausculate, ausculation
auspic	soothsay	auspice, auspiciously, inauspicious
auto	self	autocracy, autonomy, autobiographic
avi	bird	aviator, aviatrix, aviate, aviary
axiom	evident	axiom, axiomatic, axiomatically

B

Root	Meaning	Examples
bac	a staff	bacteria, bacterial, bacillus, bacillar
ball	dance	ballroom, ballad, ballerina, ballet
bapt	dipped	baptism, baptize, Baptist, Anabaptist
barb	savage	barbarian, barbarism, barbarous
bark	a ship	embark, debark, disembark
baro	weight, pressure	barometer, barograph, baroscope
bas	base, low	basic, basis, basement, bassoon
bat	battle	combat, debate, embattled, battlefield
batho	deep	bathosphere, batholith
bell(i)	war	bellicose, antebellum, belligerent

Root	Meaning	Examples
bene	well	benefit, benediction, benevolent (see 2:34)
bi	two	biennial, bigamist, binocular (see 2:24, 2:27)
biblio	book	bibliography, bibliophile, bibliotherapy
bio	life	biology, biography, biochemistry, biopsy
bla	censure	blasphemy, blasphemous, blame
bol	throw	bolt, embolism, hyperbole, parabola
bon	good	bonus, bounty, bona fide, bonny
botan	plant	botany, botanical, botanically, botanist
brac	arm	brace, bracelet, embrace
brev	short	abbreviation, abbreviate, brevity, breve
bronch	windpipe	bronchial, bronchitis, bronchia, bronchus
brut	bestial	brute, brutal, brutish, brutality
bryo	moss	bryophyte, bryology

C

Root	Meaning	Examples
caco	bad	cacophony, cacology, cacography
cad	fall	cadence, cadaver, decadence
cal	glow, heat	calorie, caloric, caldron, scald
calc	pebble	calcium, calculus, calculate
cam	field	camp, campus, encamp, campaign
camera	chamber	camera, bicameral, unicameral
camp	plain	campus, encamp, decamp, campaign
cand	shine, white	candle, incandescent, candid, candidate
cant	sing	cant, cantata, incantation
cap	head	cap, captain, capital, decapitate, caput

Corinthian   Doric   Ionic

Capitals

Root	Meaning	Examples
cap	take, seize, hold	capable, capacity, capsule, captivate
capit	head, cap	capitol, capital, capitalism, decapitate
capr	leap	caprice, capriciously, capriciousness
capt	hold	captive, recapture, capticious, caption
card	heart	cardiac, cardiology, cardiogram
carn	flesh	carnal, carnage, reincarnate, carnation
carp	seize	carp, carper, excerpt, Carpe Diem
cas	fall	cascade, casualty, occasion
cas	box	case, cassette, encase, cash, casket
caus	cause	cause, causal, causeless, causerie
caus	burn	caustic, holocaust
caut	beware	caution, incaution, precaution
caut	burn, heat	cauterize, cautery, cauterization
cav	hollow	cave, cavern, cavity, concave, excavate
caval	horse	cavalry, cavalcade, cavalier
cease	go, yield	cease, surcease, decease
cede	go, yield	concede, secede, antecedent, intercede
ceed	go, yield	proceed, exceed, succeed
ceit	take, seize	receipt, deceit
ceive	take, receive	receive, perceive, deceive, conceive
cens	appraise, judge	censor, censorious, censure, census
cent	hundred	cent, centenarian, centennial (see 2:31, 2:33)
centr	center	central, centrifugal, egocentric, eccentric
cephalo	relating to the head	cephalopod, cephalic, cephalothorax
cept	take, receive	reception, accept, conception, intercept
cerebro	of the brain	cerebrospinal, cerebral, cerebrate
cern	sift	concern, unconcern, discern
cert	sure, determine	certain, certify, ascertain, certificate
cess	go, yield	process, recess, access, concession
cha	hot, warm	chafe, nonchalant
cham	vault	chamber, chambermaid, chamberlain
chaos	abyss	chaos, chaotic
chap	hooded cloak	chapel, chaplain, chaplet, chapfallen
chapt	head	chapter
chari	grace	charity, charitable, uncharitable
chart	paper	chart, charter
chast	pure	chaste, chastise, chastity
chef	head	chef, chieftain, chief
chemo	drug	chemotherapy, chemoreflex
chiro	hand	chiropractor, chirography (see 2:44)
chloro	green	chlorophyll, chlorite, chlorosis (see 3:65)
chol	bile	cholera, choleric, melancholy
chor	sing	choral, chorus, chorister
chrom	color	chromatic, chrome, chromosome
chron	time	chronological, synchronize, chronicle
cid	fall	accident, coincide, incident

Root	Meaning	Examples
cide	cut, kill	suicide, insecticide, genocide (see 2:23)
cinc	gird	cincture, precinct, succinct
cine	movement	cinema, cinematic, cinematography
cip	take, seize	participate, participle, incipient, recipe
cipit	head, cap	precipitous, precipitate, precipitation
circ(um)	ring around	circus, circle, encircle, semicircle
cis	cut, kill	circumcise, decisive, incisor, indecisive

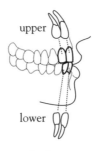

upper

lower

incisors

Root	Meaning	Examples
cit	rouse, call	cite, excite, incite, recite, resuscitate
cit	city	city, citizen, citadel (see 3:72)
civ	city	civic, civil, civilize, civilization (see 3:72)
claim	shout	proclaim, exclaim, acclaim
clam	shout	clamor, exclamation
clar	clear	claret, clarity, declare, clarify
class	rank	class, classical, classify, classification
claus	shut	claustrophobia, clause
clem	mild	clement, clemency, inclement
cler	assigned	clergy, cleric, clerk, clerkship
cline	lean	incline, recline, decline, inclination
cliv	bend, slope	acclivity, declivity, proclivity
clo	close, shut	close, disclose, enclose
clud	close, shut	include, conclude, exclude, preclude
clus	shut	recluse, inclusive, exclusion
coc	cook	concoct, concoction, precocious
cod	a tablet	code, codicil, codify, codification
cogn	know	recognize, incognito, cognition
col	care for	colony, colonial, colonization
color	hue	color, coloration, discolor, uncolored
com	festivity	comedy, comic, tragicomedy, encomium
com	with	compound, comprehend, commix
commun	common	community, communicate, communism
comp	with bread	company, companion, accompany
con	with	continue, contort, consume
concil	win over	conciliate, conciliatory, irreconcilable

Root	Meaning	Examples
contra	opposed	contrary, contrarily, contrast
copula	couple	copulate, copulation, copula
cord	heart	cordial, accord, concord, discord
corn	a horn	cornet, unicorn, cornea, cornucopia
coron	a crown	coronation, coroner, coronet
corp	body	corporation, corpse, corps, corpuscle
cosm(o)	universe	cosmonaut, cosmos, cosmopolitan
cortico	outer part	corticoid, corticolous
count	reckon	account, discount, recount, uncounted
cour	heart	courage, encourage, discourage
cour	run	course, courier, concourse, discourse
court	royally	courtly, courtesy, discourteous
cover	hide	cover, discover, covertly, undiscovered
cracy	rule, strength	aristocracy, autocracy, theocracy (see 2:29)
crat	rule	aristocrat, democratic (see 2:29)
cre	grow	accretion, crew, crescent, crescendo
cre	burst	crevice, crevasse, decrepit, discrepancy
crea	create	create, creative, procreate, recreate
crease	rise, grow	increase, decrease
cred	believe	credit, discredit, incredible, credential
cresc	rise, grow	crescendo, crescent, excrescent
cret	sift, judge	discrete, discretion, excrete, secret
crim	crime, accuse	crime, criminal, discriminate
crit	judge, distinguish	critic, criticism, criterion, critique
cru	to grow	accrue, accrual
cruc	cross	crucial, crucible, crucify
crypt	secret	crypt, cryptic, cryptogram
cub	lie down	cubicle, cubit, incubate, concubine
cul	care for	cultivate, culture, agriculture, horticulture
culp	blame	culpable, culprit, exculpate, mea culpa
cum	lie down	incumbent, recumbent, succumb
cum(u)	heap	cumulative, accumulate, cumulus
cup	take	occupy, preoccupy, occupation
cur	care	cure, manicure, pedicure, curator
cur	run	current, curriculum, concur, occur
curs	run	cursive, cursory, excursion
curt	short	curtly, curtail, curtailing, curtailment
curv	bent	curvation, curvilinear, curvity, recurve
cus	cause	accuse, accusation, excuse
cuss	shake	concussion, discuss, percussion
custom	manner	accustom, custom, customary
cyc(l)	circle, ring	bicycle, cyclone, cycle, encyclopedia
cyn	doglike	cynicism, cynosure, cynegetics
cyto	relating to cells	cytoplasm, cytostasis, cytozoon

D

Root	Meaning	Examples
damn	harm	damn, damnable, damage
dat	give	data, date, postdate, antedate, mandate
debt	owe	debt, indebted, debtor
dec	comely	decent, indecent, decorum, décor
dec(a, i)	ten	decimal, decade, December (see 2:27)
decor	to befit	décor, indecorous, decorate, decorum
dei	god	deism, deity, deify
dek	ten	dekaliter, dekameter, dekagram (see 2:27)
delet	erase	delete, deletion, deleterious
delic	delights	delicious, delicacy, delicately, indelicate
demi	half	demitasse, demigod (see 2:28)
dem(o)	people	democracy, demography, endemic
demono	devil	demon, demonology, demondatry
demn	penalize, harm	condemn, condemnation, indemnity
dendro	tree	dendrite, dendrology, dendrogram
dens	thick	condensable, condensation, density
dent	tooth	dentist, trident, dentifrice, indent
derm	skin	dermatitis, dermatology, epidermis
dext	right hand	dexterity, dexterously, dextral
di	two	dioral, dioxide (see 2:27)
di(a)	day	dial, diary, meridian, antemeridian
dic	proclaim, say	abdicate, dedicate, indicate (see 2:35)
dict	speak, say	dictate, predict, contradict, verdict
digit	finger	digit, digital, digitalis, prestidigitator
dign	worthy	dignify, dignity, indignation, condign
disci	learn	disciple, discipline, disciplinarian
dit	give	addition, edit, edition, editor, tradition
div	god	divine, divination, divinity
divi	divide	divide, divorce, division, dividend
doc	teach	docile, document, docility
doct	teach	doctrine, doctor, indoctrinate, docile
dogma	belief	dogma, dogmatic
dol	grieve, pain	doleful, dolorous, condole, indolent
dom	house	domestic, domestication, domicile
domin	master	dominate, domineer, predominate
don	give	donor, pardon, condone (see 2:30)
donat	give	donation, donate, donator
dont	tooth	orthodontist, odontoid
dorm	sleep	dormant, dormer, dormitory, dormouse
dos	give	dose, dosage, dosimeter, dossier
dot	give	anecdote, anecdotal, doting
dou	two	doubt, double, doublet, redoubtable
dox	belief, praise	orthodox, heterodox, paradox, doxology
drome	run	hippodrome, dromatery, palindrome
du	owe	due, undue, duty, dutiful
du, duo	two	dual, duel, duet, duplex, duodenum (see 2:27)

Root	Meaning	Examples
dubi	uncertain	dubiously, dubitable, indubitable
duc	lead	induce, producer, conducive
duct	lead	abduct, duct, conduct, induct, aqueduct
dur	hard	durable, duration, duress, endure
dynam	power	dynamics, dynamism, dynamite

E

Root	Meaning	Examples
ebr	drunk	ebriety, ebrious, inebriate
eco	house	economical, economize, ecology
ecto	outside	ectoderm, ectocornea, ectophyte
edi	build	edifice, edification, edify
ego	ego	ego, egocentric, egoism, egomania
electro	electric	electron, electroplate, electrostatic (see 3:65)
eleg	select	elegance, elegant, elegantly, inelegantly
elem	first principle	element, elemental, elementary
emia	blood	anemia, uremia
emp	command	empire, emperor
empt	buy, take	exempt, coempt, caveat emptor
emul	imitate	emulate, emulative, emulator, emulous
encephalo	brain	encephalitis, encephalomyelitis
endo	inside	endoral, endocardial, endoskeleton
enn(i)	year	biennial, perennial, centennial
ent	to be	absent, present, represent, entity
envi	encircle	environs, environment, environmentalist
epi	on the outside	epidermis, epidural
est	to be	interest, disinterest, uninteresting
esthe(t)	sense, perception	anesthesia, anesthetist, anesthesiologist
equ(i)	equal	equal, equality, equator, equilibrium (see 2:41)
equip	fit out	equip, equipment, unequipped
equ	a horse	equestrian, equine, equerry, equitation
erc	press	coerce, coercive, exercise, unexercised
erg	work	erg, energy, energetic, synergistic
err	wander	err, erratic, errata, error, erroneous
eroto	sexual desire	erotic, erotomania, eroticism
esot	inner	esoteric, esoterical, esotericism
esth	feeling	esthetics, estheticism, anesthesia
esti	value	estimable, estimate, inestimable
eth	customs	ethics, ethical, ethically, unethical
ethn	nation	ethnic, ethnical, ethnological
eu	good	eugenics, eulogy, euphony, euthanasia
ev	age	medieval, primeval, longevity, coeval
exam	test	examine, examinee, examiner
exem	copy	exemplify, exemplary
exo	outside	exotic, exonerate, exorbitant

Root	Meaning	Examples
exper	try	experience, experiential, experiment
ext(r)	out, outward	exterior, external, extraneous, extreme

F

Root	Meaning	Examples
fab(ul)	speak	fable, fabulous, affable, ineffable
fabr	worker	fabric, fabricate, fabrication, fabricator
fac	make, do	factory, manufacture, benefactor
fac	face	face, facet, faction
fac	easy	facile, facilitate, facsimile
facet	wit	facetious, facetiously, facetiousness
fail	deceive	fail, failure
fal	deceive	fallacy, fallible, infallible, falter, false
fam	report	famous, infamy, defame, defamation
fami	hunger	famine, famish, famishment
famil	household	familiar, familiarize, family, unfamiliar
fan	temple	fanatic, unfanatical, profane, profanity
fan	speak	infant, infantry
fant	imagine	fantasy, fantastic, fantastical
farc	stuffed	farce, farcical, farceur, farcically
fasci	enchant	fascinate, fascinator, fascinatingly
fastid	disdain	fastidious, fastidiously, fastidiousness
fat	speak	fatal, fatality, fate
fatu	silly	fatuous, fatuity, infatuate, infatuation
faul	deceive	fault, faulty, faultless, default
favor	befriend	favorable, unfavorable, favorite
feas	perform	feasible, feasibility, malfeasance
feat	do, make	features, defeat, defeated
feb	fever	febrile, febrifugal, febrifuge
fec	make, do	affect, effect, infect, perfect, perfection
fed	league	federal, federalize, confederation
feit	do, make	counterfeit, surfeit, forfeiture
felic	happy	felicity, felicitate, felicitous, infelicity
femin	woman	effeminate, femininity, feminine
fend, fen	strike, keep off	fend, fender, fence, fencing, defend
fer	bear, carry	ferry, transfer, infer, refer, confer
fer	fierce	ferocious, ferocity
ferv	boil	fervid, fervent, fervor, effervescence
fess	acknowledge	confess, profess, profession, professor
fest	joyful	festival, festoon, festive
fev	fever	fever, feverish, feverroot
fic	make, do	efficient, proficient, sufficient, beneficial
fice	make, do	office, artifice, sacrifice
fid	faith, trust	fidelity, confidence, infidel, bona fide
fig	form	figure, figment, configuration, disfigure
fil	thread	file, filament, filigree, defile, profile
fili	sibling	filial, filicide, affiliate, affiliation
fin	end	affinity, confine, define, finale, finance

Root	Meaning	Examples
finan	pay	finance, financial, refinanced
firm	securely fixed	firm, confirm, infirm, affirm, firmament
fisc	monetary	fiscal, confiscate, confiscation
fissi	cleft	fissure, fission
fit	do, make	profit, benefit, comfit
fix	fix, fasten	fix, fixture, crucifix, affix, infix, prefix
flag(r)	fire, burning	flagrant, flagrantly, flagrancy
flam	burning	flame, flamboyant, flamingo
flat	blow	flatulent, flatulence, inflation, inflate
flect	bend	reflect, deflect, reflection, inflection
flex	bend	reflex, flexible, inflexible
flic	strike	afflict, conflict, inflict, profligate
flor	flower	flora, floral, florist
flu	flow	affluence, confluence, fluent, flush
fluct	flowing	fluctuate, fluctuation
foli	leaf	foliage, folio, interfoliate
found	bottom	foundation, founder, unfounded, found
force	strong	forceful, enforce, reinforce
form	shape	form, uniform, transform, reform, formal
fort	strong	fortify, fortitude, forte, comfort, effort
fortu	chance, luck	fortuitous, fortunate, misfortune
fract	break	fracture, fraction, infraction, fractious
frag	break	fragment, fragile, fragmentary
frang	break	frangible, infrangible, refrangible
frank	free	frank, frankly, frankness
frat(er)	brother	fraternal, fraternity, fratricide, fraternize
fraud	deceit	fraud, fraudulent, fraudulently
freq	often	frequent, frequenter, frequency
fric	rub	friction, dentifrice, fricative
frig	cold	frigid, refrigerate, refrigeration, frigidity
fring	border	fringe, fringeless, infringe, infringement
front	forepart	affront, confront, front, frontier
fru	enjoy	fruit, fruition, frugal, fructose
fructi	fruit	fructiferous, fructose
fug	flee	fugitive, fugue, refuge, refugee
fulg	flash	fulgent, fulgid, effulgent
fum	smoke	fume, fumeless, fumigate, perfume
funct	perform	function, malfunction, dysfunctional
fund	bottom	fund, refund, fundament, fundamental
fur	rage	fury, furious, furiously, infuriate
fus	pour, melt	fusion, confusion, diffuse, effusion
fut	disprove	refute, confute, futile

G

Root	Meaning	Examples
gag	pledge	engage, disengagement, mortgage
gam	marriage	polygamy, monogamy, bigamy, gamete
gastr	relating to the stomach	gastronomic, gastric, gastritis
gat(e)	to ask	abrogate, interrogate, prerogative
gel	frost	gelatin, gelative, gelatinous
gen	birth, beget	generation, generate, genocide (see 2:32)
gen	do	agent, cogent, exigencies, intransigent
gent	kind	gentile, gentle, genteel (see 2:33)
geo	earth	geography, geometry, geology
germ	a sprout	germ, germinate, germane, germicide
geronto	old age	gerontology, gerontocracy
gest	bear, carry	gesture, gesticulate, congestion, digest
glor	honor	glorious, glorification, ingloriously
gloss	tongue	glossary, glossolalia, gloss
glot	tongue	epiglottis, polyglot, glottal
glu	tenacious	glue, glutinous, agglutination
glut	swallow	glut, glutton, gluttonous, gluttony
gnor	know	ignorance, ignore, ignorant
gnos	know	diagnose, prognosis, agnostic, Gnostics
gon	angle	pentagon, diagonal, trigonometry
gony	birth, begetting	cosmogony, progeny
gor	marketplace	agora, agoraphobia, category
gorg	throat	gorge, gorgeous, disgorge
govern	command	government, misgovern, regovern
gra	pleasing	graceful, disgrace, gratuitous, ingratiate
grac	thankful	gracious, disgrace, ungracious
grad	step, go	gradual, grade, gradation, centigrade
gram	letter, written	telegram, diagram, grammar, epigram
gran	grain, seed	granary, granule, granite, granola
grand	great	aggrandize, grandfather, grandeur
graph	write	photograph, phonograph, autograph
grat	thankful	gratitude, gratify, congratulate
grav	heavy	grave, gravitate, gravity, aggravate
gree	pleasing	agree, disagree, agreement
greg	gather, flock	gregarious, congregation, segregation
gress	step, go	progress, egress, regress, aggression
gri	field	pilgrim, peregrine, peregrinate
grie	heavy	grieve, grievance, grief, grievous
gru	agreeing	congruent, congruously, incongruity
gust	a tasting	gustation, gusto, disgust, disgusting
gymo	naked	gymnasium, gymnastic, gym (see 3:73)
gyn	woman	gynecologist, misogynist, monogyny (see 3:73)
gyr	revolve	gyrate, gyroscope, autogyro (see 3:65)

H

Root	Meaning	Examples
hab	have, hold	habit, habitual, habitat, cohabit
hal	breathe	inhale, inhalation, halitosis, exhalation
harmon	fitting	harmony, harmonics, harmonica
haust	draw out	exhaust, exhaustible, inexhaustible
heir	heir	heir, heir-apparent, heirloom
heli	spiral	helix, helical, helicograph, helicopter
helio	sun	heliocentric, heliotherapy, heliotrope
hem	bloodlike	hemorrhage, hemorrhoids, hematin
hemi	half	hemisphere, hemiplegiae (see 2:25, 2:28)
hepta	seven	heptagon, heptamerous (see 2:27)
her	heir	inherit, heredity, hereditary, disinherit
her	stick	adhere, cohere, incoherent
herb	a plant	herbaceous, herbal, herbalist
hero	protect	hero, heroine, heroic, unheroic
hes	stick	adhesion, cohesion, inhesion, hesitate
hetero	different	heteronym, heterogeneous, heterodox
hex	six	hexagon, hexameter (see 2:26)
hib	hold	prohibit, inhibit, exhibit
hier	sacred	hierarchy, hierology, hieroglyphic
holo	whole	catholic, holograph, holocaust
hom	man	homicide, hombre, homage
homo	same	homosexual, homogeneous (see 2:44)
hon	respect	honor, honorless, dishonor, honesty
horr	dreadful	horrify, horridness, abhorrence, horror
hort	encourage	exhort, exhortation, hortatory
hosp	guest, host	hospitality, hospital, hospice
host	guest, host	host, hostess, hostel
host	an enemy	hostile, hostility, hostage
hum	man	human, humane, humanism, humanity
hum	lowly, earth	exhume, posthumous, humble, humiliate
hydr	water	hydroelectric, hydrogen, hydrant
hyper	excessive	hyperactive, hypercritical (see 2:41)
hypn	sleep	hypnotism, hypnotic, hypnotist
hypo	too little, under	hypocrite, hypoactive (see 2:41)

I

Root	Meaning	Examples
iatr	medical care	psychiatry, podiatry, pediatrician
icon	image	icon, iconic, iconoclast, iconoclastic
idea(o)	conception	idea, ideal, idealization, ideology
ident	the same	identify, identical, identity, identification
idio	peculiar	idiocy, idiom, idiosyncratic, idiotic
ido	shape, form	idol, kaleidoscope, idolatrous
ig	set in motion	exigency, ambiguous, prodigal
ign	fire	ignition, igneous, ignite

Affixes and Roots

Root	Meaning	Examples
igno	not know	ignore, ignorance, ignorant, ignoramus
ima(g)	likeness	image, imagine, imaginative, imagery
imi	likeness	imitate, inimitable
imp	command	imperative, imperious, imperial
init	beginning	initial, initiate, initiative
insul	island	insulate, insulin, peninsula
int	within	interior, internal, intestinal, intimate
integ	whole	integrate, integral, integrity, integer
interp	explain	interpret, interpretation, misinterpret
ira	anger	irascible, irate, irritation
ire	anger	ire, ireful
iso	equal, the same	isotherm, isosceles, isotope
it	to go	circuit, ambition, exit, itinerary
iter	again	iterate, iterance, iterative, reiterate

J

Root	Meaning	Examples
ject	throw	project, inject, reject, subject, eject
jet	throw	jetsam, jetty, jet
join	join	join, joint, adjoin, conjoin, disjoin, enjoin
journ	a day	adjourn, journey, journal, sojourn
jubil	cry of joy	jubilant, jubilee, jubilation
jud	law	judge, judicial, judiciary, adjudicate
jug	yoke	abjugate, conjugal, subjugate
junct	join	juncture, conjunction, adjunct, injunction
jur	law	jurisprudence, jurist, injure, jury
jur	swear	jury, juror, conjure, perjury
jus	right, law	justice, justify, injustice, injustifiable
juven	youth	juvenile, juvenal, juvenility, juvenescent

K

Root	Meaning	Examples
kin(e)	movement	kinetic, kinesthology, telekinesis
kilo	thousand	kilometer, kilogram (see 2:25, 2:27)

L

Root	Meaning	Examples
lab(or)	work	labor, laboratory, collaborate, elaborate
lact	to do with milk	lactose, lactation
lam	wail	lament, lamentation, lamentable
langu	weak	languor, languidly, languish
laparo	abdomen	laparoscopy, laparoscope
laps(e)	slip	elapse, collapse, relapse, prolapse
lat	carry	collate, correlate, dilate, elate, legislate
lateral	side	lateral, collateral, equilateral, multilateral

Root	Meaning	Examples
lau	wash	launder, laundry, laundromat
laud	praise	laud, laudable, laudatory
lav	wash	lavatory
lax	loose	laxative, relaxation, relax, laxation
lect	gather	collect, dialect, eclectic, intellect, lecture
leg	gather	elegance, legible, illegible, legend
leg	law, ambassador	legal, illegal, legitimate, illegitimate
lege	bind, send	allege, college, allegedly
len	mild	lenient, leniency, relent, relentless
lev(i)	raise, lighten	levee, lever, levity, alleviate, elevator

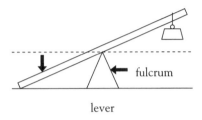

lever

Root	Meaning	Examples
lexi	speak	lexical, lexicography, dyslexic
liber	free	liberty, liberal, liberate, libertine
libr	book	library, librarian, libretto
libra	balance	libration, deliberate, equilibrium
lic	permitted	license, illicit, licentious
lig	bind	ligament, ligature, oblige, religion
limit	boundary	limit, limitless, unlimited, illimitable
line	line	line, lineal, linear, linen, delineate
lingu	tongue	lingual, linguistics, bilingual
liqu	liquid	liquid, liquefy, liquor, liquidate, liquidity
litera	letter	literal, literate, literary, literature
lith	stone	lithograph, monolith, neolithic, paleolithic
litig	strife	litigate, litigation, litigious, litigiosity
liver	free	deliverance
loc	place	location, locate, dislocate, allocate, local
locut	talk, speak	locution, circumlocution, elocutionary
log	word	prologue, dialogue, eulogy, monologue
log(y)	reason	analogy, apology, logic
logy	science of	psychology, biology, anthropology
logue	discourse	monologue, dialogue, catalogue
long	lengthen	along, longevity, oblong, prolong
loqu	speak	colloquial, eloquence, soliloquy
lu	wash	ablution, affluence, antediluvian, dilute
luc	light	lucent, lucid, Lucite, elucidate
lud(s)	deceive, play	allude, collude, elude, ludicrous, illusion
lum	light	illuminate, luminous, luminary
luna	moon	lunar, lunatic, lunette, lunacy, sublunar
lus	light, clear	luster
lustr	shine	illustrate, illustrious, lustrous, lustral

Root	Meaning	Examples
lut	wash	ablution, dilute
lys	break down	analysis, paralysis, electrolysis, catalyst

M

Root	Meaning	Examples
mach	a device	machinery, machinist, machinate
macro	long, large	macrocosm, macron, macroscopic
macul	a spot	maculate, maculation, immaculate
magn	great	magnanimous, magnify, magnificent
maj	great, large	major, majesty, majority, majestic
mal	bad	dismal, maladroit, malady, malaria (see 2:34)
man	remain	manse, mansion, manor, immanent
man	hand	manacle, manicure, manifest
mand	order	command, demand, mandate, remand
mania	madness	mania, maniacal, manic-depressive
manu	hand	manual, manufacture, manuscript
mar	border	margin, marginal
mar(i)	sea	marine, submarine, mariner, maritime
mas	chief, primary	master, masterpiece, mastermind
mater	mother	maternal, maternity
mater	matter	material, materialism, immaterial
matr	mother	matricide, matriculate, matrimony
matur	mature	mature, maturate, immature, premature
max	greatest	maximum, maxim, maximize
mech	machine	mechanic, mechanism, mechanize
medi	middle	mediate, medieval, mediocre
mega	great, million	megaphone, megalopolis, megacycle
melior	better	ameliorate, meliorate, meliorable
mem	mind	memory, remember, memorial
mend	command	commend, recommend
mend	mistake	amend, amendment, mend, emendable
menda	lying	mendacious, mandaciousness
ment	mind	mental, mention, demented, comment
mer	sea	mermaid, merman
merc	trade	merchant, merchandise, mercantile
merci	tenderness	merciful, merciless, unmerciful
merge	dive	submerge, emerge, merge, merger
merit	deserve	merit, meritorious, demerit, unmerited
mers	dive	submerse, immerse
meso	middle	mesoderm, mesocarp
meter	measure	thermometer, centimeter, diameter
metric	measure	metric, geometric, logometric
metro	mother	metronymic, metropolis
metro	measure	metronome, metrology, metroscope (see 3:170)
metry	science of measuring	geometry, symmetry, trigonometry
micro	little	microcosm, micrometer, microphone

Root	Meaning	Examples
migr	change, move	migrate, immigrant, emigrate, migratory
milli	thousand	milligram, millimeter (see 2:25, 2:27)
mim	same	mimic, pantomime, mimeograph, mime
min	small, less	mini, minimum, minor, minus, minimize
min	threats	minacious, minacity, comminatory
minen	project	eminence, pre-eminent, prominence
minis(t)	serve	minister, administer, administration
mir	wonder	miracle, admire, mirage, mirror
mis	hatred	misanthrope, misanthropic, misogamy
misc	mix	miscellaneous, promiscuous, immiscible
miser	wretched	miserly, miserable, commiserate
miss	send	missile, dismiss, mission, remiss (see 2:48)
mit	send	transmit, submit, admit, remit, permit (see 2:47)
mitig	soften	mitigate, mitigation, unmitigated
mix	mix	mixture, commix, admix, mixologist
mob	move	mobile, automobile, mobilize
mod	manner	accommodate, commodity, mode
mol	mass	mole, molar, molecule, demolish

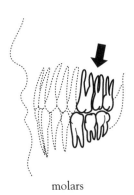

molars

Root	Meaning	Examples
molest	trouble	molest, molester, molestation
mon	advise, warn	admonish, premonition, monitor
mono	one, alone	monochromatic, monocle (see 2:24, 2:27)
mons	show	monster, demonstrate, undemonstrative
mor	manner, custom	moral, amoral, morale, demoralize
mor	bite	morsel, mordacious, remorse
morb	sickness	morbid, morbidity
morph	shape	amorphous, metamorphoses
mort	death	mortician, mortuary, mortal, immortal
mot	move	motion, motor, promote, demote, motive
mount	mount	mound, mount, mountain, amount
mov	move	movie, remove, movement, movable

Affixes and Roots

Root	Meaning	Examples
mult(i)	many	multiple, multiplication, multitude (see 2:28)
mun	gift	communal, commune, communicate
mun	an office	municipal, munificent
mus	song	muse, museum, music, musicality
mut	change	mutation, immutable, mutual, commute
mutil	maimed	mutilate, mutilator, mutilation
myst	conceal	mystery, mysterious, mystic, mysticism
myth	a fable	mythical, mythologist, mythological
myo	muscle	myocardium

N

Root	Meaning	Examples
narco	stupor	narcotic, narcolepsy, narcose
narr	tell	narrate, narration, narrator, unnarrated
nasc	born	renascence, nascent, renascent
nat	born	natal, native, nation, nativity, innate
nav	ship	navy, naval, navigate, circumnavigate
nau	ship, sail	nausea, nautical, nautilus
nec	bind	connect, disconnect, unconnected
necess	needful	necessary, necessity, unnecessary
necro	dead	necropolis, necrology, necrophobia (see 2:36)
neg	no	negation, abnegation, negative, renege
neo	new	neophyte, neoclassical, neonatal
nerv	nerve	enervate, nerve, nervous
neur	nerve	neuron, neural, neurology, neurosis
neut	neither	neuter, neutral, neutralization
new	new	new, renew, news, newspeak
nex	bind	annex, re-annex, nexus
nihil	nothing	nihilistic, nihilism, annihilate, annihilator
nobl	well known	noble, nobility, ignoble, ennoble
noc	hurt, harm	innocent, innocuous, nocuous
noct	night	nocturnal, noctuary, nocturne
nom	name	nominal, nominee, nominate
nomy	law, order	autonomy, gastronomy, economy
norm	rule	norm, normal, abnormal, enormous
not	mark	notation, notable, denote, notch
noti	know	notice, notify, notion
noun	declare	announce, pronounce, denounce
nox	harm	noxious, inoxious, obnoxious
nov	new	novel, novelty, novice, innovate, nova
nove	nine	novena, November (see 2:27)
numer	number	numeral, enumerate, numerous
nunc	declare	annunciate, enunciate, pronunciation
nur	nourish	nurse, nurture
nut	nourish	nutrient, nutrition, nutriment
nym	name	anonymous, patronym, synonym (see 2:51)

O

Root	Meaning	Examples
ob	to, against	object, obscene, oblique
oct	eight	October, octopus (see 2:27)
ocu(l)	eye	oculist, binocular, monocular
od	a way	episode, method, methodical, period
odor	smell	odor, odorous, inodorous, malodorous
olig	few	oligarchy, oligchaete
ology	study of	biology, psychology (see 2:38, 2:39, 2:40)
omin	an omen	abominate, abominable, ominous
omni	all	omnipotent, omniscient, omniformity
oner	a burden	onerous, exonerator, exonerate
onym	name	synonym, antonym, pseudonym
oper	work	operate, cooperate
opin	think	opinion, opinionated, opinionless, opine
opt	best	optimum, optimist, optimal, optimize
opt	see	autopsy, dioptic, myoptic, optical, option
ophthalm	of the eye	ophthalmologist, ophthalmology
opul	wealth	opulent, opulently, opulence, inopulent
ora	speak, plead	exorable, inexorable, oracle
orb	circle	orb, orbit, orbitary, exorbitance
ord	row, rank	order, disorder, ordain, preordain (see 2:42)
ordin	row, rank	ordinary, ordinal, extraordinary (see 2:42)
org	instrument	organ, organic, organize, disorganize
ori(g)	beginning	origin, original, originate, aboriginal
orn	furnish	ornate, adornment, suborn
ornith	of birds	ornithology, ornithologist
ortho	straight, right	orthodontist, orthodox, orthopedist
osteo	of bone	osteoarthritis, osteoporosis (see 2:44)
ov	egg	ova, oval, ovarian, ovum, ovulate

P

Root	Meaning	Examples
pac	peace	pacify, pacification, repacify, pacific
pact	bind	pact, compact, impact, recompact
pala	taste	palate, palatable, palatability
paleo	ancient	paleomagnetism, paleolithic
palp	touch	palpable, palpability, palpitation
pan	all	panacea, pancreas, pandemic
pan	spread, step	span, expand, expanse
par	appear	apparition, apparent, transparent
par	equal	par, parity, compare, incomparable
par	bring forth, birth	parent, postpartum
para	prepare	apparatus, parade, separate
para	almost	paraprofessional, paramedic (see 2:28)
parl	speak	parlance, parley, parliamentarian, parlor

Root	Meaning	Examples
part	share	part, partial, impartial, particle, partner
pass	spread, step	compass, encompass, pass, passage
pass	bear	passion, compassion, passive
past	pasture	pasture, repast, pastor, unpastoral
pat	bear	patient, impatient, compatible
pater	father	paternity, paternal
path	disease, feeling	pathology, sympathy, pathos (see 2:44)
patr	father	patricide, patriarch, patronage, patron
pau	poor	pauperism, pauper
pecca	sin	peccable, impeccable, impeccability
pect	breast	pectoral, expectorate, expectoration
pecu	property, cattle	peculiar, pecuniary, impecunious
ped	child	pedagogy, pediatrician, encyclopedia
ped	foot	pedal, pedestrian, biped, pedestal
pel	drive	propel, compel, expel, repel, repellant
pell	call	appellant, appellation
pen	punishment	penalty, penance, penitence, repent (see 3:62)
pen	feather	pen, pennant, penmanship (see 3:62)
pend	hang	pendulum, suspend, append, appendix
pene	pierce	penetrate, penetration, impenetrable
pent	five	pentagon, pentathlon (see 2:26, 2:27)
pens	hang, weigh	suspense, dispense, dispensation
peer	equal	peer, peerless, compeer
peri	try	experiment, experienced, periscope

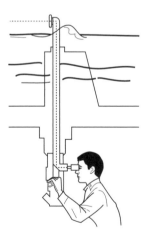

periscope

perp	entire	perpetual, perpetually, perpetuation
person	person	person, persona, impersonal
pest	plague	pest, pestering, pestilence, pestiferous
pet	seek	appetite, compete, competition
petr	stone	petrify, petrification, petrol, petroleum
phage(o)	consumer or destroyer	bacteriophage, phagocyte

Root	Meaning	Examples
phan	show	phantom, sycophant, fancy, fantasy
pharmaco	drug	pharmacology, pharmacy
phil	love	philosophy, philanthropist, philharmonic
phob	fear	claustrophobia, xenophobia (see 2:22)
phon	sound	phonograph, symphony, telephone
phos	light	phosphorous, phosphorescent
photo	light	photograph, telephoto, photosynthesis
phren	the mind	phrenologist, frenetic, frenzy
phys(ic)	nature	physical, physician, physiological
phyto	of plants	phytoplasm, phytogenesis
pie	religious	piety, impiety
pil	rob	pilfer, pillage, compile, compilation
pio	religious	pious, impious
pla	lament	complain, plaint, plaintiff, plague
pla(c)	please	placate, placid, placebo
plaint	sorrow	complaint, plaintiff
plau	applause	plausible, implausible, applaud, plaudit
ple	full, plenty	plenty, plethora, complement
ple	fold	complex, perplex, duplex, quintuple
plea	please	please, pleasant, pleasure, plea, plead
plex	unit, folds	duplex, complex, metroplex
plic	fold	applicable, complicate, explicit, implicit
plicat	interweave, fold	complicate, implication, duplication
plor	cry out	deplorable, implore, exploratory
plum	a feather	plume, plumeless, deplume, implume
plu(r)	more	plural, plurality, pluralism, pluperfect
pluto	wealth	plutocracy, plutocrat
ply	fold	ply, multiply, apply
pneuma(o)	breath	pneumatic, pneumonia
pod	foot	podiatrist, podium, tripod (see 2:44)
poe	compose	poem, poet, poetically, impoetic
pol	a pole	pole, polar, polarity, polarization
poli	city	metropolis, cosmopolitan, police (see 3:70)
poli	polish	polish, polite, impolite, polishable
poly	many	polygamy, polygram, polygraph (see 2:28)
pon	put, place	postpone, component, opponent
pond	hang, weigh	ponder, preponderant, ponderous
pont	bridge	pontiff, pontificate, pontoon
pop	people	population, popular, pop, populace
por	passageway	pore, porous, porosity, imporosity
por	pig	porcine, porcupine, porpoise, pork
port	carry	portable, transport, import, export (see 2:43)
portion	part, share	portion, proportion
pos	put, sit	pose, posture, apropos, compose
pos	able	posse, possible, impossible

Root	Meaning	Examples
pos	drink	symposium
posit	place, put	position, positive, opposition
post	demand	postulant, postulatory, expostulate
poster	after	posterior, postern, posterity
pot	able	potent, impotent, omnipotent, potential
pot	drink	potable, potion, compotation
pound	put, place	expound, impound
pov	poor	poverty, impoverished
pract	to do	practice, impractical, malpractice
prav	wrong	depraved, depravation, depravity
prec	pray	deprecate, imprecate, precarious
prec	value, esteem	appreciate, depreciate, precious
pred	plunder	predatory, depredate, depredation
preg	with child	pregnant, impregnate, pregnancy
preh	seize	apprehend, misapprehend, reprehend
prehend	seize	apprehend, misapprehend, comprehend
press	press	press, pressure, compress, express
prim	first	prime, primacy, primary, primate (see 2:28)
prin	first	prince, principal, principle
print	press	print, imprint
priv	one's own	private, privacy, privilege, privy, deprive
prob	prove, like	probable, improbable, probation
prov	prove, like	approve, disapprove, prove, improve
prop	near	propitious, propitiate
prop(e)r	one's own	proper, improper, property, propriety
proto	first	protocol, protoplasm, protozoa (see 2:28)
prox	near	approximate, proximate, proximity
psych	mind, soul	psychology, psyche, psychopath
pub	people	publicity, public, publish
pud	modesty	impudence, impudently, repudiate
pug	fight	pugnacious, pugilist, repugnant, impugn
puls	drive	pulse, compulsion, impulse, propulsion
pulv	dust	pulverable, pulverize, pulverization
punc	point	punch, punctual, punctuate, puncture
pung	point	pungent, expunge
puni	punish	punitive, impunitive, punish, unpunished
pur	cleanse	purge, purgatory, pure, purify
pur	fester	purulent, suppuration
pus	fester	pus, pustule
put	think, trim	amputate, compute, deputy, dispute
putr	rotten	putrid, putrification, unputrified
pyr	fire	pyre, pyrite, pyrotechnical, empyrean

Q

Root	Meaning	Examples
quad(r)	four	quadrangle, quadrilateral, quadriplegic (see 2:26, 2:27)

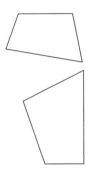

quadrilaterals

Root	Meaning	Examples
qual	kind, sort	quality, qualification, disqualify
quant	how much	quantity, quantification, quantum
quart	one fourth	quarter, quartermaster (see 2:28)
quest	ask, seek	question, inquest, request, conquest
quer	ask, seek	query, conquer
quie	quiet	quiet, quiesce, requiem
quint	five	quintuplets, quintet (see 2:26, 2:27)
quir	seek, gain	inquire, require, acquire
quisit	ask, seek	inquisitive, inquisition, requisition
quit	rest, quiet	quit, acquit, quite, requite
quot	how many	quote, quota, quotient, quotability

R

Root	Meaning	Examples
rad	ray, spoke	radius, radio, radiation, radium, radiator
radi	root	radical, radish, radix, eradicate
ranc	stale	rancid, rancidity, rancorous
rang	order	arrangement, deranged, disarranged
rap	seize	rape, rapine, rapid, rapids, rapture
ras	to scrape, rub off	rash, abrasion, erase, erasure
rat	think	rate, ratify, ratio, ration, rational
rav	seize	ravage, ravish, ravine
ray	ray	ray, rayon
re	thing	real, realist, realization, unreal
rect	straight, rule	erect, rectangle, rectify, direction
reg	rule, guide	regal, regent, regulate, regime
rend	restore	render, rendition, surrender
revere	fear, feel awe	revere, reverend, irreverence
rhe	flow, speak	rhetoric, rheumatic, rheumatism

Master List of Roots (continued)

Root	Meaning	Examples
rhino	nose	rhinocerous, rhinorrhea, rhinoplasty
rhy	measured	rhyme, rhythm, rhythmical, unrhymed
rid	laugh, to mock	ridiculous, deride, ridicule
rig	stiff	rigid, rigorousness, rigor, rigor mortis
ris	to mock	derisive, risibility, derision
rit	of rites	ritual, ritualistic, ritualize, ritualism
riv	river	arrive, derive, river, rivulet, rival
rob	strength	robust, robustness, corroboration
rod	to gnaw	erode, rodents, rodenticide
rog	ask	abrogate, interrogate, arrogance
ros	to gnaw	erosion, corrosive
roy	royal	royalist, royalties, viceroy
rub	red, ruddy	rubicund, rubric, ruby, erubescence
rud	rough	rude, rudiment, erudite, erudition
rumin	muse on	ruminant, ruminate, ruminator
rupt	break	rupture, erupt, interrupt, abrupt
rur	country	rural, ruralistic
rus	country	rustic, rustication

S

Root	Meaning	Examples
sacr	holy	sacred, sacrament, sacrifice
saga	perceive	sagacity, sagacious, presage
sal	leap	salacious, salient, salmon
sal	safe	salvage, salve, salvation
sal	salt	salt, salary, salad, salami
salu	health	salute, salutary
salv	safe, healthy	salvation, salvage
sanct	holy	sanction, sanctity, sanctuary, sanctify
san	health	sanitary, sanitation, sane, insanity
san	sound	sane, sanctuary, sanitarium, insanity
sangui	blood, red	sanguine, sanguinary, consanguineous
sap	taste	sapient, homo sapiens, sapor
sarc	the flesh	sarcoma, sarcophagus, sarcasm
sat	enough	satiate, satient, saturate, satisfy
satir	censure	satirist, satire, satirical, satirize
saur	lizard	dinosaur, brontosaurus, stegosaurus
sav	to taste, be wise	savvy, savant, savory
scal	ladder	escalade, escalator, scale
scand	disgrace	scandal, scandalize, scandalous
scend	climb, leap	ascend, descend, transcend (see 2:37)
schiz(s)	split	schizophrenia, schizoid, schism
schol	school	scholar, scholastic, unscholastic
sci	know	science, conscience, conscious
scind	to cut	abscind, prescind, rescind
scint	spark	scintilla, scintillate, scintillation
scop(e)	see	microscope, telescope, periscope
scrib	write	scribe, scribble, prescribe (see 2:45, 2:46)

Root	Meaning	Examples
script	write	script, conscript, inscription (see 2:45)
scrup	doubt	scruple, scrupulous, unscrupulous
scrut	search	scrutable, scrutiny, inscrutable
scurr	scoffer	scurrility, scurrilous, scurrilously
sec	follow	consecutive, executive, persecute
secr	holy	desecrate, execrate
secr	hidden	secret, secrecy, secretary
sect	cut	section, dissect, intersect, sect, bisect
secut	follow in order	prosecute, consecutive, execute
sed	sit, settle	sediment, sedentary, supersede
sedat	bring to rest	sedate, sedative
sema	sign	semantics, semaphore, polysemy
sembl	like, same time	assembly, resemblance, resemble
semi	half	semiannual, semicircle (see 2:25, 2:28)
semin	seed	seminal, seminary, disseminate
sen	old	senate, senescence, senility, seniority
sen	exist	essence, quintessential, presence
sens	feel	sensation, sense, sensitive, sensible
sent	feel	sentimental, assent, dissent, consent
sent	exist, to be	absent, present, nonessential, represent
sept	seven	September, septuagenarian (see 2:27)
sequ	follow	consequence, obsequious, sequel
sert	join	assert, reassert, desert, dissertation
serv	watch over	conserve, preserve, reserve, reservoir
serv	slave, serve	serve, servant, service, servile
serv	save	conserve, observation, preserve
sess	sit	assess, obsess, possess, session
sex	six	sextant, sextuplets, sexagenarian (see 2:26)
sicc	make dry	desiccate, desiccative, siccative
sid	sit	preside, presidio, president, reside
sider	star	consider, desideratum, sidereal
sign	mark, sign	signal, signature, significant, insignia
sil	leap	dissilient, resilient, transilient
sim	like	simultaneous, simulate, similar
simil	like	simile, facsimile, dissimilarity
simul	same time	simultaneous, simultaneity
sinist	left hand	sinister, sinisterly, sinistrous
sinu	winding	sinuate, insinuate, insinuation
sip	taste	insipid, resipiscence, insipience
sist	stand	consist, resist, subsist, assist
skept	doubt	skeptic, skeptical, skepticism
soci	companion	associate, sociable, dissocial, society
sol	alone	solo, solitary, desolate, soliloquy, sole
sol	comfort	console, consolation, disconsolate
sol	sun	solar, solstice, insolate, parasol
solic	anxious	solicit, solicitation, solicitude, unsolicited
solid	firm	solidity, solidarity, consolidate, soldier

Root	Meaning	Examples
solut	loose	absolute, resolution, solution
solv	loosen, solve	dissolve, solve, solvent, resolve
somn	sleep	insomnia, somnolent, somnambulist
son	sound	sonar, sonata, sonnet, unison
soph	wise	philosopher, sophomore, sophisticated
sorb	drink in	absorb, absorption, sorbent
sort	a kind	sort, assortment, consortable, resorting
spec	see, a kind	special, specify, species
spect	see, a kind	aspect, expect, inspect, spectacle
sper	hope	desperate, desperado
spers	scatter	asperse, aspersion, disperse
spher	a ball	spheroid, spherically, atmosphere
splen	to shine	splendid, splendor, resplendent
spic	look	conspicuous, perspicacity, perspicuity
spir	breathe	respiration, inspire, spirit, perspire
spoil	take from	spoil, unspoiled, despoiled
spon	promise, pledge	correspond, respond, responsible
sta	stand	stabile, stagnant, constant, establish
stat	stand	station, status, statue
stell	star	stellar, constellation, subconstellate
stereo	solid	stereophonic, stereomicroscope
still	drop	still, distill, distillery, instill
stimu	a goad	stimulus, stimulation, unstimulated
stin	fix	destine, predestine, predestination
stinct	mark, extinguish	distinct, extinct, instinct
sting	mark, extinguish	distinguish, extinguish, undistinguished
stit	stand	destitute, institute, restitution, substitute
strat	spread out	stratum, unstratified, stratagem
strict	draw tight	strict, restrict, constrict, stricture
string	draw tight	stringent, astringent
stru	construct, build	instrument, construe, instrumental
struct	build	structure, construct, instruct, destruction
stup	senseless	stupid, stupefy, stupor, stupendous
suad	advise	dissuade, persuade, impersuadable
sub	under	subordinate, subject (see 10:186)
sublim	exalted	sublime, sublimity, sublimate
suc	draw in	suck, suckle, suction, succulent
sue	following	ensue, pursue, sue
suit	to follow	pursuit, suitable, suite
sula	island	insular, peninsula, insulation
sult	leap	insult, result, exult
sum	take, cost	assume, consume, consumption
sum	highest	summit, summary, sum, summons
super	above	superb, superior, supreme, superable
supra	above, over	supranatural, supranational
sur	care	sure, assure, reassure, insure
surg	rise	surge, insurgent, resurgent

Root	Meaning	Examples
surr	rise	resurrect, insurrection, resurrection
sym(n)	alike	symbol, symbiosis, symbiotic, synonym
synchro	occurring together	synchronize, synchrotron

T

Root	Meaning	Examples
tacit	silent	tacit, taciturn
tact	touch	tactile, intact, contact, tact
tail	cut	tailor, detail, entail, retail
tain	hold	retain, contain, detain, attain (see 2:50)
tal	that kind	tally, tallying, retaliate, retaliation
tang	touch	tangible, intangible, tangent
tard	slow	tardy, tardiness, retard, retardation
tast	to feel	taste, tasteless, distaste, untasted
tax	arrangement	syntax, taxidermy, taxonomy
tec	cover	detect, protect, protectorate
techn	art, skill	technical, technology, polytechnic
teg	cover	protégé, tegument, integument
teg	touch	integer, integrate, integrity
tele	distant	telescope, telegraph, telephone
temp(o)	time	contemporary, temporary
temper	regulate	temperature, temperate (see 3:69)
tempt	try	tempt, attempt, reattempt, temptation
ten	hold	tenacious, tenure, tenant, retentive
ten	stretch	tension, tent, tense
tend	stretch	tendon, tendency, contend
tens	stretch	extension, intense, ostensible
ten(t)	hold	content, retention, discontent (see 2:49)
tenu	thin	tenuous, extenuate, extenuation
term	end	terminal, terminate, determine
ter	clean	terse, terseness, deter, detergent
terr	land, earth	territory, terrain, terrestrial, terrace
terr	fright	terror, terrible, deterred
test	witness	attest, contest, detest, protest, testify
tetra	four	tetrameter, tetrahedron (see 2:27)
tex	weave	textile, texture, text, context
the	God	atheism, theocracy, theology, pantheon
theo	observe	theorem, theory, theoretician, theoretical
therm	heat	thermometer, thermal, thermostat
thes	placing	thesis, synthesis, parenthesis
thet	put, place	epithet, parenthetical
thron	king seat	throne, dethrone, enthrone, unthrone
tic	silent	reticent, reticence
tig	touch	contiguous
tim	fear	timid, timorous, intimidate, intimidation
tin	hold	abstinence, continue, discontinue
tin	tinge	tinct, tincture
ting	touch	contingent, contingency

Root	Meaning	Examples
titl	title	title, entitled, untitled
toast	to parch	toast, toaster, toastmaster
toler	bear	tolerable, tolerant, intolerable, intolerant
tom	cut	atom, dichotomy, anatomy
ton	stretch, tone	astonish, tone, detonate, tonic
top	place	topography, utopia, topical, toponyms
tor	twist	torch, torsion, torque
torp	benumb	torpidity, torpor, torpescent, torpedo
torr	to parch	torrent, torrid, torrential
tort	twist	torture, contort, retort, tort, contortion

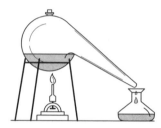

retort

Root	Meaning	Examples
total	entire	total, totality, teetotaler, totalization
tox	poison	toxic, intoxicate, intoxication, antitoxin
tract	pull, drag	tractor, attract, subtract, traction, extract
trad	hand down	tradition, traditionally
trem	quake	tremble, tremulous, tremor
tri	three	triangular, triennial, trisect, trivial (see 2:24, 2:27)
trib	give	contribute, tribute, tributary, attribute
tric	entangle	trickery, intricate, extricate
trit	rubbed	trite, attrition, contritely
trop	a turn	trophies, tropics, entropy
trud	push	intrude, protrude, intruder
trunc	cut off	truncate, detruncate, truncheon
trus	push	intrusive, obtrusive
tuber	swelling	tuberous, tubercular, protuberant
tum	swelling	tumor, tumult, tumble, tumid
turb	confusion	disturb, turbulent, perturb, turmoil
turg	swell	turgid, turgidity, turgescence
tus	bruise	contusion, obtuse, pertusion
tut	secure	tutelage, tutor, tutoress, untutored
twa	two	twice, twenty, twine (see 2:31)
type	a blow, impression	typewriter, typecast, archetype
tyra	despotism	tyrant, tyranny, tyrannical, tyrannize

U

Root	Meaning	Examples
uber	abundant	exuberance, exuberantly, ubertous
ulc	a sore	ulcer, ulceration, ulcerousness
ult	beyond	ultimate, ultimatum, ulterior, penultimate
umbr	shadow	umbrage, umbrella, inumbrate
unc	anoint	inunction, unctiousness
und	wave	undulate, inundate, abundance
uni	one	uniform, unify, union, unique (see 2:24, 2:27)
urb	city	urban, suburb, urbane, suburban
urg	press on	urge, urging, urgently, unurged
urg	work	liturgy, surgeon, metallurgy
use	use	abuse, misuse, peruse, use
ust	burn	combustion, incombustion, ustulate
uti	use	utilize, utilitarian, utility

V

Root	Meaning	Examples
vac	empty	vacant, vacation, vacate
vacu	empty	vacuum, evacuate, vacuous
vad	go	evade, invade, pervade
vag	wandering	vagabond, vagrant, vague
val	strong	valance, valor, value, prevalence, evaluate

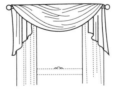

valance

vale	farewell	valedictorian, valedictory
valv	revolving	bivalve, univalve, valvular, valvelet
van	empty	vanity, evanescent
van	before	van, vanguard, advance, disadvantage
vapor	breathe	vapor, vaporize, evaporate
vari	diverse, bent	variety, invariable, unvaried, variously
vaso	tube	vasodilation, vasoconstrictor
vast	large	vast, vastness, devastate, devastation
vect	carry	vection, vector, invective
veh	carry	vehicle, vehemence
veil	to watch	surveillance, reveille
ven	come	convene, convention, advent, invent
ven	sell	vendor, vend, venal, venality

Root	Meaning	Examples
vener	reverence	venerate, venerable, unvenerable
veng	avenge	avenge, revenge, vengeance
vent	the wind	vent, ventilation, ventilator
vent	come	circumvent, invent, prevent
ventr	the belly	ventral, ventricle, ventriloquist
ver	truth	verify, verity, very, verdict, aver, veracity
ver	turn	convert, reverse, versatile, introvert
verb	word	verbal, verbatim verbiage, verbose
verber	send back	reverberate, reverberation
verd	green	verdant, verdure, verdurous, unverdant
vere	feel awe	revere, reverence, reverend, irreverence
verg	tend	verge, converge, diverge, divergingly
verm	a worm	vermin, vermicule, vermifuge
vers	turn	adverse, adversary, converse, diverse
vert	turn	advert, convert, introvert, revert
vest	clothe	divest, investment, vestment, reinvest
vestig	footprint	vestige, vestigial, investigate
vet	old	veteran, inveterate, veterinarian
via	way	deviate, trivial, via, obviate
vic	instead	vicar, vicariously, vice president
vict	conquer	victory, conviction, convict, evict, victor
vid	see	video, evidence, provide, providence
vig	to watch	vigil, vigilance, vigilante
vigor	strength	vigor, vigorously, invigorate, reinvigorate
vil	mean	vile, vilify, revile, reviling
villa	farmhouse	village, villains, villainy
vinc	conquer	convince, invincible, vincible, province
vind	avenge	vindicate, vindictive
vio	way, road	obvious, previous, impervious
viol	injure	violate, violence, inviolable, unviolated
vir	manliness	virtue, virile, virtually
viru	poisonous	virus, virulent, virulence, virulently
vis	see	advise, revise, visible, invisible
vit	to live	vita, vitality, revitalize
vitr	glassy	vitreous, vitrify, vitrescence, vitriolic
viv	life	convivial, revive, survive, vivacity, vivid
voc	voice	vocal, advocate, convocation (see 3:67)
voc	calling	vocation, avocation (see 3:67)
void	empty	void, devoid, avoid, voided, unavoidable
vok	voice, call	provoke, convoke, revoke
vol	roll	evolve, revolve, volt
vol	wish, will	volition, volunteer, voluntary, benevolent
volut	turn, roll	revolution, evolution, involute
volv	turn	revolve, involve, evolve, revolver
vor	eat	voracious, carnivore, herbivore

Root	Meaning	Examples
vot	vow	devote, devotion, vote, votive
vulg	make common, publish	divulge, vulgar, vulgate
vuls	tear out	convulse, divulse, revulsion, avulse

X

Root	Meaning	Examples
xeno	foreign	xenophobia, xenophile
xequ	to follow	execute, executive, execution
xero	dry	xerophyte, xeroderma

Y

Root	Meaning	Examples
yer	one who	lawyer, sawyer

Z

Root	Meaning	Examples
zeal	ardor	zeal, zealous, jealousy
zo(o)	animal	zoo, zoological, zoologist, zodiac

Master List of Suffixes (Meaning)

A

Suffix	Meaning	Examples
-a	plural	data, criteria, memoranda
-ability	be able	sensibility, readability
-able	is, can be	comfortable, learnable, walkable
-ably	be able	tolerably, suitably
-acious	inclined to	loquacious, mendacious, audacious
-acity	characteristics of	tenacity, reciprocity
-acy	state or quality of	supremacy, diplomacy
-ade	action or process	blockade, promenade, escapade
-ade	product or thing	lemonade, marmalade
-ae	plural	alumnae, algae, formulae
-age	action or process	marriage, voyage, pilgrimage, blockage
-al	relating to	natural, royal, maternal, suicidal
-an	relating to, person	urban, American, veteran, Hawaiian
-ance	state or quality of	repentance, annoyance, resistance
-ancy	state or quality of	buoyancy, truancy, vacancy, vagrancy
-ant	one who	servant, immigrant, assistant, merchant
-ant	inclined to	vigilant, pleasant, defiant, buoyant
-ar	one who	beggar, liar
-arch	ruler	monarch, patriarch
-archy	rule	monarchy, oligarchy
-ard	one who	drunkard, steward, coward, wizard
-arian	one who	librarian, humanitarian, libertarian
-arium	place for	aquarium, planetarium, solarium
-art	one who	braggart
-ary	place for	library, mortuary, sanctuary, infirmary
-ary	relating to	honorary, military, literary, ordinary
-ate	state or quality of	fortunate, desperate, passionate
-ate	to make	activate, fascinate, annihilate, liberate
-ation	state or quality of	desperation, starvation, inspiration
-ation	action or process	emancipation, narration, computation
-ative	inclined to	demonstrative, pejorative, talkative

B

Suffix	Meaning	Examples
-ble	inclined to	gullible, perishable, voluble, durable
-ble	repeated action	stumble, squabble, mumble, tumble

C

Suffix	Meaning	Examples
-cle	small	corpuscle, particle, icicle, cubicle
-crat	person of power	democrat, autocrat, bureaucrat
-cule	small	miniscule, molecule
-cy	state or quality of	accuracy, bankruptcy, conspiracy
-cy	action or process	truancy, diplomacy, vagrancy, privacy

D

Suffix	Meaning	Examples
-d	past tense	baked, raised, noted, spaced
-dom	state or quality of	freedom, boredom, martyrdom, wisdom

E

Suffix	Meaning	Examples
-ectomy	surgical removal of	tonsillectomy, appendectomy
-ed	past tense	talked, walked, heated
-ed	state or quality	ill-tempered, frustrated, married
-ee	object of action	payee, lessee, employee
-eer	a person	engineer, racketeer, puppeteer
-en	relating to	golden, ashen, wooden, earthen
-en	to make	strengthen, fasten, lengthen, frighten
-en	past completed action	taken, eaten, proven, stolen
-ence	state or quality of	violence, absence, reticence
-ency	state or quality of	frequency, clemency, expediency
-enne	female	comedienne, equestrienne, tragedienne
-ent	one who	regent, superintendent, resident
-ent	inclined to	competent, different, excellent
-er	action or process	murder, plunder, waiver, flounder
-er	one who	teacher, painter, seller, shipper
-er	more (comparative)	damper, smarter, closer, lighter, quicker, softer
-ern	direction	eastern, western, northern, postern
-ery	state or quality of	bravery, savagery, forgery, slavery
-ery	trade or occupation	surgery, archery, sorcery
-ery	establishment	bakery, grocery, fishery, nunnery
-ery	goods or products	pottery
-es	plural	boxes, parentheses
-es	forms third person	finishes, lavishes
-escence	forms noun of action	convalescence
-ese	state or quality of	Japanese, Chinese, Portuguese
-esque	relating to	statuesque, picturesque, Romanesque
-ess	one who (female)	princess, waitress, countess, hostess
-est	most (comparative)	smartest, closest, lightest, quickest

Master List of Suffixes
(Meaning) *(continued)*

Suffix	Meaning	Examples
-et	small	midget, sonnet, bassinet, cygnet
-eth	numbers	twentieth, fiftieth, sixtieth
-etic	relating to	alphabetic, dietetic, frenetic, athletic
-ette	small	dinette, diskette, majorette, barrette
-ety	state or quality of	gaiety
-eur	one who	chauffeur, connoisseur, masseur
-eur	state or quality of	hauteur, grandeur

F

Suffix	Meaning	Examples
-fic	making	honorific, soporific
-fication	forms noun of action	specification
-ful	full of	joyful, fearful, careful, thoughtful
-fy	to make, cause to be	satisfy, terrify, falsify, beautify, solidify

H

Suffix	Meaning	Examples
-holic	addict	chocoholic, alcoholic
-hood	state or quality of	childhood, adulthood, falsehood

I

Suffix	Meaning	Examples
-i	plural	alumni, foci
-ial	relating to	filial, commercial, remedial
-ian	relating to	barbarian, Christian, physician
-iatry	healing area	psychiatry, podiatry
-ibility	ability	responsibility, irresistibility
-ible	is, can be	gullible, combustible, horrible
-ic	relating to	comic, historic, poetic, public
-ical	relating to	comical, rhetorical, economical
-ice	state or quality of	cowardice, malice
-ician	person who	beautician, physician, politician
-ics	scientific or social	physics, economics, politics, statistics
-id	state or quality of	candid, sordid, lucid, splendid, rigid
-ide	chemical compound	fluoride, bromide, peroxide, sulfide
-ier	one who	cashier, gondolier, carrier
-ify	to make	terrify, falsify, beautify, vilify
-ile	state or quality of	virile, agile, volatile, docile, fragile
-ility	forms noun	ability, civility, agility
-ina	female	czarina, ballerina, Wilhelmina
-ine	chemical compound	iodine, chlorine, quinine
-ine	female	heroine, Josephine, Pauline

Master List of Suffixes (Meaning) *(continued)*

Suffix	Meaning	Examples
-ine	relating to	feminine, bovine, feline, marine
-ing	continuous action	singing, talking, jumping, eating
-ing	material	bedding, roofing, frosting, stuffing
-ion	state or quality of	companion, champion, ambition
-ious	state or quality of	gracious, ambitious, religious, nutritious
-ish	relating to	childish, bookish, Scottish, selfish
-ish	near, like, almost	pinkish, sevenish
-ish	action or process	finish, flourish, nourish, punish
-ism	state or quality of	baptism, heroism, racism, despotism
-ism	doctrine of	capitalism, socialism, communism
-ist	one who practices	biologist, capitalist, dentist
-ite	mineral or rock	granite, anthracite, bauxite
-ite	person	socialite, Luddite
-itis	inflammation of	laryngitis, arthritis, bronchitis
-ity	state or quality of	necessity, civility, parity
-ive	inclined to	active, passive, negative, restive
-ization	state or quality of	civilization, standardization, organization
-ize	to make	standardize, computerize, popularize

K

Suffix	Meaning	Examples
-kin	small	lambkin, napkin, manikin, munchkin

L

Suffix	Meaning	Examples
-less	without	thoughtless, tireless, joyless, ageless
-let	small	owlet, rivulet, starlet, leaflet, islet
-like	resembling	lifelike, homelike, childlike, computerlike
-ling	small	duckling, yearling, suckling, fledgling
-ly	resembling	fatherly, scholarly, motherly, sisterly
-ly	forms adverb from adjective	slowly, beautifully, happily, largely
-ly	every	daily, weekly, monthly, yearly

M

Suffix	Meaning	Examples
-man	one who works with	cameraman, mailman, doorman
-mat	automatic machine	laundromat, vendomat
-ment	action or process	government, development, experiment

Suffix	Meaning	Examples
-ment	state or quality of	amusement, predicament, amazement
-ment	product or thing	instrument, ornament, fragment
-mony	product or thing	testimony, matrimony, ceremony
-most	most	utmost, westernmost, innermost

N

Suffix	Meaning	Examples
-ness	state or quality of	kindness, happiness, goodness
-nomy	arrangement	economy, taxonomy

O

Suffix	Meaning	Examples
-ock	diminutive	hillock, bullock
-ocracy	ruling	democracy, theocracy, aristocracy
-oid	resembling	humanoid, asteroid, paranoid, planetoid
-ol	alcohols	methanol, ethanol, glycol
-olent	full of	violent
-ology	study or science of	biology, psychology
-or	one who	doctor, actor, editor
-or	state or quality of	error, stupor, candor, fervor, pallor
-orium	place for	auditorium, emporium
-ory	place for	laboratory, conservatory, purgatory
-ory	serving to, tending to	conciliatory, prohibitory
-ose	sugars	glucose, sucrose, fructose, dextrose
-ose	full of	verbose, morose, bellicose, comatose
-osis	state or condition	tuberculosis, fibrosis, hypnosis
-ous	full of	joyous, virtuous, nervous, wondrous

P

Suffix	Meaning	Examples
-phobia	fear of	claustrophobia, acrophobia

R

Suffix	Meaning	Examples
-ry	trade or occupation	dentistry
-ry	goods or products	jewelry, cutlery
-ry	state or quality of	bravery, savagery, forgery, butchery

S

Suffix	Meaning	Examples
-s	plural	pens, books, parents
-s	forms third person	runs
-'s	possession	John's, dog's
-ship	skill or art of	penmanship, showmanship

Master List of Suffixes (Meaning) *(continued)*

Suffix	Meaning	Examples
-ship	state or quality of	friendship, hardship, citizenship
-sion	state or quality of	tension, compulsion
-some	inclined to	meddlesome, awesome, tiresome
-ster	person	gangster, gamester

T

Suffix	Meaning	Examples
-teen	numbers 13–19	thirteen, fifteen, nineteen
-th	state or quality of	strength, warmth, filth, depth, length
-th	fractional numbers	fifth, twelfth, tenth, fourth = 1/4
-tion	state or quality of	caution, attention, fascination
-trix	female	aviatrix, executrix
-tude	state or quality of	gratitude, fortitude, beatitude
-ty	state or quality of	loyalty, honesty, amnesty, unity

U

Suffix	Meaning	Examples
-ular	relating to	granular, cellular, circular, popular
-ule	small	globule, pustule
-ulent	full of	turbulent, corpulent, fraudulent, truculent
-um	place	museum, auditorium, podium
-und	state or quality of	rotund, fecund, moribund, jocund
-uous	state or quality of	contemptuous, tempestuous, sensuous
-ure	action or process	censure, procure, endure, inure, secure

W

Suffix	Meaning	Examples
-ward	direction	forward, backward, eastward, upward
-ways	manner	sideways, always, longways, crossways
-wise	manner, direction	clockwise, lengthwise, counterclockwise
-wright	one who works with	playwright, shipwright, wheelwright

Y

Suffix	Meaning	Examples
-y	being or having	fruity, sunny, rainy, funny, gooey, chewy
-y	little one	Billy, Tommy, Cathy
-yer	one who	lawyer, sawyer

Suffix Grammar List

In the Master List of Suffixes, we tried to deal with suffixes as morphemes (meaning units). However, suffixes have another, perhaps more important function of grammar. They change parts of speech. For example, you can't say "the joy woman"; you have to say "the joyful woman."

The suffix *-ful* makes the noun into an adjective.

Noun Suffix	Example Word	Noun Suffix	Example Word
-a	data	-i	alumni
-ade	escapade	-ian	physician
-ade	lemonade	-ics	physics
-ae	alumnae	-ide	fluoride
-age	marriage	-ie	ladies
-al	refusal	-ier	cashier
-ance	repentance	-ina	czarina
-ancy	buoyancy	-ine	iodine
-ant	immigrant	-ine	heroine
-ar	beggar	-ing	bedding
-ard	drunkard	-ion	champion
-arian	librarian	-ish	pinkish
-arium	aquarium	-ism	baptism
-ary	library	-ist	biologist
-ation	desperation	-ite	granite
-cle	corpuscle	-itis	laryngitis
-crat	democrat	-ity	necessity
-cule	miniscule	-ization	civilization
-cy	accuracy	-kin	lambkin
-cy	truancy	-let	rivulet
-dom	freedom	-ling	duckling
-ectomy	tonsillectomy	-man	cameraman
-ee	payee	-mat	laundromat
-eer	engineer	-ment	amusement
-ence	violence	-mony	testimony
-ency	frequency	-ness	happiness
-enne	comedienne	-ocracy	aristocracy
-ent	superintendent	-ol	methanol
-er	teacher	-ology	biology
-ery	surgery	-or	actor
-ry	dentistry	-or	stupor
-es	boxes	-orium	auditorium
-ese	Chinese	-ory	laboratory
-ess	waitress	-ose	glucose
-et	midget	-osis	tuberculosis
-ette	dinette	-phobia	claustrophobia
-eur	chauffeur	-ry	jewelry
-ful	spoonful	-s	pens
-fy	beautify	-'s	John's
-hood	childhood		

Noun Suffix	Example Word		Noun Suffix	Example Word
-ship	penmanship		-trix	aviatrix
-ship	friendship		-tude	gratitude
-sion	tension		-ty	loyalty
-ster	gangster		-ure	failure
-th	strength		-wright	playwright
-tion	attention		-yer	lawyer

Adjective Suffix	Example Word		Adjective Suffix	Example Word
-able	drinkable		-ine	feminine
-acious	loquacious		-ious	gracious
-al	natural		-ish	childish
-an	urban		-istic	socialistic
-ant	vigilant		-itious	ambitious
-ary	honorary		-ive	active
-ate	fortunate		-k	panicky
-ative	demonstrative		-less	thoughtless
-ble	gullible		-like	childlike
-en	golden		-ly	fatherly
-ent	competent		-ly	weekly
-er	crazier		-most	utmost
-ern	eastern		-oid	humanoid
-ese	Japanese		-orial	editorial
-esque	statuesque		-ose	verbose
-est	fattest		-ous	joyous
-eth	twentieth		-some	awesome
-etic	alphabetic		-th	fifth
-ful	thoughtful		-ular	granular
-ial	remedial		-ulent	turbulent
-ian	barbarian		-und	rotund
-ic	comic		-uous	contemptuous
-ical	rhetorical		-ward	forward
-id	candid		-y	fruity
-ile	virile			

Verb Suffix	Example Word		Verb Suffix	Example Word
-ade	blockade		-ing	singing
-age	ravage		-ise	advertise
-ate	activate		-ish	finish
-ble	stumble		-ize	standardize
-d	raised		-k	picnicking
-ed	talked		-ly	slowly
-en	taken		-lyze	analyze
-en	strengthen		-s	runs
-er	discover		-ure	censure
-es	finishes		-ward(s)	onwards
-fy	satisfy		-ways	sideways
-ie	carried		-wise	clockwise
-ify	intensify			

Suffixes for Technical Words

Suffix	Meaning	Example
-acea	zoological classes	crustacea
-aceae	botanical families	rosaceae
-aceous	biology, resembling	herbaceous
-algia	pain	neuralgia
-ana	collection	Americana
-androus	male	polyandrous
-andry	male	polyandry
-ane	hydrocarbons	propane
-ast	one connected to	enthusiast
-ate	function	consulate
-athon	event	marathon
-cyte	cell	leucocyte
-ectomy	removal	appendectomy
-iatry	healing area	psychiatry
-ide	chemical compound	sulfide
-ine	chemical compound	iodine
-ite	mineral	granite
-itis	inflammation	arthritis
-lith	stone	paleolith
-lysis	breaking down	analysis
-ol	alcohols	glycol
-oma	tumor	melanoma
-opia	eye	myopia
-ose	sugars	glucose
-osis	condition	fibrosis
-phasia	speech disorder	aphasia
-phobia	fear of	acrophobia
-phrenia	mental disorder	schizophrenia
-phyte	plant	lithophyte
-saur	extinct reptiles	dinosaur

HOMOPHONES

Introduction

Introduction

Homophones are words that sound the same but have a different spelling and a different meaning. They used to be called "homonyms," but homonyms have a slightly different definition that could include "homographs" (words with the same spelling but different meaning and origin), but we won't go into all that.

Homophones are important because you need to know them for both reading and writing (spelling).

They need to be taught in elementary school, in secondary school, and yes, even in college. Most elementary pupils are taught the difference between "to, two, and too," but even many adults get confused between "faun and fawn" or "pedal and peddle."

Besides saving you from looking like a semi-literate when you write, studying homophones can be useful in building a meaning vocabulary. In short, if you know the homophone partner, you know many more words. This can improve your score on many types of tests.

And in addition to teaching and studying homophones in the regular progression of grades, homophones are very useful for special populations of students like English as a second language (ESL) learners and adult literacy students.

Homophones are your computer spell-checker's specific problem. Those brilliant machines are not very savvy when pointing out errors like "I can reed a book," so what this means is that the writer must know homophones to check up on the spell-checker.

Lately, some reading and writing tests, used widely to test "standards" in schools or tests for employment, sneak in some homophones in the proofreading section, spelling section, or vocabulary section.

So, I hope this chapter will find a lot of uses for students or teachers at many levels (see teaching suggestions in List 197 of this chapter).

This chapter will also be helpful as a reference. When in doubt about a homophone meaning or spelling, you can quickly look it up. Besides just a short definition, each homophone is used in a sentence.

As an additional help in learning and using these homophones, the part of speech is given. For example:

> The potter has a *wheel* (N)
> to *wheel* around quickly (V)
> *we'll,* meaning *we will* (Contr)

Last, but not least, homophones are fun. See some of the jokes under the teaching suggestions. They are also the basis of many puns. For those who love the English language, these homophones are a treasure chest.

The Vocabulary Teacher's Book of Lists

Homonym Confusion

There is a vast amount of confusion about *homonyms, homophones, homographs,* and *heteronyms* (homo = same, hetero = different, nym = name, phone = sound, graph = write). If you don't want to wrestle with the differences, just skip this discussion. But in case you do, the roots will help you, or you can also take the old-fashioned way and just call everything similar a *homonym* and go on.

A *homonym* is a word that sounds the same but has a different meaning and usually a different spelling; for example, *heir* and *air*.

A *homophone* is the same as a homonym. The words are both **pronounced the same** and have different meanings, and they can have different spellings. For example, *air* and *heir* are both pronounced the same. Homophones also can have the same spelling, for example, *bill*, as in a "*bill* for money" and a "bird's bill," but when they have the same spelling, we have listed them as homographs.

A *homograph* is like a homonym, but most have the **same spelling** and a different meaning. It **may** have the same pronunciation, like *bill*, but it may have a **different pronunciation**. For example, *bass* as in "bass fish" or a "bass voice." When it has a different pronunciation, we have listed them as heteronyms.

A *heteronym* is a special type of homograph—namely, it has the same spelling but it **must have a different pronunciation**, as in *bass*.

You can remember these better if you just look at the roots.

> Homophones (phone = sound) must sound alike.
> Homographs (graph = write) must be written the same.
> Heteronyms (heter = other) must have a different pronunciation.

However, some people, like older teachers, call all of the above homonyms. These older teachers are not all wrong either, as some dictionaries say a homonym could be either a homophone or a homograph. It is mostly some linguists who prefer to throw out the term *homonym* and use the more descriptive terms.

Term	Spelling	Pronunciation	Meaning	Example	Origin
homophone	same or different	same	different	bill, bill die, dye	different
heteronym	same	different	different	bass	different
homograph	same	same or different	different	bass bill	different

The term *homophone* tends to be used now by modern teachers instead of *homonym*. Lists of homographs and heteronyms can be found in Chapter 7, lists 156 and 158.

If you want a suggestion on where to start teaching the homophones, try the homophones in this list. The Master List of Homophones (List 199) has definitions and examples for each of these homophones and hundreds more.

add	ad	
air	heir	
already	all ready	
ant	aunt	
ball	bawl	
bare	bear	
beat	beet	
bee	be	
bin	been	
blew	blue	
brake	break	
buy	bye	by
cent	sent	
clothes	close	
creak	creek	
deer	dear	
dye	die	
eight	ate	
eye	I	
fair	fare	
feet	feat	
fined	find	
flour	flower	
four	for	
great	grate	
hear	here	
herd	heard	
high	hi	
hole	whole	
horse	hoarse	
hour	our	
inn	in	
it's	its	
knew	new	
lead	led	
loan	lone	
maid	made	
Mary	marry	merry
meat	meet	
might	mite	

missed	mist	
morn	mourn	
need	knead	
night	knight	
no	know	
oar	or	ore
one	won	
owe	oh	
pear	pair	
piece	peace	
plane	plain	
principal	principle	
rain	reign	rein
read	red	
reel	real	
road	rowed	rode
sail	sale	
seam	seem	
see	sea	
sell	cell	
sew	so	sow
shoe	shoo	
shone	shown	
side	sighed	
steel	steal	
sum	some	
sun	son	
tail	tale	
their	there	they're
threw	through	
to	two	too
tolled	told	
tow	toe	
vary	very	
wear	where	
weather	whether	
wee	we	
week	weak	
weigh	way	
wood	would	
write	right	
you're	your	

See the huge homophone list at the end of this chapter (List 199).

Rule Number 1: Don't depend on your computer's spell-check to correct homophone errors.

Rule Number 2: You learn homophones by paying attention to them. Teachers and teaching materials can call attention to homophones but finding them when you read or write anything is also important.

Here are some teaching suggestions:

1. **Have some fun;** both you and the kids can develop jokes and riddles.

   What is a large animal without its fur? (a bare bear)

   What covers a hopping animal? (hare hair)

   An insect's relative? (ant's aunt)

2. **Proofread** and correct sentences.

   Please drink sum milk.

   Turn write at the end of the street.

3. **Make flashcards**, one of a homophone pair on each side.

   Student sees one side, tries to say or to spell the other. Discuss the meaning, or use both words in a sentence.

4. **Make playing cards** for a Go Fish or Rummy type game. Use the same cards for a Concentration type game.

5. You or the students **make some worksheets**.

   Type A: Write the homophone pair: "sell/ _ _ _ _"

   Type B: Select the right word: "Dogs have (for/four) legs."

   Type C: See the sample workbook page in List 198 of this chapter.

6. **Make a game.**

   A. Bingo cards—Student marks homophone when it is called out.

   B. Crossword puzzles—Definitions guide student on how to fill in the blanks.

   C. Spinner type games

   D. Board type games; for example, racetrack and shake dice

   E. Challenge—Say one homophone meaning and opponent must say the other.

7. **A spelling test or a spelling bee** is a good way of teaching homophones. Be sure to stress the definition when dictating the word so the student spells the correct homophone. Select five or ten pairs of homophones for a weekly test. See Chapter 7, List 165, for some suggestions on how to teach spelling.

8. **Find homophones in other materials**—social studies, math, art, and so on. Have classroom teams competing for three days to see who can come up with the longest homophone list. The list should contain both matching homophones, each followed by a short definition or use in a sentence.

9. **Have a word wall** or corner of a chalkboard with a pair of homophones. Discuss them for two minutes and change them every day.

10. **Selection of homophones is important**. Choose homophone pairs that are on the growing edge of your students' vocabulary. Most of the time choose homophone pairs in which the students are apt to know one word in the pair but may not know the other, or be confused about its meaning or spelling. The homophones in the body of this book give you lots of choices. If you would like a little guidance, List 196 in this chapter has a list of relatively easy or common homophones.

one **1** won

One is the number 1, meaning a single thing. "I have one brother."

Won means to have been the best in a contest or race. "John won the race."

When you've won a game, you are number one!

Fill in the right one or won in each of these sentences.

1. I have _____ sister.

2. Lea _____ the race.

3. Our team _____ the spelling bee.

4. Will you give me _____ of your apples?

5. There is only _____ winner in this contest.

6. The girls_____ first prize.

7. Planet earth has_____ moon.

8. Who_____ the game last night?

9. _____ boy was standing by the tree.

10. The red team_____ the first race.

What can you say about the winner of his first race? (He won one.)

Practice: Write a sentence or a joke using each of the above homophones.

Master Homophone List

This master list of homophones is one of the largest you will ever see and, even so, a number of rare word homophones were omitted. Also omitted were homophones of names (Pat/pat). Since a homophone word can have several meanings, most of the time we attempted to use each of the meanings in a sentence. The letters in parentheses indicate part of speech.

> (N) = Noun; the name of a person, place, or thing
> (V) = Verb; shows action
> (Adj) = Adjective; modifies a noun
> (Adv) = Adverb; modifies a verb
> (Prep) = Preposition; shows some relationship
> (Interj) = Interjection; an exclamation
> (Contr) = Contraction; letters missing
> (Pron) = Pronoun; takes place of a noun
> (Conj) = Conjunction; joins two nouns, phrases, or clauses
> (H.V.) = Helping verb

These homophones can be used for interesting spelling lessons, for reference, and for vocabulary extension.

Acts—A formal decision. Deeds. Main division of a play. To pretend.
   The civil rights *acts* were passed through Congress. (N)
   They were *acts* of kindness. (N)
   This version of *Romeo and Juliet* was made into four *acts*. (N)
   Jill *acts* like a fool when she is with her friends. (V)
Ax—Tool for cutting trees.
   Joe used an *ax* to cut down the branches. (N)

Ad—Public announcement or description of something, short for "advertisement."
   We put an *ad* for our house in the paper. (N)
Add—To increase.
   They will *add* another room onto the house. (V)

Ads—Plural of ad or advertisements.
   They placed *ads* in the newspapers promoting their business. (N)
Adz—Heavy, broad, curved, ax-like tool used to cut timber.
   Dad used an *adz* to clear the field. (N)

Aid—To help or support.
   The Red Cross is an organization that will *aid* travelers on their journey. (V)
Aide—Assistant or helper.
   The teacher's *aide* graded our tests. (N)

Ail—To be sick.
   My grandfather has been *ailing* all week. (V)
Ale—Alcoholic beverage made from malt and hops that is more bitter than beer.
   The bartender handed him a bottle of *ale*. (N)

Air—Mixture of gases surrounding the earth, like oxygen.
   Up in the mountains, the *air* is clean. (N)
Heir—A person who inherits property and such.
   The man was an *heir* to the estate. (N)

Aisle—A passage between seats, usually in a church or theater.
   We walked down the *aisle* to the front. (N)
I'll—I will.
   I'll help you carry that. (Contr)
Isle—A small island.
   From the mainland, we could see a few *isle*s. (N)

Ale—See "Ail."

All—The whole amount, everything, entirely.
   All of the students went on vacation. (Adj)
   I am *all* worn out. (Adv)
Awl—Tool for piercing holes in leather.
   Mom used an *awl* to make more holes in her belt. (N)

Aloud—In a normal voice, but spoken loudly.
   He reads *aloud* every night to me. (Adv)
Allowed—To give permission to. To take into consideration.
   She is *allowed* to spend the night here. (V)
   My father *allowed* an hour for the traffic. (V)

Altar—A specially designed table in the church used for religious acts.
   We placed flowers on the *altar*. (N)
Alter—To change or become different.
   If I have time, I will *alter* the hem of your pants. (V)
   To avoid detention, he needed to *alter* his behavior. (V)

Ant—A small, crawling insect that lives in a colony.
   I found an *ant* in the sugar. (N)
Aunt—Father's or mother's sister or sister-in-law.
   My *Aunt* Kim came to visit yesterday. (N)

Ante—A (poker) player's stake put into the pot before the deal; an amount of money
   paid in advance to ensure an individual's share in a business venture.
   Each player *anted* up five dollars. (V)
   The *ante* was a minimum of ten thousand dollars. (N)
Auntie—Informal of "aunt."
   My mother's sister is our favorite, whom we call *Auntie* Barbara. (Adj)

Arc—Part of a circle, or curve.
   Can you see the *arc* of the rainbow? (N)
Ark—Biblical boat in which Noah saved his family and two of every animal in the flood.
   The story of the *ark* is in Genesis, the first book of the Bible. (N)

Ascent—A movement upward in rank. A way or path moving upward.
   He was congratulated on his *ascent* from assistant coach to head coach. (N)
   The mountain *ascent* was steep. (N)
Assent—To agree. Agreement.
   I will *assent* to the terms of the contract. (V)
   The *assent* was written up in the meeting's minutes. (N)

Assistance—To give help.
> May I be of any *assistance* to you? (N)

Assistants—Those who help others. Serving in the secondary position.
> Mary is one of the *assistants* at the retirement home. (N)
> The *assistant* coach was in charge when the head coach was away. (N)

Ate—Did eat. Past tense of eat.
> I *ate* a sandwich for lunch. (V)

Eight—The number 8.
> Seven plus one is *eight*. (N)
> There were *eight* people at the party. (Adj)

Attendance—The number attending.
> The *attendance* was weak, I'm afraid. (N)

Attendants—People who escort others.
> The *attendants* showed us to our seats. (N)

Aural—Referring to the ear.
> The doctor visit included an *aural* examination. (Adj)

Oral—Referring to the mouth.
> The students gave their *oral* reports. (Adj)

Aunt—See "Ant."

Auntie—See "Ante."

Away—Distant. Out of sight or possession.
> The store is five miles *away*. (Adj)
> He ran *away*. (Adv)

Aweigh—Something that is just below the bottom of something and hanging straight down.
> "Anchor's *aweigh*!" shouted the sailor. (Adj)

Awful—Unpleasant or harmful.
> This fruit tastes *awful*! (Adj)

Offal—The part of an animal that is thrown away after it is killed for food.
> The *offal* were unfit to eat. (N)

Awl—See "All."

Aye—Yes; an affirmation.
> "*Aye,* that's my boy," said Mr. Smith. (Adv)

Eye—Organ for sight. To look at or watch. A way something is viewed. Anything referred to as an eye. The calm, quiet area in the middle of a hurricane.
> My mom has to have surgery on her right *eye*. (N)
> The security guard *eyed* the suspicious character as he walked through the store. (V)
> I laced my shoestrings through the *eyes* of my sneakers. (N)
> The safest place to be in a hurricane is in the *eye*. (N)

I—Personal pronoun. The person talking.
> Jamie and *I* are going to the store. (Pron)

Ax—See "Acts."

Bail—The agreement to pay money in return for the release of someone from jail. The curved handle of a pail or kettle. Pail or scoop used to toss water from a boat.
I had to *bail* my cousin out of jail. (N)
The *bail* of the kettle was broken. (N)
It is a tedious task to *bail* water from a sinking canoe. (V)
Bale—A large bundle tied with cord or wire.
There were *bales* of hay in the fields. (N)

Bait—Food used to attract animals into traps.
The *bait* on the hook tempted the fish. (N)
Bate—To hold one's breath due to excitement. To decrease, restrain, or hold back.
The children listened with *bated* breath as she told the story. (V)
Amateur boxers use headgear to *bate* the blows of their opponents. (V)

Bald—Having no hair.
The man didn't need a comb, he was *bald*. (Adj)
Bawled—Crying loudly and uncontrollably.
The baby *bawled* for her bottle. (V)

Bale—See "Bail."

Ball—Round object of any size and material, used in games. In baseball, a pitched ball not thrown over home plate between the batter's knees and shoulders.
The *ball* rolled into the street. (N)
The count was one *ball* and two strikes. (N)
Bawl—Cry loudly and uncontrollably.
I heard the child *bawl* when she fell and hurt her knee. (V)

Band—A group that plays music. A group.
The *band* was playing jazz music. (N)
There was a *band* of thieves. (N)
Banned—Forbidden to go.
They were *banned* from the stadium. (V)

Bard—A person who writes or sings poems.
Shakespeare was a famous *bard*. (N)
Barred—Something that has bars. Forbidden to enter.
The windows were *barred*. (Adj)
The drunk was *barred* from the club. (V)

Bare—To be naked or exposed or empty. To expose.
The room was *bare*. (Adj)
The dog will *bare* its teeth when it becomes angry. (V)
Bear—A large mammal with thick hair covering its body and a short tail. To show a resemblance to someone. To carry the weight of something. To carry and birth offspring.
The *bear* woke out of hibernation. (N)
She *bears* a resemblance to her mother. (V)
Joan can't *bear* the work of having a job and three kids. (V)
It was difficult for her to *bear* children. (V)

Baring—To remove one's coverings. To be straightforward.
> When she took off her shawl, she was *baring* her shoulders to the wind. (V)
> Parents are responsible for *baring* the truth to their children. (V)

Bearing—Manner of a person. An understanding of a situation.
> This man has a dignified *bearing.* (N)
> They must hold onto their *bearings* if they want to win the race. (N)

Bark—The sharp noise a dog makes when it is excited. The covering on a tree.
> The hounds *barked* at the scent. (V)
> A pine tree's *bark* is rough and bumpy. (N)

Barque—Type of ship with three masts.
> You can see the *barque's* masts on the horizon! (N)

Baron—Important financier of low nobility.
> My great-grandpa was a *baron.* (N)

Barren—Unable to have babies. Anything that doesn't produce much of anything.
> The pig was *barren.* (Adj)
> The old factory has been *barren* for many years. (Adj)

Barque—See "Bark."

Basal—Of, at, or forming the base; fundamental, basic.
> That company publishes a *basal* reading book. (Adj)

Basil—Any of several herbs of the mint family.
> *Basil* adds such good flavor to salads and pizza. (N)

Base—The foundation of something. The biggest ingredient of something. One of four corners on a baseball diamond. A building or resting place in a specific area, mostly in the military.
> The *base* of a house is usually cement. (N)
> The casserole has a fish *base.* (N)
> Jimmy ran from second *base* to third. (N)
> Meet me here at the military *base* in three hours. (N)

Bass—A deep tone.
> My grandpa sings *bass* in the choir. (N)
> Jim plays *bass* drums. (Adj)

Basil—See "Basal."

Based—A basis that is established.
> That grocery store has shops all over the U.S., but it's *based* in Chicago. (V)
> The movie was *based* on a true story. (V)

Baste—To moisten meat by covering with juice.
> *Baste* the chicken in lemon juice before you put it on the grill. (V)

Bases—Plural of base.
> There were players on all the *bases.* (N)

Basis—Foundation or base of anything.
> Sign language was the *basis* of Helen Keller's success. (N)

Bask—To be exposed to pleasant warmth.
My favorite thing to do is *bask* in the sun. (V)
Basque—A group of people or their language from Western Spain and France.
I did a history report on ancient *Basques* and their language. (N)

Baste—See "Based."

Bate—See "Bait."

Bawl—See "Ball."

Bawled—See "Bald."

Bazaar—A place where many kinds of goods are sold, especially in the Middle East.
The local *bazaar* sold a variety of things. (N)
Bizarre—Very peculiar or strange.
Some coincidental incidents are so *bizarre*! (Adj)

Be—To exist or live. Having a position or place. To take place or happen. Used to begin a question or command. Used as a helping verb to show past or present action.
Will there *be* any lions at the zoo? (V)
The new computer will *be* over here. (V)
Where will the new store *be*? (V)
Please, *be* more considerate. (V)
Could he *be* the one who called? (V)
Bee—Insect with four legs and a stinger. A social event where people have a task or contest.
There is a swarm of *bees* near that beehive. (N)
All of the students got together for a national spelling *bee*. (N)

Beach—Sand or pebbles along a seashore. To run a boat or sea-animal onto the sand.
I collect seashells on the *beach*. (N)
The whale was *beached* on the sand. (V)
Beech—Tree with smooth, gray bark and sweet nuts.
This wood comes from a *beech* tree. (Adj)
These *beech* nuts are very good in pies. (N)

Beadle—A parish officer having various subordinate duties such as waiting on the rector.
Please ask the *beadle* to bring my vestments now. (N)
Beetle—Any of various insects characterized by hard forewings that protect the membraneous flight wings.
We found a *beetle* in the back corner of the garage when we moved some boxes. (N)

Bear—See "Bare."

Bearing—See "Baring."

Beat—To strike over and over. The sound the heart makes as it pumps blood. To defeat. A particular time kept in music. A regular route used by police officers. To be physically exhausted.
Add eggs and *beat* for two minutes. (V)
The doctor listened to the *beat* of her patient's heart. (N)
We have to *beat* this team if we're to make it to the playoffs. (V)
This song has a nice *beat*. (N)
Some officers are very friendly with the people on their *beat*. (N)
I was *beat* after a long day of hard work. (Adj)
Beet—A plant, with red roots used as a vegetable, and with white roots used for sugar.
We had red *beets* for dinner. (N)

Beetle—See "Beadle."

Beau—A man dating a woman. A man who is very concerned about his clothing.
Joe is Mary's *beau*. (N)
A tailor fitted the *beau*. (N)
Bow—Decorative knot that is curved. Stringed wooden device used to propel arrows.
The package had a *bow* on it. (N)
A *bow* and arrows are required for the game of archery. (N)

Bee—See "Be."

Beech—See "Beach."

Been—Past participle of be.
It has *been* a cloudy day. (V)
Bin—Box used for storing.
Put your toys in the *bin*. (N)

Beer—Alcoholic drink made with fermented hops and barley.
My dad enjoys a good *beer* while watching a baseball game. (N)
Bier—A coffin stand.
The coffin was laid out on a *bier*. (N)

Bell—A hollow cup that makes a ringing sound when its rim is struck.
The *bell* in church sounded like a million tinkling drops of water. (N)
Belle—Woman with charm and beauty, and sometimes popularity.
Christie was so admired by everyone, some called her a *belle*. (N)

Berry—Small, juicy fruits, like strawberries or blackberries.
The *berry* pie was delicious. (N)
Bury—To dig a hole and put something in the ground and then put dirt over it.
We had to *bury* our dog after she died. (V)

Beet—See "Beat."

Berth—Place to rest. A dock.
The ship was *berthed* at the dock. (N)
Birth—The act of being born or any beginning.
The *birth* of the United States of America was July 4, 1776. (N)

Better—Superior or of greater value.
    This sweater is of *better* quality than that one. (Adj)
Bettor—Someone who bets.
    The *bettor* won all of the money. (N)

Bier—See "Beer."

Bight—Looped or curved part of a rope or river.
    There was a *bight* on the river's shoreline. (N)
Bite—To grip or tear a section of something with the teeth. A wound made by a bite. A small amount of food.
    I took a *bite* of my lunch. (V)
    After the camping trip, I was covered with mosquito *bites.* (N)
    All I want is a *bite* of your cookie. (N)
Byte—An information unit in data processing, composed of 8 bits, usually representing a letter or numeral.
    This will only need a few *bytes* of memory on your computer. (N)

Billed—Past tense of bill.
    I was *billed* for my purchases. (V)
Build—To put together materials or parts. To strengthen. To mold or form.
    The construction workers were hurrying to *build* the corporate building. (V)
    Hard work *builds* character. (V)
    By working out with weights, Trey was able to *build* up his muscles. (V)

Bin—See "Been."

Birth—See "Berth."

Bizarre—See "Bazaar."

Bite—See "Bight" and "Byte."

Blew—Past tense of blow.
    The wind *blew* down Gina's house. (V)
Blue—Color between green and violet in the spectrum. To be unhappy.
    The new shirt is *blue.* (N)
    The team was *blue* when they lost the game. (Adj)

Bloc—Group with similar interests in politics.
    To win the election the people must vote as a *bloc.* (N)
Block—Anything made into or shaped like a cube. Preventing the passageway or progress. An object that prevents something from being done. An area in a city that has streets on all sides of it.
    A *block* of ice is needed to keep the food cold. (N)
    The barricades served to *block* anyone from entering. (V)
    A *block* in traffic made us miss the opening act. (N)
    We live on the same *block* as a woman whom I went to college with. (N)

Blue—See "Blew."

Boar—Male hog or pig that is uncastrated.
The *boar* on the farm won the blue ribbon at the state fair. (N)
Bore—To make a hole using a revolving tool. Making a hole by chewing, pushing, or digging. To make someone uninterested by being dull. A tiresome, dull thing. Past tense of bear.
I will *bore* a hole into the wall. (V)
The dog *bore* a hole under our fence. (V)
You are beginning to *bore* me with your tall tales. (V)
This party is a *bore*. (N)
She *bore* a son. (V)

Board—Piece of wood sawed thin. Daily meals. An official group of persons. To go onto. To cover something up with pieces of wood. A flat piece of wood or other material used for a specific purpose.
Nail this *board* to the wall. (N)
At college I will get my room and *board* living in the dorm. (N)
The *board* of trustees agreed on a new housing plan. (N)
If we don't hurry, we'll not be able to *board* the train! (V)
All of the windows on the abandoned building were *boarded* up. (V)
My friend bought a chess *board* made of ivory. (N)
Bored—Past tense of bore.
Do you ever get *bored* on weekends? (V)

Boarder—One who rents from another. A person whose duty it is to board an enemy ship.
We have a *boarder* living in our guest quarters. (N)
When I was in the navy, no one wanted to be a *boarder*. (N)
Border—A line separating one piece of land from another. Decorative threads on a piece of fabric.
Those white fences are a good *border* for your yard. (V)
The satin created a wonderful *border* on the quilt. (N)

Bore—See "Boar."

Bored—See "Board."

Border—See "Boarder."

Born—Delivered at birth. Anything that is by nature or natural.
The puppies were *born* on Saturday. (Adj)
My nephew is a *born* athlete. (Adj)
Borne—To carry or bring. Past participle of bear.
I have *borne* the baby around town all day. (V)
Bourn—To set a point where something ends. To set a point to reach.
Every farm land has a *bourn*. (N)
The runner set a *bourn*. (N)

Borough—Town with its own local government.

    She lives in the *borough* of Brooklyn in New York City. (N)

Burro—A pack animal of the same family as the donkey in southwest U.S. and Mexico.

    The farmer had a *burro* to carry supplies. (N)

Burrow—A tunnel in the ground or the process of making one.

    You can fall if your foot gets stuck in a *burrow*. (N)

    A mole will *burrow* down into the ground if it sees sunlight. (V)

Bough—Branch of a tree.

    If you are not watching, you can get hit by a low *bough* when walking in the forest. (N)

Bow—Front of a ship. To bend at the waist.

    Is that whale to the stern or to the *bow*? (N)

    The conductor gave a deep *bow* after his performance. (V)

Bouillon—Clear, seasoned broth made from meats like beef or chicken.

    Drink this *bouillon*; it's good for you. (N)

Bullion—Uncoined gold or silver.

    The pirates struck it rich when they uncovered a chest filled with *bullion*. (N)

Bourn—See "Born" and "Borne."

Bow—See "Beau."

Boy—Male child. An exclamation of excitement or exasperation!

    Mrs. Phyllis gave birth to a baby *boy*. (N)

    Oh, *boy,* here we go again! (Interj)

Buoy—Floating marker that shows a channel or dangerous area.

    The *buoy* showed where the water was very deep. (N)

Brake—A pedal or gadget used to stop a vehicle. The action itself. A thicket of shrubs, bushes, and the like.

    Dan's bike *brake* is not working well. (N)

    The car *braked* at the intersection. (V)

    The boys lost their baseball in the *brake* by the field. (N)

Break—To make something come apart. A place that is broken. To ruin something. To crack a bone. The inability to keep a promise. To force something to go your way. A brief rest or interruption from a task. To decrease the force of something. To stop something.

    The vase will *break* if you drop it. (V)

    There was a *break* in the window. (N)

    Why did you let him *break* my radio? (V)

    If that falls on your leg, you will surely *break* your leg. (V)

    I hate to *break* a promise, but I have to cancel our date. (V)

    I'll need help if I'm going to *break* into the music industry. (V)

    The supervisor gave us all a one-hour lunch *break*. (N)

    The rubber mats will serve to *break* your fall. (V)

    It is very difficult to *break* the bad habit of smoking. (N)

Bread—Food made of dough or batter and baked.
   I buy my *bread* at the grocery store. (N)
Bred—Designed for a specific purpose. To produce offspring. Cultivated.
   This dog was *bred* for shows. (V)
   Most endangered animals are *bred* in captivity. (V)
   The teacher *bred* an interest in music for his students. (V)

Break—See "Brake."

Bred—See "Bread."

Brewed—Made a beverage by boiling or soaking in water. Formulated a plan or plot. Anything that went through a process of forming.
   I *brewed* some coffee for breakfast. (V)
   The thief *brewed* an ingenious plan to steal the diamonds. (V)
   This situation has *brewed* for a long time. (V)
Brood—Young birds that are hatched at the same time in a nest or are cared for all together. Young people or animals who have the same mother or are taken care of by the same person. The act of an animal sitting on eggs to hatch them. To ponder or worry about something for a long period of time.
   While at the zoo, we saw a *brood* of ducklings. (N)
   Mothers are very protective of their *broods*. (N)
   Hens are very aggressive when they *brood*. (V)
   Don't *brood* over your loss for too long. (V)

Brews—Present participle of brew.
   Sally *brews* coffee every morning. (V)
   El Niño still *brews* in some parts of the country. (V)
Bruise—To injure without breaking skin. A bump.
   The older you get, the easier you *bruise*. (V)
   When the ball hit me, I got a *bruise*. (N)

Bridal—Things having to do with a wedding or the bride.
   We had a *bridal* shower for a friend. (Adj)
Bridle—Headgear for a horse. To control.
   You have to hook your horse to a *bridle*. (N)
   Bridle your anger! (V)

Broach—To bring up or mention for the first time. To open something by making a hole in it. A tapered, sharp tool used for enlarging and shaping holes. A slender, sharp pointed rod that's used to hold meat while it's roasted.
   I will *broach* the subject at our next meeting. (V)
   The soldiers attempted to *broach* the fort. (V)
   The belt maker used a *broach* to enlarge the holes in the belt. (N)
   The chickens were placed on a *broach* to be roasted. (N)
Brooch—A pin.
   That *brooch* is gorgeous! (N)

Brood—See "Brewed."

Brows—Plural of brow (the ridge over the eye).
    In the 1940s, women used eye pencil on their *brows*. (N)
Browse—To look through or glance at casually.
    He *browsed* the shelves looking for something to read. (V)

Browse—See "Brows."

Bruise—See "Brews."

Build—See "Billed."

Bullion—See "Bouillon."

Bundt—A ring-shaped cake baked in a tube pan with fluted sides.
    My sister's lemon *bundt* cake won the prize at the fair. (Adj)
Bunt—To bat very gently so that the ball rolls in the infield close to home plate.
    He was told by the coach to *bunt* his next time up at bat. (V)

Bunt—See "Bundt."

Buoy—See "Boy."

Burro—See "Borough."

Burrow—See "Borough" and "Burro."

Bury—See "Berry."

But—On the contrary. Except. However.
    You can use it, *but* return it when you're done. (Conj)
    I bought everything for the barbecue *but* the meat. (Prep)
    Yes, I see you *but* I don't remember you. (Conj)
Butt—The end of something. One made fun of. To thrust.
    The cigarette *butt* was lying in the street. (N)
    Why am I always the *butt* of a joke? (N)
    Goats *butt* heads. (V)
    Don't *butt* in to our conversation. (N)

Buy—To pay money for something. A bargain.
    Mom needs to *buy* milk at the store. (V)
    What a great *buy*! (N)
By—On the side of. The means used. By the measure of. A particular time. In accordance with. Done as steps continuously. The difference between.
    Let's walk *by* the field. (Prep)
    They arrived *by* train. (Prep)
    I like to buy meat *by* the pound. (Prep)
    I plan to be there *by* noon. (Prep)
    You should always play *by* the rules. (Prep)
    I followed the instructions step *by* step. (Prep)
    They lost the game *by* five points. (Prep)

Bye—A tournament participant being allowed to advance to the next round without having to face an opponent like other participants.
> I was lucky enough to get a *bye* in the first round of the tennis match. (N)

Byte—See "Bight" and "Bite."

Cache—Hiding place for wealth or other important items. To conceal or hide.
> There's an old *cache* underground that was used for treasure. (N)
> The robbers *cached* the money up in the rafters. (V)

Cash—Coined or paper money. To give or get cash for something.
> I don't have any *cash* on hand. (N)
> We *cashed* the check. (V)

Callous—To be mean and insensitive. Rough texture of work-worn hands.
> Old Miss Hannigan was *callous* toward the orphan. (Adj)
> Miguel's *calloused* hands ached from the long day's work. (Adj)

Callus—Hard tissue.
> The *callus* on her hand was as hard as stone. (N)

Cannon—A huge gun set on a stand that shoots out explosives.
> The pirate ship had four *cannons*. (N)

Canon—A rule that is used to judge something. A law that governs the church. An official listing of the books of the Bible. A listing of an author's accepted writings. An authentic list of saints. Any list that is official. A part of a church service that takes place after the collection of offerings. A musical composition that has different voices singing the same piece of music one after the other either at the same or different pitch. An official member of a clergy that belongs to a church that has more than one minister.
> It is important that we follow the *canons* of good parenting. (N)
> Ministers must follow all sacred *canons* if they expect their followers to do so. (N)
> There is a *canon* of all of the books of the Bible in the almanac. (N)
> Mother Teresa is on the *canon* that is at the Vatican. (N)
> All of the senators were on the *canon* to vote on the new bill. (N)
> Reverend Gaines gave a beautiful sermon during the *canon* on Sunday morning. (N)
> Our church choir sang a *canon* at the Christmas celebration. (N)
> The selection committee chose him to become a *canon* member. (N)

Can't—Not able to; cannot.
> I *can't* go to sleep. (Contr)

Cant—Insincere statement. Inclination or slant. Special language.
> His *cant* was a total lie. (N)
> Our floor *cants* to the left a bit. (N)
> The Gypsies spoke in a specific *cant*. (N)

Canvas—A heavy, durable cloth made for oil paintings, tents, sails, and so on. A picture painted on canvas.
> Uncle Rex's sail is made of strong *canvas*. (N)
> How much do you think a Picasso *canvas* is worth? (N)

Canvass—To go door-to-door getting votes or support, usually for political purposes.
> The Republicans have *canvassed* the town. (V)

Capital—Money or property wealth able to produce more wealth. A city used as the center of government for a specific state or country. A letter written in a large form used at sentences' beginnings and for proper names.

A company wanting to expand may need to borrow *capital*. (N)

The *capital* of Kansas is Wichita. (N)

Always use a *capital* letter at the beginning of your name. (Adj)

Capitol—The building in D.C., our nation's capital, where Congress holds meetings. Any building used by state representatives.

We visited the *Capitol* in Washington, D.C., our nation's capital. (N)

The president is coming to the *capitol* building tomorrow. (N)

Carat—Unit of weight for precious stones that equals about 1/5 gram.

The diamond weighs 1 *carat*. (N)

Caret—A mark (^) made to show something should be added.

Today, we learned how to use a *caret* in editing our writing. (N)

Carrot—A vegetable with a long, orange root.

Carrots are very nutritious. (N)

Carol—A joyous song or hymn, usually one of Christmas. A practice from the Middle Ages of dancing in a ring to music. The act of singing joyously. A first name.

My favorite *carol* is "Silent Night." (N)

Adam comes from a long line of *carolers*. (V)

My family goes Christmas *caroling* every year. (V)

Give *Carol* her present.

Carrel—Study space in a library or class, sometimes boxed in on three sides.

I used the *carrel* in the library to study for the test. (N)

Carrot—See "Carat" and "Caret."

Cash—See "Cache."

Cast—To fling, hurl, or toss something away. To throw something to the side or off of something. The complete distance that something is thrown. To shape a thing by pouring or squeezing something into a mold to harden. A soft or hard protective covering used to support or shape a broken limb. The action of selecting participants in a play or movie. All of the actors who participate in a play or movie.

Todd loved to *cast* stones across the lake. (V)

Mr. Jones, who is so tall, *casts* a long shadow in the sun. (V)

My dad taught me how to make a long *cast* line while fishing. (N)

Metal has to first be melted before it is *cast*. (V)

The basketball player was able to play with a soft *cast* on her hand. (N)

The director was very careful not to *cast* any amateurs in his play. (V)

The entire *cast* was invited to the governor's mansion. (N)

Caste—A social class in the Hindu culture. A distinctive, exclusive social class. A system that socially separates according to position, wealth, rank, and birth.

In India, people are born into a *caste*. (N)

Many people are against the numerous *caste* systems that exist around the world. (N)

Cause—Anything that makes something happen. The act of making something happen. The reason something is done. Anything that interests a lot of people and they tend to support.

Loud music is the *cause* of your bad hearing. (N)

The brisk wind *caused* me to be cold. (V)

Having a birthday is a *cause* for celebration. (N)

Defeating illiteracy is a *cause* she believed in. (N)

Caws—The cry of a crow.

That crow *caws* from the telephone pole. (V)

Cede—To yield or surrender.

They had to *cede* their land to the bank. (V)

Seed—A pit from which a plant grows. To spread seeds over an area.

We planted flower *seeds* in our garden to have flowers for spring. (N)

The woman *seeded* her garden with tulips. (V)

Ceiling—Overhead lining on the inside of a room.

The lamp hung down from the *ceiling.* (N)

Sealing—A type of wax or glue used to hold two things together without cracks.

The *sealing* kept all the moisture inside. (N)

Cell—Small room in prison. The fundamental microscopic unit of any living thing.

The prisoner stayed in a *cell* for six months. (N)

Your body is made up of billions of tiny *cells.* (N)

Sell—To exchange an object for currency. Having goods for purchases. Anything that is on sale.

Hilda wanted to *sell* her house. (V)

My sister plans to *sell* flowers. (V)

These bananas *sell* for a great price. (V)

The car is such a good bargain, it will *sell* itself. (V)

Cellar—A room underground underneath the house.

Grandma keeps food in her *cellar.* (N)

Seller—A salesman, dealer, or any person who sells merchandise.

The *seller* came peddling his ware down the road. (N)

Censer—A container in which incense is burned, usually at religious services.

The priest had *censers* around the room at the funeral. (N)

Censor—One who cuts out harmful or improper parts. The action of doing this.

My neighbor is a *censor* at a local television station. (N)

A prisoner's letters will be *censored.* (V)

Sensor—Detection device.

Many people have motion *sensors* in their homes. (N)

Cent—A unit of money (penny) that's equal to 1 percent of one dollar in the U.S.

In the United States, if you have one penny, you have one *cent.* (N)

Scent—A certain smell, usually pleasant. A traceable odor left by an animal or person.

The *scent* from the kitchen told me that Mom was baking cookies. (N)

The bloodhounds quickly caught the *scent* of the thief. (N)

Sent—Did send. Past tense and past participle of send.

I *sent* a letter to my friend. (V)

Cents—Pennies, a hundredth part of a U.S. dollar.
   I bought a notebook for twenty-five *cents.* (N)
Sense—One of the five senses (smell, touch, sight, hearing, taste). Ability to understand.
   Ability to think clearly. A vague awareness.
   My *sense* of smell is very sharp. (N)
   I think she has a good *sense* of style. (N)
   It doesn't take much *sense* to touch a hot stove. (N)

Cereal—An edible grain used for a breakfast food.
   I had oat bran *cereal* for breakfast. (N)
Serial—A movie or story written or seen as a series.
   The second part of the *serial* is on tonight. (N)

Cession—To hand over or surrender something to another.
   I am going to *cession* my car to my brother for the evening. (N)
Session—Meeting of a group to conduct business. The time it takes to have a meeting.
   Periods of lessons and study that the school year is divided into.
   The investors had a group *session* to talk about their stock growth. (N)
   This *session* of Congress has a lot of work to get done. (N)
   In our state, the school year is divided into four *sessions.* (N)

Chance—An opportunity; a possibility. Anything that is a risk.
   Now is your *chance* to make big money. (N)
   There's a good *chance* that I will not be back. (N)
   Your winning the lottery is all due to *chance.* (N)
   You'll be taking a big *chance* if you call her. (N)
Chants—Stylized way of speaking or singing.
   The tribe sang *chants* around the fire. (N)

Chased—Did chase; past tense of chase.
   Our dog Spot *chased* a fox around the yard. (V)
Chaste—To have pure morals.
   The princess was *chaste* in her ways. (Adj)

Cheap—Inexpensive; costing little. Made poorly. Someone who is unwilling to spend
   money.
   Fast-food restaurants are usually *cheap.* (Adj)
   My ring was so *cheap* that it broke the day I got it. (Adj)
   My uncle has always been *cheap.* (Adj)
Cheep—To chirp.
   Baby birds *cheep* when they are hungry. (V)

Chews—To grind with the teeth.
   Haley *chews* her food twenty times before swallowing. (V)
Choose—To make a choice.
   The coaches will *choose* who will be on the team. (V)

Chic—Stylish and sophisticated.
   You look so *chic* in that outfit. (Adj)
Sheik—Arab chief or religious leader.
   The *sheik* is considered very wise. (N)

Chili—The pod of a pepper, usually dried and used for seasoning. A seasoned dish of chopped meat, beans, peppers, and tomato broth. Also correctly spelled "chile."
A *chili* will add spice to the dish. (N)
I eat *chili* twice a week for lunch.
Chilly—Slightly cold.
The air is very *chilly* tonight. (Adj)

Choir—Singing group.
The church *choir* will now sing. (N)
Quire—Set of twenty-four sheets of paper.
Our printer needs a *quire* of paper. (N)

Choose—See "Chews."

Choral—Music written for a choir.
The choir will now sing a beautiful *choral* piece. (Adj)
Coral—A hard skeleton of tiny sea animals, usually pink, white, or red.
Angie saw many *coral* reefs on her vacation to Florida. (N)

Chorale—A hymn; a chorus.
The whole choir hummed the *chorale*. (N)
Corral—Pen for livestock. The act of directing animals into a holding area. To besiege or surround someone.
Saddle up a horse in the *corral*. (N)
It is your job to *corral* the horses. (V)
The movie star was *corralled* when she came out of the restaurant. (V)

Chord—Harmonious blend of three or more musical notes.
The harmonious *chord* gave way to a splendid finale. (N)
Cord—A thick rope, usually of yarn or leather. Electrical wire that is insulated.
The white *cord* was tied to the tree. (N)
Please do not step on the *cord* from the television. (N)

Chute—Sloping tube, used like a slide, to deposit objects from one place to another.
The laundry went down the *chute* and into the basement. (N)
Shoot—To aim for and fire at an object with a gun or other weapon. To send something quickly. The act of attempting to score a goal in either hockey or basketball. Taking a picture with a camera. To come forth from something.
The cowboys had to *shoot* the poisonous snake. (V)
I am going to *shoot* you a letter as soon as possible. (N)
I learned to *shoot* a basketball when I was a child. (V)
May I please *shoot* your photograph? (V)
It is an amazing sight to see water *shoot* from a geyser. (V)

Cite—To summon to appear before a court of law. To offer in support of.

Ms. Bailey was *cited* to appear in court Monday morning. (V)

Most lawyers *cite* cases that will help their case in court. (V)

Sight—The ability to use the sense of seeing. The act of looking or seeing. Something that can be seen. Something that is enjoyable to see. Something used to guide your vision when taking aim at something.

My *sight* was better when I was younger. (N)

I loved my first *sight* of the green grass at Wrigley Field. (N)

Some people get sick at the *sight* of blood. (N)

A sunset at the beach is a beautiful *sight*. (N)

You have to adjust the *sight* on the rifle. (N)

Site—A particular place.

Yankee Stadium has been the *site* for many exciting baseball games. (N)

Clause—Grammatical part of a sentence using a verb and a subject. One part of a law or treaty.

Your sentence doesn't have a main *clause*. (N)

You are in violation of a *clause* in your contract. (N)

Claws—Sharp nails on animals' feet, usually curved and pointed. The act of using claws to scratch or mark. The part of the hammer that's used to pull nails.

Falcons use their *claws* to pierce their prey. (N)

Her cat *claws* at the door when he wants to come in. (V)

Be sure to use the *claws* to remove that broken floorboard. (N)

Click—Sharp, small sound. The act of making a clicking sound. The act of pressing a button on a mouse to give instructions to a computer.

I heard a *click* when she put the key in the lock. (N)

The key *clicked* when I tapped the table with it. (V)

You have to *click* on the icon to bring the program up. (V)

Clique—A small, exclusive group of people.

There are many tight little *cliques* at our school. (N)

Climb—To move upward by using the feet or hands. To travel upwards. The action of traveling upwards. To move up higher. A place that has to be climbed.

I *climbed* the stairs with no problem. (V)

At Wrigley Field, the vines *climb* up the wall. (V)

Her *climb* up the social ladder has been the stuff of legends. (N)

The price of beef has *climbed* steadily over the past five years. (V)

The mountain will be a very difficult *climb*. (V)

Clime—Climate or weather condition. A country or area that is pleasant to live in.

It was a sunny *clime*. (N)

The *clime* in Australia is very nice this time of year. (N)

Clew—Ball of thread or yarn. The lower corner of a sail. A metal ring that is fastened to the lower corner of a sail that has lines attached to it.
　　What color *clew* are you selecting to knit the sweater? (N)
　　There was a hole in the *clew* of the sail. (N)
　　The fisherman bought new *clews* for his sailboat. (N)
Clue—A bit of evidence or hint used in partly solving a mystery or problem.
　　Here, I'll give you a *clue*. (N)

Close—To shut something. To end something. Not open for business.
　　Please *close* the door after you leave. (V)
　　The semester will *close* with a final exam. (V)
　　The store was *closed* all weekend. (N)
Clothes—Coverings on the body (pants, shirts, skirts, etc.).
　　Do you like my new *clothes*? (N)

Clue—See "Clew."

Coal—A black mineral used as fuel for burning. A piece of wood or coal used for burning.
　　We needed *coal* for the stove. (N)
　　A *coal* is still hot long after it has been removed from fire. (N)
Cole—Cabbage-like plant.
　　If you buy *cole* at the store you will have it for the slaw. (N)

Coarse—Anything consisting of large parts. Anything that is rough.
　　I enjoyed running through the *coarse* sand. (Adj)
　　My, that cloth is *coarse*! (Adj)
Course—Any direction that is taken. Moving ahead. A run of classes on any given subject. A portion of a meal served separately from another. An area for games or races.
　　Our *course* was already mapped out for us. (N)
　　The detectives followed the *course* of the suspect from Friday to Monday. (N)
　　I plan to take an English *course* this semester. (N)
　　I didn't particularly care for the first *course* of the meal. (N)
　　I'll meet you at the golf *course* on Wednesday. (N)

Cole—See "Coal."

Colonel—Army rank above lieutenant and below brigadier general.
　　A *colonel* is a higher ranking officer than a captain. (N)
Kernel—Grain of corn. The soft inner part of a hard shell of a nut or fruit.
　　There were a few *kernels* at the bottom of the popcorn bowl. (N)
　　Some snacks are made from the *kernels* of fruits. (N)

Complement—Something used to complete or bring together.
　　The party was a good *complement* to the year. (V)
Compliment—Comments of praise or approval. The act of making a compliment.
　　She received many *compliments* on the cake she baked. (V)
　　Please, allow me to *compliment* you on a job well done. (V)

Coop—Pen used to cage chickens, rabbits, pigs, or other small animals.
Guard the chicken *coop* from the foxes! (N)
Coupe—Two-doored car, much like a sedan of the same model.
Did you see that *coupe* driving down Manchester Avenue? (N)

Coral—See "Choral."

Core—Center or innermost part of anything. The middle of a fruit that contains its seeds. To remove the middle of fruit.
What exactly is the *core* of your argument? (N)
How did this apple *core* get on the ground? (N)
You should *core* the apples before baking them. (V)
Corps—Any group of people that are specially trained. Specially trained soldiers used by the military.
The *corps* of medical doctors were all bustling around. (N)
Have you ever heard of the Signal *Corps*? (N)

Corral—See "Chorale."

Cord—See "Chord."

Correspondence—Writing of letters to a friend or business relation. Relationship, as in similarity or sameness.
Our *correspondence* lasted for over a year. (N)
There is little *correspondence* between this book and the movie. (N)
Correspondents—People who write to one another. Someone used to report news from a faraway place.
My *correspondents* always write to me. (N)
They have been *correspondents* on this network for many years. (N)

Council—Legislative body called together to discuss important issues and laws. People called together to give advice or settle differences.
The city *council* met to discuss the new law. (N)
The citizens' *council* was called to decide if the city should build a new stadium. (N)
Counsel—One who advises or gives advice to another. A lawyer. The act of giving advice.
You must seek good *counsel* immediately. (N)
I suggest you get *counsel's* advice before signing that contract. (N)
Will you *counsel* my friend before he makes a mistake? (V)

Coupe—See "Coop."

Course—See "Coarse."

Creak—Making a loud or squeaking noise. Grating or squeaking noise.
The step *creaked* when I walked on it. (V)
That *creak* is a sign that the door needs to be oiled. (N)
Creek—Small stream of fresh water.
The slow-moving *creek* was perfect for finding frogs. (N)

Crewel—A type of stitching used for embroidery.
She used a *crewel* stitch in the hem of my shorts. (N)
Cruel—Being purposely mean or hurtful. Causing pain.
Her intentions were *cruel.* (Adj)
Standing or walking all day can be *cruel* to your feet. (Adj)

Crews—Groups of workers.
The *crews* were able to service all of their customers. (N)
Cruise—A pleasure trip on a boat. Wandering without a specific purpose.
He took a wonderful *cruise* on the Seine. (N)
Many people *cruise* the Internet for ways of getting information. (V)

Cruel—See "Crewel."

Cue—A signal, usually by action or words, made for something to happen. A long stick used to hit pool balls.
That line was my *cue* to appear on stage. (N)
The *cue* hit the pool ball right into the pocket. (N)
Queue—Line of people.
There was a long *queue* waiting to get into the theater. (N)

Currant—Small raisin used in cooking. A small berry used in jams.
Put some *currants* in the pie. (N)
Current—Recent happenings. Fast part of a stream.
This is my most *current* magazine. (Adj)
The *current* speeds up around the bend. (N)

Curser—One who curses.
Why does that *curser* swear so much? (N)
Cursor—Moving pointer on a computer.
Put your *cursor* in the field, then click. (N)

Cymbal—Round percussion instrument.
I want to learn to play the *cymbals.* (N)
Symbol—Sign or mark used to represent something.
The *symbol* for love is a heart. (N)

Dam—A hand-built or natural wall used to hold back water.
Beaver *dams* hold back water from flowing. (N)
Damn—To condemn or curse something. To swear at by saying "damn."
I don't believe a *damn* thing you say. (Adj)
"Damn you!" said the woman. (N)

Days—Plural of day.
The conference lasted seven *days.* (N)
Daze—A dazed condition; state of bemusement.
After meeting the author, I was in a *daze* for weeks. (N)

Dear—Anyone or anything that is much loved. Darling. Someone who is very respected. Word used to express surprise or worry.
Her cats were very *dear* to her. (Adj)
"You are so *dear* to me," said Phillip to Margaret. (N)
When you write a formal letter always use *Dear* at the beginning. (Adj)
Oh *dear,* I thought you would be late. (Interj)
Deer—Swift animal that is related to the elk or moose.
I saw a *deer* in the front yard. (N)

Desert—To abandon.
Come back! Don't *desert* me! (V)
Dessert—Sweets that follow main course of meal.
My, this rice pudding is the best *dessert* I've ever tasted! (N)

Dew—Small drops of moisture, condensing on cool surfaces at night.
There is *dew* on the grass every morning. (N)
Do—To perform or carry out as an action. To work out, solve.
We watched him *do* a jig. (V)
He is *doing* the crossword puzzle. (V)
Due—Anything that needs to be paid. What someone earns. A fee for membership to a club. An expected arrival.
Tom picked up the money that was *due* him for two weeks. (Adj)
She has finally received his *due* respect. (N)
Most club members have to pay *dues* to remain members. (N)
Jack is *due* to arrive tomorrow morning. (Adj)

Die—To become dead; stop living. Something that stops working. To lose strength or force. A single dice.
Everyone has to *die* sooner or later. (V)
My car *died* on the highway. (V)
After a while, the excitement will *die* down. (V)
Each *die* has six sides. (N)
Dye—Liquid color used to change the color of something else. To change the color of something.
Blueberries make for a rich blue *dye*. (N)
The woman paid a hefty price to *dye* her hair. (V)

Disburse—To pay out or spend.
I *disbursed* money to the owner of the store. (V)
Disperse—To drive off or scatter.
The sheep *dispersed* from the meadow when they saw the wolf. (V)

Disc—Flat circular object, but with computer or phonograph storage.
Where do I insert the compact *disc*? (N)
Disk—A flat round plate used to store information and instructions for computer. A flat circular object.
I saved all of my information on a *disk*. (N)
The boys played with the rubber *disk* during recess. (N)

Disperse—See "Disburse."

Do (V)—See "Dew."

Do (N)—Beginning musical note on the musical scale
    Do is the first and last note on the scale. (N)
Doe—Female deer, antelope, or rabbit.
    Did you know that a *doe* can be a female rabbit? (N)
Dough—Bread mixture of flour, water, yeast, and other ingredients.
    Dough needs yeast to make it rise. (N)

Done—Finished, completed. The past participle of do.
    I am *done* painting the wall. (Adj)
    I have *done* all of my work. (V)
Dun—To demand for payment many times. Dull brown.
    I have *dunned* $5 from you. (V)
    The house was *dun*-colored on the outside. (N)

Dough—See "Doe."

Dual—Double occupancy, ownership; two of something.
    They had a *dual* partnership. (Adj)
Duel—Contest or fight between two people.
    They fought a *duel* to the death. (N)

Ducked—Did duck. Avoiding a hit or hiding under something.
    I *ducked* just before the ball came soaring over my head. (V)
Duct—Tube for carrying liquid or air. Referring to ducts in glands.
    There was a series of air *ducts* in the walls. (N)
    Everyone has *tear* ducts. (N)

Due—See "Dew."

Duel—See "Dual."

Dun—See "Done."

Dye—See "Die."

Earn—Work for wages; work toward a goal. To get what's deserved.
    I'll *earn* $5 an hour for my summer job. (V)
    In this world, you get what you *earn*. (V)
Urn—Decorative container, used as a vase, for holding ashes, or making tea or coffee.
    The flower *urn* was dark blue with gold edging. (N)

Eave—Overhang on the edge of a roof.
    Icicles were hanging down from the *eaves*. (N)
Eve—Day before a holiday, evening, or the time before an event.
    It was the *eve* of the new year. (N)

Eight—See "Ate."

Epic—Pertaining to a long, poetic composition, usually centered on a hero, in which a series of great achievements or events is narrated; of unusually great size or extent.
Homer's *Iliad* is an *epic* poem. (Adj)
Epoch—A particular period of time marked by distinctive features, events.
The treaty ushered in an *epoch* of peace and goodwill. (N)

Ewe—A female sheep.
There was a black *ewe* at the fair. (N)
Yew—Evergreen tree of Europe, Asia, and Central America.
The table was made of a rich brown *yew*. (N)
You—Personal pronoun. People in general. The person referred to.
Why don't *you* come with me? (Pron)
You can never tell whom *you* can trust. (Pron)

Eye—See "Aye" and "I."

Eyelet—Small hole for thread or cord to go through, or used for decoration as in embroidery.
The thread slipped easily into the needle's *eyelet*. (N)
Islet—Very small island.
That *islet* is surrounded by sharks! (N)

Eve—See "Eave."

Fain—Feeling happily or merrily about something. Doing something contentedly or willingly.
The actress *fain* accepted the Oscar for her role in the movie. (Adv)
The elderly couple were *fain* about selling their home. (Adj)
Feign—To pretend in order to deceive.
She *feigned* sickness to get out of school. (V)

Faint—Something that isn't plain or clear. Anything that is weak. To fall unconscious for a short time. Feeling as if you're about to fall unconscious.
There was a *faint* sound coming from the garage. (Adj)
There was a *faint* chance of us winning the game. (Adj)
The woman *fainted* from all of the excitement. (V)
All of a sudden, I feel *faint*. (Adj)
He felt *faint* from losing that much blood. (Adj)
Feint—To attack from one direction to distract attention from another direction.
He made a *feint* of working up a disturbance in the town square. (N)

Fair—Treating everyone the same. Going by the rules. To be neither good nor bad. To have a light color. Referring to sunny or clear weather. To do something honestly. To be attractive. In baseball, a ball hit within the baselines. A show taking place outside featuring farm animals. A place where buyers and sellers gather. A sale or presentation held with a particular focus.
It is important to be *fair* to everyone. (Adj)
It's not *fair* to lie if you're playing truth or consequences. (Adj)
Blondes have *fair* hair. (Adj)
We've had *fair* weather all weekend. (Adj)
The judge was *fair* with her ruling. (Adv)
She has a *fair* smile. (Adj)
The ball was hit in *fair* territory. (Adj)
I'm looking forward to going to the state *fair* this year. (N)
I bought this painting at the art *fair*. (N)
Our school had a science *fair*. (N)
Fare—Cost of transportation. To progress.
He paid a cheap bus *fare*. (N)
My daughter did not *fare* well on her first day of school. (V)

Faun—Mythical creature of human upper body and horse-like lower body, with horns.
My story is about a *faun* and a unicorn. (N)
Fawn—Baby deer.
The *fawn* stumbled and fell at its first step. (N)

Faze—To cause to be embarrassed, confused, upset, or worried.
He wasn't *fazed* at the loss of his money. (V)
Phase—Stage or condition in process of development. One part of something.
He's just going through a *phase*. (N)
This is the beginning *phase* of the trial. (N)

Feat—A brave or difficult accomplishment.
Climbing the mountain was a great *feat*. (N)
Feet—Plural of foot. Unit of measurement.
Our *feet* are weary from the hike. (N)
He was three *feet* tall. (Adj)

Feign—See "Fain."

Feint—See "Faint."

Find—Discover by chance. To look for or come upon. To learn something. To come to a decision. Something that is found.
I hope I *find* some buried treasure. (V)
Please, help me *find* my car. (V)
We will all *find* out how ice cream is made. (V)
I *find* you to be very beautiful. (V)
This old clock was a great *find*. (N)
Fined—To demand for payment
He was *fined* $100 for littering. (V)

Fir—Evergreen tree with thick needles.
Drew has a *fir* tree in his backyard. (N)
Fur—Coat of an animal, usually fine, soft, thick. Clothing made of animal hair.
The stray's *fur* was matted and wet. (N)
My Aunt Ruth has a *fur* coat. (N)

Flair—Unusual talent or ability for something.
He has a *flair* for writing. (N)
Flare—To enflame briefly. A brief, bright blaze. A signaling device that burns for a short time. To exhibit spontaneous aggression. Something that continuously flares out.
A small brush fire *flared* up but was immediately extinguished. (V)
The fire from a match is only a *flare*. (N)
We have to be careful not to use all of our *flares* on the first day. (N)
Constant frustration will cause a person to *flare* up in anger. (V)
The bedspread *flares* out at the end of the bed. (V)

Flea—Bloodsucking parasite, living on animal flesh.
There were a dozen or so *fleas* in my bed from the dog. (N)
Flee—To run away from or to.
I watched the woman *flee* from the burning building. (V)

Flew—Did fly. Past tense of fly.
The frightened bird *flew* away. (V)
Flu—Abbr. Influenza. Contagious disease causing throat and sinus inflammation, aches, fever, and upset stomach.
A lot of people have had the *flu* this year. (N)
Flue—A shaft that allows hot air or smoke to get out.
Be sure to open the *flue* before you start a fire in the fireplace. (N)

Floe—Large sheets of floating ice.
The solid ice had broken off into chunks of *floe*. (N)
Flow—Moving along smoothly. A movement of water. To pour out of. Any movement that is not difficult.
When I lost, anger *flowed* through my veins. (V)
There is a constant *flow* of water coming from the faucet. (N)
The children *flowed* out of school and into the street. (V)
The dancers *flowed* to the music all night long. (N)

Flour—Fine, ground-up wheat and/or other grains. The act of dusting with flour.
Bread has *flour* in it. (N)
Be sure to *flour* the pan before putting the dough on it. (V)
Flower—A part of the plant that blooms. To produce flowers.
Aunt Lottie has more *flowers* than you've ever seen in your life! (N)
The cacti in the desert *flower* with bright red blossoms in the spring. (V)

Flow—See "Floe."

Flower—See "Flour."

Flu—See "Flew" and "Flue."

Flue—See "Flu" and "Flew."

For—To take the place of. To support. The price of. Because of something. With the purpose or object of. Needed to get, have, keep, or become. Supposed to be used with or by. It's meant to be for. Regards to. Due to. To honor. Used to describe how far. Used to describe how long. As it is. Concerning the amount of.
  I thanked him *for* his donation. (Prep)
  She went *for* a drive in her new car. (Prep)
  I bought a sweater *for* $30.00. (Prep)

Fore—At or toward the front part. A call that is shouted by golfers to warn of an impending shot.
  He paced the deck *fore* and aft. (Adv)
  The golfer shouted *"fore"* to warn his partner that he was in danger of being hit by a ball. (Interj)

Four—A number that is three plus one.
  There were *four* ducklings in a line. (Adj)

Foreword—Preface or introduction.
  The *foreword* introduced the characters in the book. (N)

Forward—Ahead or moving to the front. Sending something toward the front. Being overconfident. A player on a basketball or soccer team.
  Please move *forward* to the front of the line. (Adv)
  I'll *forward* the information as soon as possible. (V)
  She is very *forward* when she meets new people. (Adj)
  My sister plays *forward* on her high school soccer team. (N)

Fort—A solid protective building surrounded by walls, ditches, etc., used by soldiers to be safe and fight the enemy.
  The soldiers shot at the enemy from the *fort*. (N)

Forte—The part of a sword that is between the middle and the hilt, the strongest part of the sword.
  The *forte* has beautiful etching. (N)

Forth—Forward.
  From that day *forth,* he never teased again. (Adv)

Fourth—After third.
  This is the *fourth* phone call I've received today. (Adj)

Foul—Anything that is nasty or dirty. Make something nasty. Anything that is mean or wicked. Not following the rules. A sports term. A play that violates the rules of the game. A baseball rule. A ball that is hit outside of the lines of fair play.
  The bathroom in the abandoned building is very *foul*. (Adj)
  The mud *fouled* up her new dress. (V)
  She is a *foul* person. (Adj)
  My uncle had a *foul* review on his evaluation. (Adj)
  The basketball player received a *foul* for his aggressive play. (N)
  The baseball player hit the ball *foul* down the third-base line. (Adj)

Fowl—A hen, chicken, turkey, or any other bird.
  The *fowl* are kept in the coop. (N)

Four—See "For."

Fourth—See "Forth."

Fowl—See "Foul."

Franc—The official money of France, Switzerland, and many African and European countries.
  He came from France with three *francs* in his pocket.
Frank—Being honest and sincere. An envelope marking for free postage. To mark anything with a frank, meaning free.
  Frankly, that dress does not flatter you. (Adj)
  That package was *franked,* so it was free of charge. (V)

Freeze—To harden to a solid. To lose heat. To become immobilized due to fear.
  The meat will *freeze* if you leave it in there overnight. (V)
  You will *freeze* out here without your jacket on. (V)
  I tend to *freeze* up when I have to go on stage to speak. (V)
Frieze—Band of decoration around the top of the walls.
  The floral *frieze* was glued to the wall. (N)

Friar—Brother in religious order of the Roman Catholic Church.
  Friars live in monasteries. (N)
Fryer—A young chicken for frying. One who fries the chicken.
  James was given the duty of chicken *fryer* at the family reunion. (N)

Fur—See "Fir."

Gait—A manner of walking, stepping, or running.
  The horse kept a steady *gait* throughout the entire race. (N)
Gate—A movable barrier, usually on hinges.
  We have to keep the *gate* closed so that the dog doesn't run out of the yard. (N)

Gamble—To play at any game of chance for money or other stakes; to stake or risk money, or anything of value on the outcome of something involving chance.
  He *gambled* all his money away in one night. (V)
Gambol—To skip about as in dancing or playing.
  The children *gambolled* in the yard at recess. (V)

Gambol—See "Gamble."

Gate—See "Gait."

Gene—A small part of a chromosome containing DNA.
  Your parents' *genes* determine many things about you. (N)
Jean—Pants made from cotton cloth.
  You can wear your *jeans* to school on Friday. (N)

Gilt—The gold or gold-like covering on a surface. A female hog before her first litter.
  The ring appeared to have a *gilt* finish. (Adj)
  The farmer raised a *gilt* for breeding. (Adj)
Guilt—Being responsible for an offensive act.
  The drunk driver felt *guilt* for his actions. (N)

Gnu—A large antelope found in Africa.
  On a safari to Africa we saw a large antelope-like animal called a *gnu*. (N)
Knew—Past tense of know.
  I know you *knew* the correct answer on the test yesterday. (V)
New—Something that has never existed before.
  New shoes sometimes hurt until you break them in. (Adj)

Gorilla—Largest of hairy, man-like apes living in western Africa and surviving on plants
  and fruits.
  A baby *gorilla* just came into the zoo yesterday. (N)
Guerrilla—Soldier included in a small band infamous for quick surprise attacks or
  sabotages.
  The *guerrilla* sneaked up on the unsuspecting soldier. (N)

Grate—A metal frame used for holding firewood or coals in a fireplace. To rub vegeta-
  bles or cheese against a rough surface to make smaller pieces. A harsh sound.
  Our firewood rests on a metal *grate* in the furnace. (N)
  I have to *grate* the cheese before I continue. (V)
  The old trunk *grated* as it was finally opened. (V)
Great—Big in size or number. Anything that is outstanding. Very important.
  We have a *great* oak tree in our yard. (Adj)
  The food at this restaurant is *great*. (Adj)
  We made a *great* decision when we decided to move. (Adj)

Groan—To utter or express by moaning. Making a deep or unusual sound.
  He *groaned* in pain when he fell down. (N)
  While climbing the stairs in the old house, I heard them *groan*. (N)
Grown—Arriving at a certain age or point by maturing. Reared or cultivated in a
  specific way.
  When you reach your eighteenth birthday people consider you *grown*. (Adj)

Guerrilla—See "Gorilla."

Guessed—A judgment or opinion formed with little knowledge.
  He *guessed* the answer because he did not study. (V)
Guest—Someone entertained or received whose needs are provided for. A person
  invited to participate in an activity or event.
  As a *guest* at the country club, everything you need will be provided. (N)
  The movie star was the *guest* of honor at the parade. (N)

Guilt—See "Gilt."

Hail—A combination of ice and snow formed into a small ball that falls like rain. A gesture or motion used to attract attention.
The *hail* dented the car. (N)
It is very difficult to *hail* a taxi in New York City. (V)
Hale—To be free from sickness. To carry or support.
The flu did not affect the children because they were *hale* and hardy. (Adj)
The crowd *haled* their allegiance to the king. (Adj)

Hair—Thin strand-like growth covering the skin of a person or animal.
She brushed her *hair* daily. (N)
Hare—A small, timid mammal resembling a rabbit with long ears.
In the story, the *hare* was much faster than the tortoise. (N)

Hale—See "Hail."

Hall—A large building or room used for a specific purpose. A passageway to travel through a building or house.
The feast was held in the dining *hall*. (N)
It was very dark walking down the narrow *hall*. (N)
Haul—To drag or pull something with force. To carry something from one place to another.
We will need the tractor to help us *haul* the tree out of the front yard. (V)
Together, we can *haul* the branches that fell down in the yard from the storm last night. (V)

Handsome—To be good-looking or dashing in appearance. A tremendous or vast amount.
The tall young man was *handsome*. (Adj)
Winning the lottery gave them a *handsome* sum of money. (Adj)
Hansom—A horse-drawn carriage with two wheels where the reins pass over the top and the driver sits up high behind the carriage.
Riding in a *hansom* around Central Park was very enjoyable. (N)

Hangar—A building used to house and repair aircraft.
The airplane will be in the *hangar* until it is repaired. (N)
Hanger—Something that is used to hang something on. (N)
Please hang your coat on the *hanger* in the closet. (N)

Hansom—See "Handsome."

Hare—See "Hair."

Hart—A red, male deer.
A *hart* is a red, male deer that is found in Europe. (N)
Heart—The body organ that pumps the blood through the body.
If your *heart* is not healthy, it will have trouble pumping blood throughout your body. (N)

Haul—See "Hall."

Hay—Grass that is grown, cut, and dried, then used as food for horses and cattle.
One of Tom's chores was to stock the horses' stalls with *hay.* (N)
Hey—Sound used to ask a question, attract attention, or express oneself.
Hey, you surprised me. (Interj)

Heal—To cure or remove illness.
Many people hoping to be *healed* from an illness travel to holy places. (V)
Heel—The bottom, back portion of a person's foot. Anything rounded or squared and placed at the end of something.
The *heel* of my shoe has a hole in it and my foot is getting wet. (N)
The first and last slices in a loaf of bread are called *heels.* (N)
He'll—He shall. He will.
He'll be sure to join us. (Contr)

Hear—To perceive sound by the ear. To listen to something.
I did not *hear* you come in last night. (V)
I can *hear* music coming from your house when I am outside. (V)
Here—At this particular place or up to this point in time.
I will meet you *here.* (Adj)
We are *here* in the twenty-first century. (Adj)

Heard—Sound perceived by the ear. The past tense of hear.
Yesterday, we *heard* loud music coming from the party. (V)
Herd—A gathering of animals of one kind. A large crowd.
The cattle farmer has a large *herd* of cattle. (N)

Heart—See "Hart."

He'd—He would. He had.
He'd enjoy himself at the zoo. (he would) (Contr)
He'd wanted the trophy for a long time. (he had) (Contr)
Heed—To pay very special attention to something.
I always *heed* the advice my parents give me. (V)

Heel—See "Heal" and "He'll."

Heir—See "Air."

He'll—See "Heal" and "Heel."

Herd—See "Heard."

Here—See "Hear."

Hertz—A unit of frequency equal to one cycle per second.
Did you know that *hertz* is a unit of frequency? (N)
Hurts—Painful. Wounded or injured. To be distressed mentally.
An infected cut *hurts.* (V)
It *hurts* to see a loved one in pain. (V)

Hew—To cut or carve with an ax or sword.
  The logger *hewed* the bark from the log. (V)
Hue—Color ranging from red, yellow, or blue along with other regions of the color spectrum.
  The house was decorated with different *hues* of blue. (N)

Hey—See "Hay."

Hi—Hello. A call used for greeting.
  The word hello is often shortened to *hi.* (Interj)
  When I saw my friend, I shouted, *"Hi!"* (Interj)
Hie—To move quickly or hurried.
  If you want to catch your flight, you will have to *hie* to the gate. (V)
High—Something of more than usual height.
  The birds landed *high* atop the Golden Gate Bridge. (Adj)

Higher—Something above someone or something else.
  Since I bought my tickets a week later than you, I am sitting *higher* up in the balcony. (Adj)
Hire—To employ or put to work.
  We are looking to *hire* more people next week. (V)

Him—Objective case of he.
  I like *him.* (Pron)
Hymn—Song that praises God.
  In church on Sunday, I sing *hymns.* (N)

Hire—See "Higher."

Hoarse—Having a rough or deep voice.
  The man had a *hoarse* laugh. (Adj)
Horse—Large four-legged mammal with a long tail, mane of hair, and hoofs. A frame or structure used for support.
  I enjoy riding a *horse.* (N)
  The builder supported the lumber on a saw *horse.* (N)

Hole—An opening or space within something.
  The pool company dug a *hole* in the backyard for the new swimming pool. (N)
Whole—Full or complete.
  I was full after eating the *whole* meal. (Adj)

Holey—Something that has many holes.
  My old jeans were *holey.* (N)
Holy—Something used for God's purpose. Considered saint-like.
  A church is a *holy* place. (Adj)
  Mother Teresa was thought of as a *holy* person. (Adj)
Wholly—Entirely complete or full.
  Graduating from law school helped me to feel *wholly* successful. (Adj)

Hoard—To save and store away for future use.
    A squirrel knows winter is long, so it *hordes* nuts so it won't go hungry. (N)
Horde—A great or large quantity of something.
    Do you have a *horde* of money? (N)

Horse—See "Hoarse."

Hostel—A place used to lodge young people.
    Young people needing a place to stay in Europe often sleep in a *hostel*. (N)
Hostile—To be unfriendly or unfavorable. An enemy.
    In war, people are *hostile* to each other. (Adj)

Hour—Amount of time equaling sixty minutes.
    A day is made up of twenty-four *hours*. (N)
Our—Form of we that is possessive.
    Our wedding was the happiest day of my life. (Adj)

Hurdle—A barrier or obstacle. To jump over something.
    The accident caused a *hurdle* in the road that needed to be cleaned up. (V)
    In track and field, some events require that participants jump over a *hurdle*. (V)
Hurtle—To rush forward with great force.
    The man *hurtled* himself across the room to keep the dog from running out the
        door. (V)

Hue—See "Hew."

Hurts—See "Hertz."

Hymn—See "Him."

I—See "Eye" and "Aye."

Idle—Preferring to do nothing. Unwillingness to work.
    I find it relaxing to be *idle*. (Adj)
    Lazy people are often *idle*. (Adj)
Idol—Something or someone that is worshiped.
    The people in the Old Testament worshiped the golden calf as an *idol*. (N)
Idyll—A small writing or poem charmingly describing a scene or event.
    The young lover wrote an *idyll* about his girlfriend. (N)

I'll—See "Aisle."

In—Within.
    Please come *in*. (Prep)
Inn—Small public place used for lodging.
    We decided it would be cozier to spend the night at the *inn* instead of the large
        hotel. (N)

Incite—To cause or persuade an act or thought.
   The action of the men will *incite* a riot. (V)
Insight—An understanding of internal self. Having information about dealing with people, things, or information.
   Going on the retreat helped me to gain a better *insight* of myself. (N)
   As a personnel director you will need to have *insight* into the individual needs of your employees. (N)

Inn—See "In."

Insight—See "Incite."

Intense—Something that is very strong or extreme.
   Her feelings for her children were *intense*. (Adj)
Intents—Things that are intended.
   I don't know his *intents* for going into that business. (N)

Isle—See "Aisle" and "I'll."

Islet—See "Eyelet."

It's—It is. It has.
   It's time to go! (it is) (Contr)
   It's never been this cold in July before. (it has) (Contr)
Its—Form of "it" that is possessive.
   The large, black dog wagged *its* tail. (Adj)

Jam—A fruit preserve used as jelly. The act of compressing or shoving something between two surfaces.
   Strawberry *jam* is great on toast. (N)
   I *jammed* everything into the drawer so I could shut it. (N)
Jamb—A part of a doorway or window that forms the sides.
   Paint the *jamb* around the windows and doors white. (N)

Jean—See "Gene."

Kernel—See "Colonel."

Knead—To mix or press together and shape with the hands.
   You have to *knead* the dough with your hands. (V)
Need—Something that is essential or required.
   You *need* to feed your pets daily. (N)

Knew—See "New."

Knight—A man given an honorable military rank.
   I would have loved to have been a *knight* in King Arthur's court. (N)
Night—The dark period between evening and morning.
   When it gets dark at *night* you should be home. (N)

Knit—To join or loop yarn together with a long needle.
  Grandmother used to *knit* mittens for all of her grandchildren. (V)
Nit—A louse egg. An insect.
  The egg of a louse is called a *nit.* (N)
  A *nit* that is so small can be a big pest. (N)

Knot—Tying rope or cloth together.
  The Boy Scout knew how to tie a square *knot.* (N)
Not—Negative. Another way of saying no.
  You will *not* be able to run with a sprained ankle. (Adv)
  I will *not* answer the phone the next time it rings. (Adv)

Know—To have information about.
  Since I studied for the test I *know* all the answers. (V)
No—To deny. To refuse.
  No, I don't cheat! (Adv)
  No, I don't want any more! (Adv)

Lam—Hiding or evading.
  The crook was on the *lam* from the police. (V)
Lamb—A small sheep.
  I have never had the opportunity to order *lamb* while eating out. (N)

Lain—Past participle of lie.
  The woman has *lain* down for the evening. (V)
Lane—A small passage between areas.
  You will have to switch *lanes* if you want to get on the expressway. (N)

Lay—To reduce or move into a certain position.
  The mother *lay* beside the baby. (V)
Lei—Hawaiian ornament of flowers worn around the head or neck.
  When you land in Hawaii a *lei* will be placed around your neck. (N)

Lead—A soft metallic element.
  Divers use *lead* weights. (N)
Led—Past tense of lead.
  The teacher *led* the children from the playground back to the classroom. (V)

Leak—A crack or hole that lets something in or out.
  The water will *leak* out of the hole in the bottle. (V)
Leek—A vegetable resembling an onion.
  Using a *leek* in the soup will give it a nice flavor. (N)

Lean—To bend or slope something. To rest against something else. Very thin.
  The storm caused the branches to *lean.* (Adj)
  If you are tired just *lean* against the tree. (V)
  The diet caused her to look very *lean.* (Adj)
Lien—A claim made legally by one person on another's property.
  If you can't pay your bills on time, the bank may put a *lien* against your house.

Leased—Something rented out for a certain length of time.
We *leased* a cabin in the mountains for a few weeks last summer. (V)
Least—The smallest number of amount.
Select the hotel that costs the *least* amount of money. (Adj)

Led—See "Lead."

Leek—See "Leak."

Lei—See "Lay."

Lein—See "Lean."

Lessen—To decrease and make less.
Cutting calories along with exercise will help you *lessen* your weight. (V)
Lesson—An exercise of instruction that is taught.
The teacher used visual aids to make her *lessons* more interesting. (N)

Levee—Embankment built to prevent the overflowing of a river.
The rising river caused the townspeople to work together to build a *levee*. (N)
Levy—Funds collected by force or authority.
The Boston Tea Party was caused because the British tried to *levy* a tax on the colonists. (V)

Liar—A person who intentionally says things that are untrue.
If you tell lies, people will think of you as a *liar*. (N)
Lyre—A small harp-like instrument.
Nicholas learned to play the *lyre* while away at school. (N)

Lichen—A combination of fungus and algae that grows on trees and rocks.
Spraying the tree trunk should kill *lichen* growing on it. (N)
Liken—To compare something to something else.
The young girl prefers to *liken* herself to a movie star. (V)

Lie—An untruth told by someone who knows it is untrue. To lay something or someone flat against a surface.
It is always better to tell the truth rather than *lie*. (N)
When are you planning to *lie* down? (V)
Lye—A mixture of sodium hydroxide and potassium hydroxide that makes a strong alkaline solution.
Lye is a dangerous chemical that you need to use carefully. (N)

Lightening—To make lighter or brighter.
Lightening the driveway will make it easier to get into the garage. (V)
Lightening your hair will make you look younger. (V)
Lightning—Electrical discharge between clouds causing flashing light in the sky.
During a rainstorm, you should be careful of *lightning*. (N)

Liken—See "Lichen."

Links—Chains or loops that connect something to something else in a chainlike manner. Anything that joins in a uniting fashion.
The mischievous children broke the chain *links* in the fence. (N)
Old photographs are often *links* to our past. (N)
Lynx—A northern North American wild cat with thick soft fur and a short tail.
During our camping trip, our campsite was often visited by a *lynx*. (N)

Lo—To behold. Look or see.
I could not find the Mona Lisa in the Louvre; then *lo* and behold I was standing in front of it. (Interj)
I was so thirsty; then *lo* and behold he brought me a cold drink. (Interj)
Low—Anything that is shorter than ordinary height. Something that is below something else in stature. The opposite of a high musical note.
The coach has *low* expectations for his team this season. (Adj)
The music student has trouble identifying the *low* notes. (Adj)

Load—A physical or mental burden that a person must carry.
You have a heavy *load* dealing with a friend who is terminally ill. (N)
Lode—A vein of metal ore found in a rock.
Under a microscope, you will be able to see *lode* in the rock. (N)

Loan—Anything given that must be returned.
If you check out a library book on *loan* it must be returned within two weeks. (N)
To buy a car you might need to take out a *loan* from the bank. (N)
Lone—Alone.
Michael was the *lone* representative of his school at the local spelling bee. (Adj)

Loch—A landlocked portion of a body of water.
I love to sail the *loch* near my home. (N)
Lock—A way of securing a door, window, or box. To keep something or someone in or out.
The door is secured with a *lock*. (N)
You can *lock* the computers in the storage room. (V)

Locks—Plural of lock.
The locksmith installed new *locks* on all the doors. (N)
Lox—Salty salmon that is soaked to remove the salt.
Lox and cream cheese makes a nice breakfast or lunch. (N)

Lode—See "Load."

Loot—Anything of value taken by force or stolen.
The robbers had trouble getting rid of the stolen *loot*. (N)
Lute—A pear-shaped instrument used in the 1500s and 1600s that was played by plucking its strings.
You can see a *lute* in the musical exhibition of the history museum. (N)

Low—See "Lo."

Lox—See "Locks."

Lute—See "Loot."

Lye—See "Lie."

Lynx—See "Links."

Lyre—See "Liar."

Made—Something that is formed, created, or built.
  The candlemaker *made* the candles by repeatedly dipping the wick in the paraffin. (V)
Maid—A paid female servant.
  She worked as a *maid* during her summer away from school. (N)

Mail—Packages or letters sent through the postal service. The system that is used to send mail. To send packages or letters through the postal service.
  The mail carrier delivers the *mail* at noon every day. (N)
  Many people buy appliances through the *mail*. (N)
  I intend to *mail* the letter today. (V)
Male—The sex of a boy or man.
  Blue is usually the color people select for a *male* child. (Adj)

Main—Something that holds importance over everything else. A big pipe used for electricity, water, and sewage.
  The *main* acts at the circus are usually held in the center ring. (Adj)
  The street was flooded because the water *main* broke. (Adj)
Maine—A state in the northeast part of the United States.
  Augusta is the capital of *Maine*. (N)
Mane—Long thick hair.
  The horse's *mane* was decorated for the parade. (N)

Maize—Yellow, ripe Indian corn.
  Maize was an essential part of the American Indian's diet. (N)
Maze—A difficult or confusing pathway.
  You need to select the correct path if you want to walk through the *maze*. (N)

Maine—See "Main."

Male—See "Mail."

Mall—A walk or lane that is shaded. A large area used for shopping by many people.
  The large shade trees created a *mall* area. (N)
  There's no use going to the shopping *mall* if we have no money. (N)
Maul—To savagely beat or plunder. A heavy hammer or mallet used for driving stakes.
  A fierce dog could *maul* the baby. (V)
  The cattle rancher used his *maul* to drive the stakes in the ground for the new fence. (N)

Mane—See "Main" and "Maine."

Manner—A way or style of doing something.
  Her *manner* was very proper. (N)
Manor—A portion of property set aside for the owner.
  On southern plantations, the owner lived in the *manor.* (N)

Mantel—A shelf located above a fireplace.
  The *mantel* above the fireplace held the children's trophies. (N)
Mantle—A long gown or cloak without sleeves.
  The widow wore a black lace *mantle* when she went to church. (N)

Marry—The joining of man and woman as husband and wife.
  Hopefully, we will *marry* soon. (V)
Merry—To be happy or joyful.
  My neighbor, Mr. Wilson, is usually a very *merry* fellow. (Adj)

Marshal—A law officer of various types. A person who directs a ceremony or event.
  The *marshal* enforced the laws in his area. (N)
  The Grand *Marshal* of the parade was a local celebrity. (N)
Martial—Ready for war.
  A *martial* arts class will prepare the soldiers for hand-to-hand combat. (Adj)

Massed—Something grouped together into a mass.
  The sheep were *massed* together. (V)
Mast—A tall wooden or metal bar that extends from the keel of a sailboat that's used to support the sails.
  The sailors hoisted the sails up the wooden *mast.* (N)

Mat—A floor covering, usually made of coarse fibers. Something that has grown tightly packed together.
  Please wipe your feet on the *mat* at the front door before coming in. (N)
  The horse's hair has grown into a nasty *mat.* (N)
Matte—Having a dull or slightly roughened surface.
  The pottery has a *matte* glaze. (Adj)

Maul—See "Mall."

Meat—Mammal flesh that is used for food.
  Veal is *meat* from a young calf. (N)
Meet—To come face-to-face or make contact with.
  Let's *meet* tonight at eight o'clock. (V)
Mete—To distribute equally.
  The lawyers will *mete* out the estate funds equally. (V)

Medal—An award or commendation usually in the shape of a coin with a special inscription on it.
  Receiving the Olympic gold *medal* was a great achievement. (N)
Meddle—Being concerned with the affairs of another, although not needed.
  People should not *meddle* in their neighbors' affairs. (V)

Meet—See "Meat" and "Mete."

Merry—See "Marry."

Mete—See "Meat."

Might—Great strength or power.
    Hercules had great *might*. (V)
Mite—A small insect-like parasite on plants or animals.
    A *mite* bite will leave a mark on your skin. (N)

Miner—A mine worker.
    Since he was a little boy, Joe has always wanted to be a *miner*. (N)
Minor—Something that is less important to something else. A person below the legal age of responsibility.
    Not getting to go on the trip would only be a *minor* disappointment. (Adj)
    It is illegal to drink alcohol as a *minor*. (Adj)

Missed—To fail or suffer the loss of. The inability to grasp.
    The little boy *missed* his mother terribly on his first day of school. (V)
    He *missed* the mark in the archery tournament. (V)
Mist—The presence of water in the air that results in fog.
    The *mist* made the air very damp. (N)

Mite—See "Might."

Moan—A deep, low sound.
    Did you hear him *moan*? (N)
Mown—Something that has been cut down.
    The grass was *mown* yesterday. (V)

Morn—The morning.
    I plan to rise early in the *morn*. (N)
Mourn—The expression of grief or sorrow.
    Most people *mourn* the loss of a pet. (V)

Morning—The early portion of a day that's followed by noon.
    I enjoy getting up early in the *morning*. (N)
Mourning—The process of grieving.
    The *mourning* period for people who suffer a loss is different in many cultures. (N)

Mown—See "Moan."

Muscle—Body tissue composed of fiber that allows the body to move.
    You need to exercise and watch what you eat if you plan to build *muscle*. (N)
Mussel—Shellfish that resembles a clam.
    I ordered *mussels* while dining out last night. (N)

Naval—Anything used by the Navy.
    The general traveled in a *naval* vehicle. (Adj)
Navel—The place where the umbilical cord was attached before birth.
    Another name for your *navel* is belly button. (N)

Nay—A vote of no.
    Since I did not agree with the proposal, my vote was *nay*. (Adv)
Neigh—A drawn-out sound made by a horse.
    When visiting the horse farm in Kentucky, I could hear the horses *neigh*. (N)

Need—See "Knead."

New—See "Gnu" and "Knew."

Night—See "Knight."

Nit—See "Knit."

No—See "Know."

None—Void of anything or anyone.
    If you are looking for food, we have *none*. (Pron)
Nun—A woman who forsakes all possessions and devotes her life to religion.
    The *nun* did many good things for the community center. (N)

Not—See "Knot."

Oar—A long pole used to paddle a boat.
    To win the canoe race you will need to use your *oar* more effectively. (N)
Or—Expressing the only available choice. Expressing the consequences of something
    not happening. Explains that two things are similar.
    Do as I say *or* else. (Conj)
    You have to study *or* you will fail the test. (Conj)
    You can have coffee *or* tea. (Conj)
Ore—Metal content found in rocks or minerals.
    You should analyze the *ore* in the rocks and find out the value before selling it. (N)

Ode—A tribute in the form of a poem.
    The poet wrote an *ode* to his mother. (N)
Owed—Something that was indebted.
    Mr. Thomas *owed* the bank for several unpaid loans. (V)

Offal—See "Awful."

Oh—An expression of emotion resulting from anger, pain, fear, or surprise.
    Oh, I am surprised to see you up this early! (Interj)
Owe—To be indebted to someone or something.
    I *owe* you so much for all you've done for me. (V)

One—The first whole number. A single person or thing.
>The first whole number is *one*. (N)
>You are my *one* and only true friend. (N)

Won—To be victorious.
>If you finish first you will have *won* the race. (V)

Oral—See "Aural."

Our—See "Hour."

Overdo—To do something more than is necessary.
>You can hurt yourself if you *overdo* your exercise program. (V)

Overdue—Something that should have happened but has not.
>Cleaning the house was long *overdue*. (Adj)

Overseas—A location that is across the sea.
>Hopefully, the company will send me *overseas* to work. (Adv)

Oversees—To monitor or manage.
>The teacher *oversees* the students' progress. (V)

Owe—See "Oh."

Owed—See "Ode."

Pail—A container used for carrying liquid.
>Jack and Jill used a *pail* to carry the water down the hill. (N)

Pale—Something that doesn't have much color.
>The ill man looked *pale*. (Adj)

Pain—A sense of ache, hurt, or suffering.
>Severing his Achilles' tendon caused him a lot of *pain*. (N)

Pane—A sheet of glass in a window.
>You need to clean the *pane* of glass in the large window. (N)

Pair—Two of anything that are used together.
>Shoes are purchased in a *pair*. (N)

Pare—To remove the outer shell of something by shaving, trimming, or cutting.
>If you pay extra, the butcher will *pare* your meat for you. (V)

Pear—A rounded, sweet fruit.
>Apples, oranges, and *pears* are all fruits I enjoy eating. (N)

Palate—The roof of the mouth.
>Sherbet is served to clean your *palate* between courses in fancy restaurants. (N)

Palette—A painter's board that is thin and circular and used to mix and lay colors.
>The artist mixed his paints carefully on his wooden *palette*. (N)

Pallet—A shaping tool used by sculptors or potters. A low platform for storing goods.
>A sculptor uses a *pallet* to help shape his creations. (N)
>All the boxes in the warehouse were on *pallets*. (N)

Pale—See "Pail."

Pane—See "Pain."

Pare—See "Pair" and "Pear."

Passed—Past tense of pass.
   The new crime bill was *passed* last week. (V)
Past—A point in time that has already happened.
   The photo album is full of memories of the *past*. (Adj)

Patience—The ability to remain calm or disciplined.
   The first graders will test the *patience* of any teacher. (N)
Patients—People under a doctor's care.
   All of the *patients* were not covered by Medicare. (N)

Pause—A brief halt.
   When the song stops please push *pause* on the tape recorder. (V)
Paws—Animal feet.
   The big bear caught the fish with its *paws*. (N)

Peace—Being free from stress or restraint.
   All I need is a little *peace* and quiet. (N)
Piece—A portion of something.
   May I please have a *piece* of candy? (N)

Peak—A pointed top of a hill or mountain. The highest point of something. The best
   state or position.
   The mountain climbers climbed to the *peak* of the mountain. (N)
   Not many athletes retire while at the *peak* of their careers. (N)
   The presentation by the ballet company was a *peak* performance. (Adj)
Peek—To take a quick, secret glance or look.
   Please, cover your eyes and do not *peek*. (V)
Pique—To be upset, offended, or angered. To excite or arouse.
   I was *piqued* to find out that I was not awarded the promotion. (V)
   The movie's ad *piqued* my curiosity. (V)

Peal—A long, loud burst of noise.
   The *peal* from the explosion was enough to wake the whole town. (N)
Peel—To remove skin or bark from something. The rind or skin that has been removed
   from certain fruits. A long-handled shovel used to put bread or pies into an oven or
   take them out.
   It is always best to *peel* an orange before eating it. (V)
   I almost slipped on the banana *peel*. (N)
   The restaurant has an old *peel* to remove pizzas from the oven. (N)

Pearl—A gem that is the calcium deposit formed in certain types of oysters.
   Doris received a *pearl* necklace for her twentieth anniversary. (N)
Purl—A style of knitting that changes the stitch from one side to the other.
   She learned the *purl* in knitting class. (N) (Adj)

Pedal—A lever used to move or operate machinery. A motion used to ride a bicycle.
Tom claimed his gas *pedal* was stuck when he was stopped for speeding. (N)
When riding a bicycle, the faster you *pedal* the faster you go. (V)
Peddle—To sell something while moving from place to place.
In order to *peddle* merchandise within city limits, you must have a peddler's license.

Peek—See "Peak" and "Pique."

Peel—See "Peal."

Peer—A person of the same age, class, or rank.
Peer pressure is one of the leading causes of juvenile mischief. (N)
Pier—A structure that extends out into the water and is used as a place for ships to dock.
Many boats are docked at Navy *Pier* in Chicago. (N)

Per—For all.
The limit is two bags *per* customer. (Prep)
Purr—The sound that a cat makes when it is satisfied.
I awake to the sound of my cat's *purr* every morning. (N)

Phase—See "Faze."

Pi—The sixteenth letter of the Greek alphabet. A mathematics ratio equal to approximately 3.141592.
If you study Greek, you learn that the sixteenth letter in the alphabet is *pi*. (N)
You have to learn the function of *pi* before passing this class. (N)
Pie—A baked food that contains fruit, meat, cheese, or vegetable ingredients and covered with a pastry crust.
Alex was awarded third place in the *pie*-baking contest. (N)

Piece—See "Peace."

Pier—See "Peer."

Pique—See "Peek" and "Peak."

Plain—Something that is easily seen, understood, or heard. Anything without design or accessory. Food without much seasoning or flavor. The simple manner of someone or something. Ordinary features. An area of land that is flat.
It is *plain* to see that you are in love with her. (Adj)
I'm one of the few people who likes my oatmeal *plain*. (Adj)
I don't like *plain* eggs. (Adj)
I enjoy reading *plain* mystery novels. (Adj)
I have a *plain* face compared to most other people. (Adj)
Buffalo have roamed across the Colorado *plain* for generations. (N)
Plane—A tool with a blade that's used to shape or smooth wood. Any surface that is level and flat. Abbreviated form of airplane.
The carpenter used a *plane* to smooth the wood. (N)
The merchandise was laid across a *plane* surface. (Adj)
Our *plane* had to land in Cleveland to refuel. (N)

Plait—A braid or pleat. To braid or pleat.
   I bought a straw *plait* at the crafts fair. (N)
   Katie loves to *plait* her horse's mane. (V)
Plate—A flat, smooth, sometimes round dish. A piece of metal used for armor. A large mass of rock that makes up the earth's crust.
   Bob orders a *plate* of fried catfish every Friday. (N)
   It was the *plate* of armor that saved the young officer's life. (N)
   The earth's crust is made up of several giant *plates* of rock. (N)

Plane—See "Plain."

Plate—See "Plait."

Pleas—Plural of plea. To make requests or appeals.
   David made *pleas* to several banks for loans. (N)
Please—To make satisfied or give enjoyment to. A word used to politely ask for something.
   It would *please* me to see you happy. (V)
   Would you *please* close the door when you leave? (Adv)

Plum—A small, purplish, sweet, edible fruit that has one large seed.
   I have a taste for a cold, ripe *plum*. (N)
Plumb—A small weight that's attached to the end of a line and is used to determine depth of water or to determine if a wall is vertical.
   The *plumb* was attached to a line and dropped to the bottom of the lake. (N)

Pole—A piece of wood or steel that is usually long and slender. The most northern and southern points of the earth.
   The wire fence in the backyard is attached to a wooden *pole*. (N)
   There is not much difference in temperatures between the North and South *poles*. (N)
Poll—The place where voting or voter registration takes place. To gather opinions from a specific or nonspecific group.
   I plan to take my mother to the voting *poll* early in the morning. (N)
   The school staff took a *poll* of the student body concerning their attitudes about drinking and driving. (V)

Pore—To dwell on or consider something intently. Small opening in the skin where absorption and perspiration take place.
   I'll have to *pore* over this one for a couple of days and let you know my answer. (V)
   You have to keep your *pores* clean to be free of acne. (N)
Pour—To allow liquid or a soft solid to flow freely from a container. The act of letting something flow freely.
   May I *pour* you a cup of tea? (V)
   Alan allowed his feelings for Betsy to *pour* out. (V)

Pray—Communication with a god in a worshipful manner.
   I will *pray* for you on Sunday. (V)
Prey—Anything that is hunted and caught for food.
   Gazelles are *prey* for many animals in the African wilderness. (N)

Presence—The fact of being present somewhere.
My mother's *presence* was felt in our home long after she died. (N)
Presents—Gifts that are given or received.
The little girl received many *presents* for her birthday. (N)

Principal—The most important part of something. A person who runs an elementary, middle school, or high school.
Eggs are the *principal* ingredient when making quiche. (Adj)
Mr. Washington is a *principal* known for getting good results from his students. (N)
Principle—A standard law or rule.
Respect is the *principle* rule in this classroom. (N)

Profit—Any advantage or reward gained.
You will *profit* from hard work and determination. (N)
Prophet—A person who expresses the will of a god.
The wandering man spoke like a *prophet*. (N)

Purr—See "Per."

Queue—See "Cue."

Quire—See "Choir."

Rack—A frame that has shelves, pegs, or bars and is used to display or hold things. A device of torture used to stretch a person's body.
Please place the boxes on the *rack* in the garage. (N)
Many people were placed on the *rack* for opposing the king. (N)
Wrack—Destruction or wreckage.
The tornado placed the small town into *wrack* and ruin. (N)

Rain—Water drops that fall to the ground that are condensed from atmospheric vapor.
The forecaster says it will *rain* all weekend. (N)
Reign—A period of sovereign rule.
The Queen of England has had a long *reign*. (N)
Rein—A long leather strap attached to a bridle and used by a rider to control a horse or other animal.
Susie held the *reins* tightly while riding her horse. (N)

Raise—To move or lift something up to a higher position or worth. To make something go up. To increase the amount or size of something. To collect or gather something. To tend to something to help it grow. Building something.
Will you please *raise* your right hand. (V)
The only way to *raise* bread dough is to add yeast to it. (V)
Sally tends to *raise* her voice when she becomes angry. (V)
The literature serves to *raise* the awareness of breast cancer. (V)
All parents should *raise* their children to be responsible adults. (V)
The university intends to *raise* a tribute to its most accomplished alumni. (V)
A good rule in poker is to never *raise* a raiser. (V)
Rays—Thin beams of radiation in the form of heat or light.
Flowers need *rays* of sunlight to grow. (N)
Raze—To destroy or tear down level to the ground.
Many buildings in my community have been *razed*. (V)

Rap—To hit swiftly or sharply. A style of music with the vocalist talking rhythmically instead of singing.
I heard someone *rap* on the door. (V)
Many young people today listen to *rap* music. (N)
Wrap—To cover or conceal something by folding or coiling.
It took me a long time to *wrap* your birthday present. (V)

Rays—See "Raze" and "Raise."

Raze—See "Raise" and "Rays."

Read—Past tense of read.
I *read* the book and liked it a lot. (V)
Red—A group of colors that vary in saturation and brightness whose hue resembles blood.
I have a *red* jacket with shoes to match. (N)

Read—To grasp the meaning of something through examination of words or articles.
My uncle *reads* the newspaper every morning. (V)
Reed—Tall grass with jointed stalks that grows in wet areas. A strip of metal or cane placed in the mouthpiece of a woodwind instrument.
It was tough walking through the *reeds* and weeds in the water. (N)
My sister has a new *reed* for her saxophone. (N)

Real—Something that is authentic.
It was discovered that the dinosaur bones were *real*. (Adj)
Reel—A circular spool that turns on an axis and is used to wind rope, tape, or any other flexible material. To be knocked off balance or forced to retreat.
The box contains many *reels* of old game footage. (N)
Tom *reeled* when he was struck in the head. (V)

Red—See "Read."

Reed—See "Read."

Reek—Smells strongly.
The room *reeks* of garlic and onions. (V)
Wreak—To inflict punishment or vengeance on a person.
The boy intended to *wreak* as much havoc as possible. (V)

Reel—See "Real."

Reign—See "Rain" and "Rein."

Rein—See "Rain" and "Reign."

Rest—The state of refraining from all activity or motion. What remains after something has been taken away.

I plan to get a lot of *rest* this weekend. (N)

You may have the *rest* of the pie. (N)

Wrest—To take something by force.

Control of the border was *wrested* away from the northerners. (V)

Review—The process of going over a subject again in order to memorize. A critical article or report as in a periodical, on a book, play, recital or the like; critique, evaluation. To reexamine.

I had to *review* my notes many times before the test. (V)

The play got an excellent *review* in the *Times*. (N).

Revue—Any entertainment featuring skits, dances, and songs.

The show was a musical *revue* of Sondheim songs. (Adj)

Revue—See "Review."

Right—To be in agreement with what is fact, reason, or truth. The opposite of left.

It is always *right* to tell the truth. (Adj)

Move the couch a little to the *right*. (Adj)

Rite—The customary way of performing a ceremony.

Getting a driver's license is a *rite* of passage for many young people into adulthood. (N)

Write—The act of making letters, words, or figures on a surface with a tool such as a pen or pencil.

I have many letters to *write* this weekend. (V)

Rhyme—A poem or verse that ends with sounds that sound the same.

Most poems that you hear have end words that *rhyme*. (N)

Rime—A coating on grass or trees that is frost or granular ice.

There was a beautiful coat of *rime* on the grass this morning. (N)

Ring—A circular object, arrangement, or form that also has a circular center. A small band made of precious metal and worn on the finger. An enclosed area where sports or exhibitions take place. The sound a bell makes when it is being used. Collection of people who privately conduct illegal activities. The act of calling attention to.

The moss formed a *ring* around the maple tree. (N)

Bo gave his girlfriend a beautiful engagement *ring*. (N)

The main event of the circus takes place in the center *ring*. (N)

When the bell *rings,* that means it's time to eat. (V)

The undercover police officer cracked the *ring* of car thieves. (N)

I thought I heard my telephone *ring*. (V)

Wring—To compress, twist, or squeeze with force.

Please *wring* out the towels before using them again. (V)

Rime—See "Rhyme."

Rite—See "Right" and "Write."

Road—An open space that's used by vehicles, people, and animals for travel.
   I took a shortcut home by taking the back *roads*. (N)
Rode—Past tense of ride.
   Cowboy Bill *rode* all the way to New Mexico without stopping. (V)
Rowed—Past tense of row.
   The ship's captain *rowed* his way to safety. (V)

Roe—The eggs of a fish that are found in the ovary. A small European or Asian deer.
   Many *roe* were found in the fish we caught. (N)
   The *roe* is distantly related to the American deer. (N)
Row—Objects lined up next to each other in a straight line. To propel or steer about with oars.
   You should find your seat in the second *row*. (N)
   You must be strong in order to *row* a canoe. (V)

Role—A character portrayed by an actor in a dramatic performance.
   This *role* is the best character I've ever portrayed. (N)
Roll—To move or push forward on a surface by constantly turning over. To envelop or wrap in a covering. A small piece of baked, rounded yeast dough.
   The boy *rolled* the barrel uphill. (V)
   My father prefers to *roll* his own cigarettes. (V)
   My mother serves *rolls* every Sunday. (N)

Roomer—Someone who pays rent for a room.
   The landlord collected rent from several *roomers* this month. (N)
Rumor—Information that is not verified but is spread anyway by word of mouth.
   There is a *rumor* going around about my favorite player being traded. (N)

Root—The underground part of a plant that contains food and water for the plant. The most important part of something. To passionately support or cheer for someone or something.
   In order to kill a weed, you must kill the *root*. (N)
   Some people say that money is the *root* of all evil. (N)
   I am very proud to *root* for my home team. (V)
Route—A highway or street used for traveling from one place to another. An established course of travel.
   In order to get to town, you must take *Route* 69. (N)

Rose—A flower that comes in many different colors that has thorns on its stems. Past tense of rise.
   My girlfriend loves large yellow *roses*. (N)
   The young executive *rose* quickly through the ranks within the company. (V)
Rows—Plural of row.
   There are *rows* of people lined up to buy concert tickets. (N)

Rote—A process for memorizing using routine. A stringed instrument from the medieval times.
   She used *rote* memory skills to help her study for her final exam. (N)
   Anyone who could play the *rote* was revered in medieval times. (N)
Wrote—Past tense of write.
   I *wrote* to the newspaper last week. (V)

Rough—Something that is uneven, ungentle, or crude. The unmowed section on a golf course.
> The basketball coach was very *rough* with his players when they made a mistake. (Adj)
> The golfer had to go into the *rough* to get his golf ball. (N)

Ruff—A pleated, starched circular collar worn by men and women in the 16th and 17th centuries. Playing a trump on a card when one can no longer follow suit. A European fish related to the perch that is found in fresh water.
> Many men and women wore *ruffs* in the 16th and 17th centuries. (N)
> It is customary in bridge to *ruff* an opponent's trick when possible. (V)
> Michael caught many *ruff* while fishing this weekend. (N)

Route—See "Root."

Row—See "Roe."

Rowed—See "Road" and "Rode."

Rows—See "Rose."

Rude—Impolite or uncivilized.
> It is not polite to be *rude* to people. (Adj)

Rued—To feel remorse or regret for.
> I *rued* the day I lied to my mother. (V)

Ruff—See "Rough."

Rumor—See "Roomer."

Rung—Past participle of ring. A crosspiece between the legs of a chair or ladder.
> The man missed a *rung* on the ladder and fell to the ground. (N)
> The telephone had *rung* several times before I answered it. (V)

Wrung—Past tense and past participle of wring.
> The wet towels were *wrung* out before being used again. (V)

Rye—A cereal grass with seeds that are valued as grain.
> I love toasted *rye* bread with grape jam. (N)

Wry—Something that is abnormally twisted or bent. Ironic humor.
> She had a *wry* neck due to the poor seating. (Adj)
> The stand-up comedian had a *wry* sense of humor. (Adj)

Sac—A baglike structure in an animal, plant, or fungus, as one containing fluid.
> The infection caused a *sac* to form on Johnny's arm. (N)

Sack—A bag; a loose fitting dress. To go to bed. To tackle (as in football). To dismiss or discharge.
> We will need lots of potatoes, so buy a full *sack*. (N)
> After driving cross country, all he wanted to do was hit the *sack*. (N)
> The underdogs *sacked* the quarterback and made the touchdown. (V)
> Greg was *sacked* when the company found out about the errors. (V)

Sack—See "Sac."

Sail—A piece of fabric attached to a boat and used to catch wind to push the boat.
Traveling on water by sailboat. Controlling a sailboat.
The sailors raised their *sails* to catch the approaching wind. (N)
I plan to take lessons to learn to *sail*. (V)
I plan to *sail* from Miami to Jamaica in the winter. (V)
Sale—The selling of goods for a discounted price.
Every year, department stores have a 20-percent-off *sale*. (N)

Scene—The place where something happens.
The police sectioned off the *scene* of the crime. (N)
Seen—Past participle of see.
Tina was *seen* leaving the library at six. (V)

Scent—See "Cent" and "Sent."

Scull—An oar used to propel or steer a boat. A small, light boat used for racing for one or more rowers.
Bill used a *scull* to steer his boat. (N)
Many people turned out to see the *scull* races. (N)
Skull—The hard bony shell that covers and protects the brain.
Your brain is protected by your *skull*. (N)

Sea—Large bodies of fresh or salt water that are completely or partly enclosed by land.
Many people believe that the Red *Sea* is actually red. (N)
See—To acknowledge with the eye. To tend to or address something.
I *see* a difference in the way you cut your hair. (V)
I will *see* to it that all obligations are met. (V)

Sealing—See "ceiling."

Seam—A line formed when two pieces of fabric are sewn together.
There is a small tear in my pants along the *seam*. (N)
Seem—The impression of appearing to be.
She *seems* to have lost weight since she began exercising. (V)

Sear—To make something dry up. To burn or scorch something with a hot instrument on the surface.
The desert heat *seared* our throats. (V)
The rancher will *sear* his logo onto the backside of each animal. (V)
Seer—One who sees into the future.
At the carnival, I met a woman who claims to be a *seer*. (N)

See—See "Sea."

Seed—See "Cede."

Seem—See "Seam."

Seen—See "Scene."

Seer—See "Sear."

Sell—See "Cell."

Seller—See "Cellar."

Sensor—See "Censer" and "Censor."

Sent—See "Cent" and "Scent."

Sense—See "Cents."

Serf—A feudal servant bound to the land owned by someone else.
    The *serf* tilled the lord's fields. (N)
Surf—Waves of the sea that break on the shore or reef.
    The swimmers became lost in the *surf*. (N)

Serial—See "Cereal."

Session—See "Cession."

Sew—The process of mending or making with a thread and needle.
    Before you go, let me *sew* that button back onto your coat. (V)
So—In the manner or condition indicated.
    You need to go to college *so* you can get a good job. (Adv)
Sow—Spreading seed across the ground to grow.
    Farmers *sow* seeds in the spring. (V)

Shake—To move a thing swiftly from side to side, up and down, or back and forth. To scatter by moving. The grasping of someone's hand when greeting them. To make something tremble or vibrate. To disturb something. The act of shaking something. A cold beverage made with milk, ice cream, and flavoring that is prepared by shaking.
    Tom told his son not to *shake* his little sister. (V)
    I watched my neighbor *shake* all of the snow off of her coat. (V)
    When going for an interview, always *shake* hands with the interviewer. (V)
    That movie was so scary, it made me *shake* with fear. (V)
    Because you lied, my trust in you has been *shaken*. (V)
    If you agree, just give a *shake* of your head,(N)
    I'll have a hamburger and a *shake,* please. (N)
Sheik—Arab chief or religious leader.
    The *sheik* is considered very wise. (N)

Shear—To remove by clipping or cutting.
    The farmer will *shear* the sheep tomorrow. (V)
Sheer—Something that is very thin; transparent.
    I prefer shirts that are made of *sheer* material. (Adj)

Sheik—See "Chic" and "Shake."

Shoe—A durable covering for the human foot that usually has a rigid heel and sole.
    I had to get a new heel put on my left *shoe*. (N)
Shoo—To scare or drive away animals or birds.
    Every now and then, I have to *shoo* the birds away from my back porch. (Interj)

Shone—Past tense and past participle of shine.
The sun *shone* brighter yesterday. (V)
Shown—Past participle of show.
The movie was *shown* to audiences all over the world. (V)

Shoo—See "Shoe."

Shoot—See "Chute."

Shown—See "Shone."

Side—A surface of something. A position maintained in a contest or dispute.
Your job is to paint this *side* of the garage. (N)
In any dispute, always *side* with the truth. (N)
Sighed—Past tense of sigh. To emit a sound of exhalation.
The woman *sighed* when she heard her son would survive his accident. (V)

Sight—See "Cite" and "Site."

Site—See "Cite" and "Sight."

Skull—See "Scull."

Slay—To deliberately kill.
The representatives sought to *slay* the new tax reform bill. (V)
Sleigh—A small, light vehicle used on snow or ice and usually pulled by a horse.
I love to go for *sleigh* rides in the winter. (N)

Sleight—Accomplished or crafty, dexterity.
The magician proved to be very *sleight* of hand. (N)
Slight—Something small in amount, size, or importance.
I have a *slight* problem with our arrangement. (Adj)

Slew—Past tense of slay. A large number or amount.
In the Bible, David *slew* Goliath. (V)
Michael Jordan has won a *slew* of awards during his basketball career. (N)
Slue—To twist or turn something to the side without removing it from its axis.
Will you please *slue* the fan this way? (V)

Slight—See "Sleight."

Slue—See "Slew."

So—See "Sew" and "Sow."

Soar—To fly high with little effort.
It is a beautiful sight to see eagles *soar* so effortlessly. (V)
Sore—A source of distress, irritation, or pain. Experience pain or discomfort.
Michael bought some ointment for the cold *sore* on his lip. (N)
Theodore was *sore* after his first night of lifting weights. (Adj)

Sole—The bottom portion of the foot or shoe. Anything that is the one and only. A small-mouthed flat fish with close-set eyes.
The *sole* of my left shoe has a hole in it. (N)
I am the *sole* provider for my family. (Adj)
While in Europe, I had the chance to catch a lot of *sole*. (N)
Soul—The essential part of people. The critical part of something.
Every person invests his or her *soul* into something at one time or another. (N)
David grew to be the *soul* of his soccer team. (N)

Some—A specified or unspecified part of something.
Yes, I would like *some* water. (Adj)
Sum—An amount achieved by adding.
I would like the *sum* of the two bills. (N)

Son—A male child.
The Murphys had a *son* last night. (N)
Sun—A bright star that sustains life on earth.
It takes a full year for the earth to rotate around the *sun*. (N)

Sore—See "Soar."

Soul—See "Sole."

Sow—See "Sew" and "So."

Staid—Something that is very conservative in style. Permanent.
The recent graduates wore *staid* outfits on their first job interviews. (Adj)
The experience left a *staid* impression on me. (Adj)
Stayed—Past tense of stay.
He *stayed* at my house last night. (V)

Stair—A single step of a stairway.
Just go up one *stair* at a time and don't look down. (N)
Stare—To look fixedly.
It is very rude to just *stare* at someone. (V)

Stake—A vertical post of wood or metal that's driven into the ground. A place where prisoners are burned. Money or property that is put up for gambling. An interest in the outcome of something.
To fix the broken fence, a new *stake* is needed. (N)
In Colonial America, witches were tied to a *stake* and burned. (N)
When you bet on a team to win, you have a *stake* in the game. (N)
Parents invest a lot of time in their children; thus they have a *stake* in their future. (N)
Steak—A piece of meat, usually beef, that's cut across the muscle grain.
That restaurant serves the best *steak* in town. (N)

Stare—See "Stair."

Stationary—Being still without movement.
　　If you see a snake, remain *stationary*. (Adj)
Stationery—Writing materials (paper, pens, and ink).
　　Stationery is always a nice gift for someone who enjoys writing letters. (N)

Stayed—See "Staid."

Steak—See "Stake."

Steal—To take illegally.
　　It is wrong to *steal* anything from any person or place. (V)
Steel—A hard alloy containing iron and carbon, used to make tools and machinery.
　　The large building has a *steel* frame. (N)

Straight—Traveling continuously in the same direction with no waves or curves. The sequential order of five cards in a poker game.
　　Get on Highway 1 in New York and you can drive *straight* to Key West, Florida. (Adj)
　　A *straight* in the card game of poker is hard to beat. (Adj)
Strait—A narrow body of water that joins two larger bodies of water.
　　While in the Mediterranean, I visited the *Strait* of Gibraltar. (N)

Stile—A collection of steps used to cross a wall or fence.
　　A *stile* is often used by farmers to cross over a stone wall. (N)
Style—The method used to express, say, or do something. A particular type of fashion.
　　The candidate's *style* of delivery won her many supporters. (N)
　　People can express their own individuality by the *style* of clothing they select. (Adj)

Style—See "Stile."

Serge—Twilled wool cloth used for suits.
　　The tailor selected a *serge* material to use for making the new suit. (N)
Surge—To excitedly rush forward as if in waves.
　　The audience *surged* toward the stage and the rock band. (V)

Suite—A set of rooms that connect and are used by one person or a family.
　　A *suite* at the hotel will give us more room. (N)
Sweet—Something that has a sugary taste. Someone who is pleasant to be around.
　　The candy is definitely very *sweet*. (Adj)
　　Everyone enjoys being around Granny because she is so *sweet*. (Adj)

Sum—See "Some."

Sun—See "Son."

Surf—See "Serf."

Surge—See "Serge."

Symbol—See "Cymbal."

Tacks—Short, flat-headed nails with sharp tips. Large, loose stitches used to mark something. Plural of tack. Applying a tack to something.
    You should use *tacks* to secure your posters to your wall. (N)
    The tailor *tacks* in the alterations until the final fitting. (V)
Tax—Money that is paid by citizens to support the government.
    Our *tax* check must be postmarked by April 15, or it is late. (N)

Tail—The rear appendage of an animal. Any appendage that is to the bottom or rear of something. Someone following someone else while documenting his or her movements and actions.
    When I arrive home, my dog's *tail* is always wagging. (N)
    The *tail* of her dog has a few scratches on it. (N)
    The detective *tailed* the suspect. (N)
Tale—A retelling of something that has happened. A lie.
    Often, Grandpa would tell us a *tale* from his childhood. (N)
    Mother knew he was telling her a *tale*. (N)

Taper—To become smaller or thinner at one end. To diminish. A candle, especially a slender one.
    The arrowhead *tapered* to a very sharp point. (Adj)
    The storm began to *taper* off after an hour. (Adv)
    Mom lit the *tapers* in the candlesticks on the dining table. (N)
Tapir—A large, stout, three-toed animal found in Central and South America resembling a swine and having a long snout.
    Tapirs are an endangered species. (N)

Tapir—See "Taper."

Taught—Past tense and past participle of teach.
    Your teacher *taught* you that last year. (V)
Taut—Drawn or pulled tight.
    A bow held her hair *taut*. (Adj)

Tax—See "Tacks."

Tea—Dried leaves of the tea plant that are used to make a beverage that people drink hot or cold. A serving of refreshments, usually in the afternoon, consisting of small sandwiches and cakes served with tea.
    I enjoy a good cup of hot *tea*. (N)
    Afternoon *tea* is still served at the Drake Hotel in Chicago. (N)
Tee—A small peg inserted into the ground and used to hold a ball to be hit.
    I carry an extra golf *tee* in my pocket. (N)

Team—A group of people working together. More than two animals harnessed together to work.
    The members of our *team* work well together. (N)
    Many Amish farmers still use a *team* of horses to pull the plow when they are cultivating their fields. (N)
Teem—To be full.
    A *teem* of mosquitoes swarmed over the stagnant water. (V)

Tear—A clear drop of liquid that moisturizes the eyeball and eyelid.
    Cutting onions can cause a *tear* to form in your eye. (N)
Tier—One of many rows that are placed one after another.
    If the committee decides on a *tier* seating plan, everyone will have a better view of the stage. (N)

Teas—Plural of tea.
    Most restaurants offer you a wide selection of different *teas.* (N)
Tease—To make fun of. To entice. To comb hair from the end to scalp to fluff the hair. To separate the fibers of fabric.
    Children often *tease* other children. (V)
    The free popcorn and cola will *tease* many people to attend this showing of the new movie. (V)
    A hairdresser can *tease* your hair to create a different look. (V)
    To *tease* the fabric will allow you to separate the fibers. (V)

Tee—See "Tea."

Teem—See "Team."

Tern—Sea bird with a forked tail resembling a gull. A set of three.
    The *tern* is due to give birth any day now. (N)
    A set of three layers on a cake is referred to as a *tern.* (N)
Turn—To have something make the same motion a wheel does. An opportunity to do something. To change something from one state to another. To make something face a new direction. To get from one side of something to another.
    You have to *turn* the lock to the right to open it. (V)
    It is my *turn* to use the computer. (N)
    I found out that caterpillars *turn* into butterflies. (V)
    The brisk wind made the weather vane *turn* to the east. (V)
    When you *turn* the corner, the mailbox should be right there. (V)

Their—Showing ownership of something.
    Their car is parked in the garage. (Adj)
There—Located in a certain spot. At a certain place. A specific point in time.
    There are swings at the park. (Adv)
    Your car keys are over *there.* (Adv)
    When you reach twenty-one, *there* will be more places to go. (Adv)
They're—They are.
    They're busy tonight. (Contr)

Theirs—Showing ownership by them.
   Theirs is the big yellow house on the hill. (Pron)
There's—There is.
   There's hope for everyone to learn if they just try. (Contr)

There—See "They're" and "Their."

They're—See "There" and "Their."

Threw—Past tense of throw.
   Yesterday, I *threw* the ball through the school window. (V)
Through—From one end to the other. From start to finish. In, over. From. Finished.
   We drove *through* the Holland Tunnel. (Prep)
   She read *through* the instruction manual. (Adv)
   We walk *through* the rain. (Prep)
   I got your address *through* your brother. (Prep)
   Without food, we will be *through* soon. (Adv)

Throe—A twitching muscle, severe pain.
   When he over-exercised he felt the *throe* in his muscles. (N)
Throw—Using your arm to hurl an object through the air. The act of hurling something through the air. The act of making someone fall.
   The pitcher is warming up so that he can *throw* a winning game. (V)
   If you catch the ball, *throw* it to first base. (N)
   The instructor showed the class how to *throw* someone for a fall. (V)

Throne—The name given to the special chair on which a king, queen, or other very important person sits. The special power of a ruler.
   At the coronation, the king sat on his *throne*. (N)
   The *throne* of England is respected throughout the world. (N)
Thrown—Past participle of throw.
   Mother has *thrown* away your old toys. (V)

Through—See "Threw."

Thrown—See "Throne."

Thyme—A spice used for seasoning.
   Using spices like *thyme* will add taste to the chicken. (N)
Time—Yesterday, today, and tomorrow. Past, present, and future. A certain span in history. Beat in music. To get the speed.
   Now is the *time* to plan your schedule. (N)
   A *time* capsule today will be opened in the future. (N)
   The Colonial Period was a *time* of expansion. (N)
   The conductor helps the members of the orchestra keep *time* to the music. (N)
   They *timed* the birth of the new baby. (V)

Tic—An uncontrollable movement of the muscles, usually in the face.
> Tourette's syndrome is a neurological disorder that causes people to have involuntary *tics* and sudden outbursts. (N)

Tick—A small insect having eight legs related to a spider that lives by sucking blood from animals. A sound made by a clock.
> It is hard to find the small *tick* on your dog after he has been in the woods. (N)
> I could hear the *tick* of the clock as I lay in the bed. (V)

Tide—Every twelve hours the coming in and going out of the ocean caused by the gravitational pull of the sun and moon.
> When you are swimming in the ocean, you need to watch for the *tide*. (N)

Tied—Past tense of tie. Putting two pieces of string together in a knot or a bow.
> She *tied* her shoestrings together. (V)

Tier—See "Tear."

Time—See "Thyme."

To—Going in a direction. Going along. To agree with. Comparing.
> Please park your car *to* the left. (Prep)
> We exercised *to* the music. (Prep)
> Being lazy is not the way *to* win the game. (Prep)
> He left at a quarter *to* nine. (Prep)

Too—Wanting to also go. Next to. Having more than enough.
> I want to go *too*. (Adv)
> We *too* went on a picnic. (Adv)
> I had *too* much candy. (Adv)

Two—Adding one more to one.
> If you have one apple and one orange, you have *two* pieces of fruit. (Adj)

Toad—A small animal with rough brown skin that lives mostly on land and looks similar to a frog.
> It will be easier to find a *toad* on land rather than in water. (N)

Towed—Past tense of tow. Pulling something by a rope or chain. The action of towing.
> We *towed* the car out of the snow bank using chains. (V)
> Without the right equipment, *towing* another car is difficult. (V)

Toe—One of the terminal digits of the human foot.
> Playing baseball, I hurt my big *toe*. (N)

Tow—Pulling something by a rope or chain. The action of towing.
> The only way to move the old car is to *tow* it. (V)

Told—Past tense and past participle of tell.
> You *told* me that yesterday. (V)
> The police officer *told* me to wait. (V)

Tolled—Past tense of toll. Sounding a bell.
> The teacher *tolled* the bell to signal the end of recess. (V)

Too—See "Two" and "To."

Tool—A device that helps you to do a job. A person or a thing used like a tool. Using a device used to shape something.
The hammer is a *tool* that will help you to pound in the nails. (N)
Your textbook is a learning *tool*. (N)
The leather crafter *tooled* a beautiful design in the leather. (V)
Tulle—Thin fine silk net that can be used for veils.
The seamstress used *tulle* to make the bride's veil. (N)

Tow—See "Toe."

Towed—See "Toad."

Tray—A flat piece of plastic or metal with a rim around it used for carrying dishes or other things.
Your meal in a hospital is delivered on a *tray*. (N)
Trey—A card, a die, or a domino that has three dots.
Do you have a *trey*? (N)

Troop—An assemblage of persons or things; company; band; a great number.
The new army recruits went as a *troop* to get measured for their uniforms. (N)
Troupe—A company, band, or group of singers, actors, or other performers, especially one that travels about.
The acrobatic *troupe* we saw this summer at the Renaissance Festival was great! (N)

Troupe—See "Troop."

Trussed—To tie or fasten closed.
Grandmother *trussed* the turkey's cavity after stuffing it with dressing. (V)
Trust—To have a firm belief. To have a firm commitment to honesty and truth. To count on a person or a thing. To allow a person to use or borrow something. To have hope or a belief. Property or money managed for someone by someone else.
I have *trust* in God. (N)
I have *trust* that you are honest. (N)
I *trust* that you won't let me down. (V)
I *trust* you, so I will let you borrow my jacket. (V)
I *trust* the belief that you will have bad luck if you walk under a ladder. (V)
My *trust* is being handled by the bank. (N)

Tulle—See "Tool."

Turn—See "Tern."

Two—See "Too" and "To."

Urn—See "Earn."

Vain—Having a lot of confidence in your looks or your abilities. Trying, but not successful.

If you are too *vain,* many people will have a difficult time liking you. (Adj)

I only made a *vain* attempt to complete my assignment. (Adj)

Vane—A paddle or blade that can be seen on a windmill or a propeller.

The birds sit on the wind *vane* on the roof. (N)

Vein—A vessel in your body that carries blood from the heart throughout your body. The center line and branches in a leaf. A crack in a rock filled with mineral or metal ore.

The car accident I had last month damaged a *vein* in my leg. (N)

Put a piece of paper over the leaf, color the paper, and you will clearly be able to see the leaf's *veins.* (N)

After analyzing the rock, I learned that metal ore could be found in the *vein* of the rock. (N)

Vale—A valley between two hills or mountains.

Margaret lives in Australia in a little *vale* by the stream. (N)

Veil—A covering for the head. To hide.

In Spain, a *veil* is often worn by a woman when going to church. (N)

He hid in a *veil* of secrecy. (V)

Vane—See "Vain" and "Vein."

Vary—To change or make different.

I often *vary* my hairstyle. (V)

Very—An extra amount. Exactly on target. Absolutely, complete.

She has a *very* large amount of money. (Adv)

You are *very* accurate. (Adj)

Vein—See "Vain" and "Vane."

Vice—Doing something harmful on a repeated basis; a bad habit.

Drinking can quickly become a *vice.* (N)

Smoking is a *vice.* (N)

Vise—A tool with a wide opening that screws down to hold something firmly.

The carpenter used his *vise* to hold the two pieces of wood firmly in place. (N)

Wade—To go on foot through water, mud, or snow. Something that blocks you moving freely. To go with trouble.

Wear your high boots if you plan to *wade* through the water. (V)

To *wade* through the book is difficult due to the small print. (V)

I can *wade* through the assignment without your help. (V)

Weighed—Past tense of weigh.

Yesterday, I *weighed* myself. (V)

Wail—Pain or sorrow causing a person to cry out. To make a sharp sound. To be sorrowful for.

A loud *wail* came from the mourning parents. (V)

The *wail* was loud and sharp. (V)

She *wailed* for her lost child. (V)

Whale—A large mammal that lives in the sea.

Did you know that the *whale* is related to the dolphin? (N)

Waist—The narrow part above your hips.
  Exercise will help make your *waist* smaller. (N)
Waste—To use things inefficiently. Spending money frivolously.
  You will *waste* electricity if you don't turn the lights out when you leave the room. (V)
  Credit cards can cause you to *waste* your money. (N)

Wait—To stop what you are doing until a person or thing happens. Prepared for.
  Wait until the other students have finished before you leave for lunch. (V)
  I will *wait* for you outside. (V)
Weight—How heavy a person or thing is. A burden.
  What is your *weight*? (N)
  Her husband's illness is a huge *weight* to bear. (N)

Waive—To forego your claim. Not enforced.
  You will *waive* your rights to the lottery if you lose your ticket. (V)
  The police can *waive* the policy for a variety of reasons. (V)
Wave—A moving ridge of water. Energy being changed. A motion of movement.
  If the *wave* is high, get your surfboard. (N)
  You can get a shock from an electric *wave*. (V)
  Wave your hand so they will see you. (V)

Want—To hope for. To be without something. To have police looking for you.
  I *want* to buy a new dress. (V)
  Because they are very hungry, the family *wants* food. (V)
  If your face is on a wanted poster, the police *want* you. (V)
Wont—A ritual or a comfortable habit; to be accustomed.
  She is *wont* to rise early. (Adj)

Ware—Items that are for sale that have been manufactured. Pottery items.
  The school gets a discount on the plastic *ware* that it buys. (N)
  Mrs. Smith bought several pieces of *ware* to display in her gallery. (N)
Wear—Having something on your body. Things that are made to be worn. To bring
  something to a particular point through usage. Exhibiting a certain facial expression.
  If it is cold outside, you can *wear* my jacket. (V)
  This summer, I will be in desperate need of more athletic *wear*. (N)
  My car has a lot of *wear* and tear on it. (N)
  You *wear* a look of surprise on your face every time you see me. (V)
Where—In or at what place. In what position or situation. From what source or place.
  To what place or toward what end. At which place. In a place in which. In a situa-
  tion or place in which. To a place or situation in which.
  Where is your mother? (Adv)
  He moved to the city *where* his girlfriend lives. (Conj)

Warn—To give notice or advice of danger, impending evil, possible harm, or anything
  else unfavorable.
  They *warned* him of a plot against him. (V)
Worn—Past tense of wear. Lessened in value due to use, wear, handling.
  From the marks on the soles we knew the shoes had already been *worn*. (V)
  We bought the used car in spite of its *worn* tires. (Adj)

Waste—See "Waist."

Watt—A unit used to measure electrical power.
 I use a 100-*watt* light bulb in my bedroom. (N)
What—Word used when asking questions about people or things. Word used to show shock or surprise.
 What is the price of that shirt? (Pron)
 What a movie! (Interj)

Wave—See "Waive."

Way—A particular style. How a task is completed. A direction to travel from place to place. The direction of something. The distance of something.
 My sister is wearing her hair in a new *way*. (N)
 I have found a new *way* to make vanilla milk shakes. (N)
 Is this the *way* to your mother's house? (N)
 When you hear the cue, please look this *way*. (N)
 My birthday is still a long *way* off. (N)
Weigh—Finding out the weight of something. To consider something carefully.
 You have to *weigh* the box before mailing it. (V)
 I'll *weigh* my options before deciding which college I'll attend. (V)
Whey—The watery part of milk that separates from the curd when cheese is made.
 The milk was out so long, the *whey* has begun to separate from the curd. (N)

We—Someone who's speaking and whom he or she is talking to.
 We will soon be out of money.
Wee—Anything that is extremely tiny or small. Very early hours in the morning.
 The recipe calls for only a *wee* amount of paprika. (Adj)
 The commotion outside awoke me in the *wee* hours of the morning. (Adj)

Weak—Without power or strength. Something that is easily broken. Anything that does not function well. Lacking authority or support.
 Due to his illness, he was too *weak* to continue exercising. (Adj)
 The hammer went through a *weak* spot in the plaster wall. (Adj)
 You can't stress him because he has a *weak* heart. (Adj)
 Due to a lack of support from its people, the government was *weak*. (Adj)
Week—A period of seven days, one after another.
 I plan to take a vacation for a full *week*. (N)

Weal—For the betterment of something. A welt or streak appearing on the skin.
 Teachers act for the *weal* of the entire community. (N)
 The lash left a large *weal* on his back. (N)
We'll—We shall. We will.
 We'll not spend any more money than we have to. (we shall) (Contr)
 We'll be there any minute now. (we will) (Contr)
Wheel—A round disk-like frame that turns on an axle or shaft in the middle. Anything similar to a wheel in shape or movement. The motion of turning. To move something by placing it on something else that has wheels.
 These *wheels* are too small for my bike. (N)
 I laid the keys on the potter's *wheel* before I left. (N)
 There was a look of anger on her face as she *wheeled* around to face me. (V)
 Please *wheel* these boxes out to the truck. (V)

Wear—See "Ware" and "Where."

Weather—Climate conditions outside at a particular time and place. Change occurring from the effects of the weather. To endure a difficult situation successfully.
Watch the news and find out what the *weather* will be like today. (N)
Barbed wire loses some of its sharpness once it has *weathered* a few seasons. (V)
The defendant *weathered* the storm of questions from the prosecutor. (V)

Whether—Used to express possibilities or choices. Representing "if."
I don't know *whether* I'll go or stay. (Conj)
I would like to know *whether* you're coming or going. (Conj)

Weave—To make cloth from fibers or threads. To make things such as clothing from the same material. To travel by turning or twisting. A method of weaving.
It takes a skilled person to *weave* fibers from the cotton plant into cloth. (V)
My mother *weaves* rugs to be sold at the local mart. (V)
The drunken driver was *weaving* in and out of traffic. (V)
There are three basic types of *weave*. (N)

We've—We have.
We've seen all we need to see. (Contr)

We'd—We had. We would.
We'd needed to accomplish our goal. (we had) (Contr)
We'd love to hear you sing. (we would) (Contr)

Weed—An unwanted plant that grows in great numbers. The act of removing unwanted plants.
There are a lot of *weeds* growing in my backyard. (N)
I'll have to pay the boy next door to *weed* my garden. (V)

Wee—See "We."

Week—See "Weak."

Weigh—See "Way."

Weighed—See "Wade."

Weight—See "Wait."

Weir—A dam built to raise the water level while stopping it in order to direct the water to a mill. A fence made of broken branches put into a stream to catch fish.
I was lucky to land a job on the crew that is building a *weir*. (N)
The fisherman showed the boy how to place a *weir* in the stream. (N)

We're—We are.
We're lucky to be alive after that accident. (Contr)

We'll—See "Wheel" and "Weal."

Wet—To be soaked with water or any other liquid. Something that is not very dry. The act of making something wet.

It is not wise to put on *wet* clothes and go out in the cold. (Adj)

Stanley made a mistake and sat on the *wet* paint. (Adj)

Please go *wet* a cloth and bring it to me. (Adj)

Whet—To make sharp. To stimulate something. Something used as an appetizer.

In order to cut the meat properly, the butcher has to *whet* his knives everyday. (V)

The food served to *whet* my appetite. (V)

The *whet* served before dinner proved to be very tasty. (N)

We've—See "Weave."

Whale—See "Wail."

What—See "Watt."

Wheel—See "We'll" and "Weal."

Where—See "Wear" and "Ware."

Whet—See "Wet."

Whether—See "Weather."

Whey—See "Way" and "Weigh."

Which—Word used to ask questions about people or things. Word used to connect a group of words to another word in a sentence. The one that . . .

Which plane are you taking to New York? (Pron)

Be careful *which* road you take on your way back. (Pron)

Which will you vote for? (Pron)

Witch—A woman believed to have magical, supernatural power.

The *witch* in the story helped the children find their way home. (N)

While—A period of time. During a specific time. Different from the fact that.

I have been waiting a long *while* to hear from you. (N)

While you were gone, I cleaned your room. (Conj)

While I like you, I don't want to marry you. (Conj)

Wile—Deceiving in a cunning way. To lure or coax away.

The con artist, by her *wiles,* persuaded the man to hand over his watch. (N)

The promise of millions *wiled* the young football star from college into the pros. (V)

Whine—To make an unhappy, high crying sound. A high, sharp cry or sound. The act of complaining in a childish way.

The child *whined* when she became sleepy. (V)

We heard the *whine* of the car engine from next door. (N)

Some people always *whine* when their team loses. (V)

Wine—An alcoholic beverage made from fermented juice of grapes.

I prefer red *wine* to white. (N)

Whit—An extremely small amount.
> I don't give a *whit* what you have to say. (N)

Wit—The ability to say or think things that are extraordinary or funny.
> His sharp *wit* came in handy in his stand-up comedy routine. (N)

Whole—See "Hole."

Wholly—See "Holy" and "Holey."

Who's—Who is. Who has. Conjunction or shows possession.
> This is the woman *who's* going to pay your fee. (who is) (Contr)
> This is a man *who's* seen the world. (who has) (Contr)

Whose—Something that is of or belongs.
> I need to know *whose* car this is parked behind mine. (Pron)

Wile—See "While."

Wine—See "Whine."

Wit—See "Whit."

Witch—See "Which."

Won—See "One."

Wont—See "Want."

Worn—See "Warn."

Wood—What lies beneath the bark of a tree. Trees that have been chopped down, cut up, and stored for use.
> *Wood* from an oak tree is best for making certain things. (N)
> You need to chop some *wood* for the fireplace. (N)

Would—Past tense of will. Word used to express what someone said. To express something done over and over again in the past. To express a circumstance that might have been had something else happened.
> He said he *would* send it right over. (H.V.)
> Mom said it *would* be okay to wear your new jeans to school. (H.V.)
> She *would* work on her computer for hours with no break. (H.V.)
> We *would* be done by now if we had started on time. (H.V.)

Worst—Anything that is in more distress or bad shape than its comparison. Anything that is in the worst degree or manner.
> That is the *worst* dress I have ever seen you in. (Adj)
> The children are at their *worst* when we go out. (Adj)

Wurst—Sausage from Germany.
> Cynthia brought some *wurst* for the barbecue this weekend. (N)

Wrack—See "Rack."

Wrap—See "Rap."

Wreak—See "Reek."

Wrest—See "Rest."

Wring—See "Ring."

Write—See "Right."

Wrote—See "Rote."

Wrung—See "Rung."

Wry—See "Rye."

Wurst—See "Worst."

Yew—See "You" and "Ewe."

Yoke—A frame made of wood that is placed over the necks of work animals. A pair of work animals fastened together. The act of placing a yoke on work animals.
The mules ran astray when the *yoke* broke. (N)
It will take a *yoke* of oxen to get the cart out of the mud. (N)
You'll have to *yoke* some cows and hitch them to the wagon. (V)
Yolk—The part of the egg that is yellow.
I do not like the taste of raw *yolk*. (N)

Your—Belonging to you. Concerning you. Part of a title. What is well-known.
It will cost you five dollars to wash *your* car. (Adj)
What is the name of *your* dog? (Adj)
I am in full agreement, *Your* Honor. (Adj)
Your average professional athlete makes a lot of money. (Adj)
You're—You are.
You're the only person I have ever truly loved. (Contr)

REFERENCES— THE ULTIMATE LIST

Ultimate does not mean "best," but it does mean "last."

Agnes, M. (Ed.) (1998). *Webster's new world basic dictionary of American English*. Cleveland, OH: Wiley.

Barnhart, R.K. (Ed.) (1988). *The Barnhart dictionary of etymology*. Bronx, NY: H.W. Wilson Company.

Bartlett, J. (2002). *Bartlett's familiar quotations* (17th ed.). Boston: Little, Brown.

Bauman, J.R., Kameenui, E.J., & Ash, G.E. (2003) Research on vocabulary instructions: Voltaire redux. *Handbook of research on teaching the English language arts*. Mahway, NJ: Lawrence Earlbaum.

Bear, D.R., Invernizzi, M., Templeton, S., & Johnston, F. (2000). *Words their way*. Upper Saddle River, NJ: Merrill.

Beeler, D. (1988). *Book of roots: A full study of our families of words*. Chicago: The Bernstein Design Group.

Blackwell, C.W. & Blackwell, A.H. (2002). *Mythology for dummies*. New York: Hungry Minds.

Bonk, M.R. (1977). *Acronyms, initializations & abbreviations* (22nd ed.). Detroit, MI: Gale Research.

Bowler, P. (1982). *The superior person's book of words*. Boston: David R. Godine.

California driver handbook. (1998). Sacramento, CA: State of California Department of Motor Vehicles.

Carnevale, L. (2001). *Hot words for the SAT* I*. Hauppauge, NY: Barron's.

Carroll, J.B., et al. (1971). *Word frequency book*. New York: American Heritage.

Cevasco, G.A. (1977). *New words for you*. St. Paul, MN: Carillon Books.

Claman, C. (Ed.) (2003). *10 real SAT's* (3rd ed.). Plano, TX: College Board Publications.

Corbell, U.C. (1968). *The facts on file visual dictionary*. New York: Facts on File Publications.

Crystal, D. (1995). *The Cambridge encyclopedia of the English language*. Cambridge, UK: Cambridge University Press.

Dale, E., O'Rourke, J., & Bamman, H.A. (1971). *Techniques of teaching vocabulary*. Palo Alto, CA: Field Educational Publications.

Davies, P. (1983). *Reader's Digest success with words: A guide to the American language*. Pleasantville, NY: Reader's Digest.

Erdoes, R., & Ortiz, A. (Eds.) (1984). *American Indian myths and legends*. New York: Pantheon Books

Fernald, J.C. (1947). *Funk & Wagnall's standard handbook of synonyms, antonyms, and prepositions*. New York: Funk & Wagnall's.

Flesch, R. (1977). *A deskbook of American spelling and style*. New York: Barnes and Noble.

Flexner, S.B., & Hauck, L.C. (Eds.) (1987). *The random house dictionary of the English language* (2nd ed.). New York: Random House.

Flood, J., Lapp, D., Squire, J.R., & Jensen, J.M. (Eds.) (2003). *Handbook of research on teaching the English language arts*. Mahway, NJ: Lawrence Earlbaum.

Fry, E.B. (1957) Developing a word list for remedial reading. *Elementary English*.

Fry, E.B. (1999a). *How to teach reading*. Westminster, CA: Teacher Created Material.

Fry, E.B. (1999b). *1000 instant words: The most common words for teaching reading, writing, and spelling*. Westminster, CA: Teacher Created Materials.

Fry, E.B. (1999c). *Phonic patterns: Onset and rhyme word lists*. Westminster, CA: Teacher Created Material.

Fry, E.B. (2000). Vocabulary drills, middle level. Chicago, IL: Jamestown-Glencoe McGraw-Hill.

Fry, E.B., Kress, J.E., & Fountoukidis, D.L. (2002). *The reading teachers' book of lists* (4th ed.). Paramus, NJ: Prentice Hall.

Ganske, K. (2000). *Word journeys: Assessment-guided phonics, spelling, and vocabulary instruction*. New York: The Guilford Press.

Gibbs, N. (2003). The real magic of Harry Potter. *Time, 161*(25).

Glassman, B.S., (1996). *The Macmillan visual almanac*. New York: Macmillan.

Glazier, S. (1997). *Random House word menu*. New York: Random House.

Graves, M.F., & Watts-Taffe, S.M. (2002). The place of word consciousness in a research-based vocabulary program. In A.E. Farstrup & S.U. Samuels (Eds.), *What research has to say about reading instruction* (3rd ed.). Newark, DE: International Reading Association.

Greene, H.A. (1954). *The new Iowa spelling scale*. Iowa City, IA: State University of Iowa.

Gulland, D.M., & Hinds-Howell, D.G. (1986) *Dictionary of English idioms*. Harmondsworth, Middlesex, England: Penguin Books.

Hanks, P., & Hodges, F. (1988). *A dictionary of surnames*. Oxford, England: Oxford University Press.

Hanna, P.R., Hanna J.S., Hodges, R.E., & Rudorf, E.H. (1966). *Phoneme-grapheme correspondences as cues to spelling improvement*. Washington DC: U.S. Department of Health, Education, and Welfare.

Hairston, M., & Ruskiewicz, J.J. (1991). *The Scott, Foresman handbook for writers* (2nd ed.). Austin, TX: HarperCollins

Hirsch, Jr., E.D., Kett, J.F., & Trefil, J. (2002). *The new dictionary of cultural literacy* (3rd ed.). New York: Houghton Mifflin.

Kamil, M.L., Mosenthal, P.B., Pearson, P.D., & Barr, R.L. (2000). *Handbook of reading research* (Vol. III). Mahway, NJ: Lawrence Earlbaum.

Kissel, T., Weaver, W., & Lundin, D. (2002). *How to prepare for the SAT 9* (7th ed.). Glendale, CA: Carney Educational Services.

Lederer, R. (1989). *Crazy English: The ultimate joy ride through our language.* New York: Pocket Books.

Levey, J.S., & Greenhall, A. (Eds.) (1983). *The concise Columbia encyclopedia.* New York: Columbia University Press.

Lewis, N. (1949). *Word power made easy: The complete three-week vocabulary builder.* New York: Pocket Books.

Lewis, N. (Ed.). (1961). *Roget's thesaurus.* New York: Pocket Books.

Lewis, N. (1982). *Instant word power.* New York: Amsco College Publications.

Lundmark, T. (2002). *Quick qwerty: The story of the keyboard @ your fingertips.* Sydney, Australia: University of New South Wales Press.

Lutz, W. (1983). *Doublespeak.* New York: Harper and Row.

Lutz, W. (Ed.). (1989). *Beyond* Nineteen Eighty Four. Urbana, IL: National Council of Teachers of English.

Maggio, R. (1990). *How to say it: Choice words, phrases, sentences, and paragraphs for every situation.* Paramus, NJ: Prentice Hall.

McCormick, C. (1996). *Hippocrene dictionary and phrasebook: British-American American-British.* New York: Hippocrene Books.

McGeveran Jr., W. (Ed.) (2002). *The world almanac and book of facts.* New York: World Almanac Books.

McGeveran Jr., W. (Ed.) (2003). The *world almanac and book of facts.* New York: World Almanac Books.

Monson, S.C. (1965). *Word building* (2nd ed.). New York; Macmillan.

Moore, B., & Moore, M.C. (1997). *Dictionary of Latin and Greek origins.* Lincolnwood, IL: NTC Publishing Group.

Muschla, G.R. (1991). *The writing teacher's book of lists.* Englewood Cliffs, NJ: Prentice Hall.

Nagy, W.E. (1988). *Teaching vocabulary to improve reading comprehension.* Urbana, IL: ERIC Clearinghouse on Reading and Communication Skills.

National Geographic. (2000). *National geographic atlas of the world* (7th ed.). Washington, DC: National Geographic.

National Reading Panel. (2000). *Report of the National Reading Panel; Reports of the subgroups.* Washington, DC: National Institute of Child Health and Human Development Clearinghouse.

Nixon, M. (Ed.) (1999). *The Oxford mini-reference thesaurus* (2nd ed.). New York: Oxford University Press.

Norton, M.B., Katzman, D.M., Escott, P.D., Chudacoff, H.P., Paterson, T.G., & Tuttle, Jr., W.M. (1990). *A people & a nation: A history of the United States* (3rd ed.). Boston: Houghton Mifflin.

Peter, L.J. (1977). *Peter's quotations: Ideas for our time.* New York: Bantam Books.

Royce, P.M. (1982). *Sailing illustrated.* Ventura, CA: Western Marine Enterprises.

Sakiey, E.H. (1977). Syllables: A weighted graphemic inventory. Unpublished dissertation. New Brunswick, NJ: Rutgers University.

Sebranek, P., Kemper, D., & Meyer, V. (2001). *Writers inc: A student handbook for writing and learning.* Wilmington, MA: Write Source.

Siegel, A., & Basta, M.M. (1992). *The information please kids' almanac.* New York: Houghton Mifflin.

Thorndike, E.L. (1942). *Thorndike century senior dictionary.* New York: Appleton–Century-Crofts.

Thorndike, E.L., & Barnhart, C. (1979). *Scott, Foresman intermediate dictionary.* Glenview, IL: Scott, Foresman.

Thorndike, E.L., & Lorge, I. (1944). *The teacher's book of 30,000 words.* New York: Teachers College Press.

Venezky, R.L. (1999). *The American way of spelling.* New York: The Guilford Press.

Wallechinsky, D., Wallace, I., & Wallace, A. (1977). *The people's almanac presents the book of lists.* New York: Bantam Books.

Watkins, C. (Ed.). (1985). *The American heritage dictionary of Indo-European roots.* Boston: Houghton Mifflin.

INDEX

Italic terms are words that have been defined within the lists. A hyphen before a letter cluster designates that the cluster is a suffix; a hyphen after a letter cluster indicates that the cluster is a prefix.

occupations, 4–5; onomastics, 6; from places, 5; seasonal names, 5; variations on Smith, 5; variations on "son of", 5

Latin alphabet, 70

Latin phrases, 136

Latin words, 128

Law/lawyers, words related to, 95–96

League, 185

Lederer, Richard, 3

Legion, 35

Length, measuring, 180

Lengthening words, 143

-less, 234, 277, 281

-let, 277, 280

Letter doubling. *See* Geminates (double letters)

Letters, words for, 102–103

Lewis, Norman, 17

lieutenant, 48

light year, 185

-like, 277, 281

Linear mathematics, 21

Linear measurements, 181

-ling, 277, 280

lingu-, 98

Linneaus, Karl, 80

Liquid measurements, 181

liter, 81

-lith, 282

Local norms, 12

Longitude and time, 182

Love (ama-), 71

lumen, 81

Lutz, William, 19

lux, 81

-ly, 234, 277, 281

-lysis, 282

-lyze, 281

M

mach, 185

macro-, 240

magni-, 240

maintain, 48

Major languages, 134

mal-, 38, 240

Malapropism, 112

male-, 240

malediction, 39

malevolent, 39

malign, 38

man-, 53

-man, 235, 277, 280

manuscript, 47

Maps, 199

March, 65

marinate, 90

-mat, 277, 280

May, 65

Maze, difference between labyrinth and, 75

Measurements: circular, 181; cubic, 181; dry, 181; geometric figures, 186–189; linear, 181; liquid, 181; longitude and time, 182; metric system, 180; old measuring units, 185; scientific measurement units, 81, 185; square, 181; super numbers, 183–184; temperature conversion formulas, 182; U.S. weights and measures, 181–182

Medical specialties, 97

mega-, 183, 240

Megabyte, 184

megalopolis, 73

Megaton, kiloton vs., 21

-ment, 234, 277–278, 280

meta-, 240

Metaphors, 108, 112; definition by, 217

meteorology, 42

meter, 81

Methods: of defining a word, 217–218; direct instruction, 207; flashcards, 214; glossing, 211; graphic organizers, 220–221; group work, 213; new words, encouraging use of, 210; new words, paying attention to, 206; old-fashioned vocabulary lesson, 225; polysemy, 215–216; reading, 206; rewards, 212; systematic self-instruction, 209; teachable moments, 208; teacher enthusiasm and fun, 209; testing, 212; time, 207; visualization, 224; vocabulary instruction, integrating with every subject, 208; vocabulary workbooks, 222–223; word-a-day, 226; writing, 213

Metonym, 50, 112
Metric system, 180
Metronymic names, 5
Metronyms, 50
metropolis, 73
Mexico: maps of, 204; states of, 197
micro-, 240
microbiology, 40
mid-, 230, 240
mili-, 31
Military officers, 93
millennium, 31
milli-, 34, 183, 240
milligram, 31
millimeter, 34
million, 34
millipede, 31
minerals, 189
Minimum U.S. history terms, 11
minute, 81
mis-, 230, 240
misanthrope, 68
miss-, 48
mission, 48
missives, 48
mit-, 48, 53
Modern science words, and word origins, 69
mole, 81
mon-, 240
monarchy, 36
Monday, 65
mono-, 30, 33
month, 65
-mony, 278, 280
More or less (hyper-, hypo-, equi-), 43
Morphemes, 36, 218; bound, 234; free, 217
-most, 278, 281
Moving around (travel), words related to, 86
multi-, mult-, 35, 240
multifold, 35
multifulor, 35
multiplication, 35
Musical instruments, words related to, 87–89
musicology, 42

myria-, 240
Myriad, 35
Myth, words related to, 84

N

nano-, 183, 240
Nanometer, 21
Nanoscience, 21
Nanotechnology, 21
nat-, 53
National Council of Teachers of English (NCTE), 19
National norms, 12
National Spelling Bee words, 148
Nations/capitals of the world, 190–194
Native American Indian words, 125
Nature, last names based on things found in, 6
naturopath, 46
naut-, 53
nautical mile, 185
ne-, 240
necro-, 39
neo-, 240
-ness, 234, 278, 280
net-, 240
Neurologist, 97
neurorosis, 69
New words, paying attention to, 206
newton, 81
-nomy, 278
non-, 230, 240
Non-numerical amounts, prefixes for, 35
non-reoccurring, 36
Non-SI measurement units, 81
nondescript, 47
Nonlinear mathematics, 21
Notebook, of new words, 206
nove-, 34, 240
November, 34, 65
Numbers: counting in Latin and Greek, 32; non-numerical amounts, 35; quad-, penta-, quint-, hex-, sex-, 32; semi-, hemi-, mili, kilo-, cent-, demi-, 31; uni-, bi-, tri-, mono-, poly-, 30
-nyms, 50

Turkish words, 130
-ty, 234, 279, 281

U

-ular, 279, 281
-ule, 279
-ulent, 279, 281
ultra-, 243
-um, 279
un-, 229, 230, 243
-und, 279, 281
under-, 230, 243
Underlining, new words, 206
uni-, 30, 33, 54, 243
uniform, 30
United States, 195–196; capitals/postal
    abbreviations, 195; cities, by population,
    196; map of, 202
-uous, 279, 281
-ure, 279, 281
Urologist, 97
U.S. history terms, 11
U.S. weights and measures, 181–182

V

val-, 54
valedictory, 39
Vascular, 97
vassal, 111
ven-, 55
Venn diagrams, 221
vert-, 54
Very hard words, 3
ville, 73
Virgule, 116
Visualization, 224
voc-, 55
Vocabulary: biology, 80; chemical, 80; on the
    Internet, 219; old-fashioned vocabulary
    lesson, 225; popular science, 21; and
    reading, 206; SAT vocabulary words,
    7–8; word-a-day, 226; workbooks,
    222–223; and writing, 213
Vocabulary instruction, integrating with
    every subject, 208

vocation, 71
Voice (voc-), and word origins, 71
volt, 81
Volume, measuring, 180
Vowels, phonics, 150

W

-ward, 279, 281
watt, 81
-ways, 279, 281
Weasel words, 20
weber, 81
Webster's Dictionary, 17
Webster's New World Basic Dictionary, 224
Wednesday, 65
Weight, measuring, 180
-wise, 279, 281
with-, 243
Word-a-day method, 226
Word names (-nyms), 50
Word origins, 57–75, 57–99; cities (cit-, civ-),
    74; cities (poli-), 72; city areas, 73; days
    and months, 65; demimonde, 66; double,
    68; eponyms, 61–63; Greek and Roman
    gods, 59; Greek and Roman mythology,
    59; gym-, gymno-, gyn-, 74; labyrinth,
    difference between maze and, 75; love
    (ama-), 71; modern science words, 69;
    old English counting system, 67; old
    Greek words, 68; onomatopoeia, 60;
    pen, 67; place names, 64; Runes, 70;
    Shakespearean phrases, 66; temper
    (temp-), 72; voice (voc-), 71
Word pairs, 14
Words: body parts, 98; foreign, 119–136; fun
    with, 3; for letters, 102–103; misspelled
    words, 153; of the Old West, 82; origins
    of, 57–75; oxymorons, 16, 20; SAT 9
    (Stanford Achievement Test, 9th Edi-
    tion), 11; SAT (Scholastic Aptitude Test)
    math words, 9; SAT vocabulary words,
    7–8; shortest words, 13; with similar
    spellings, 104–107; very hard words, 3;
    weasel words, 20
World capitals, 190–194
World map, 201

-wright, 281

Writing, 101–118; confusing words (words with similar spellings), 104–107; derogatory terms, 111; idioms, 110; metaphors, 108; opposite writing terms, 113; printers' symbols, 117; proofreaders' symbols, 117; punctuation, 113–116; scribe-, 47; secret writing, 118; similes, 109; terms, 112; and vocabulary, 213; words for letters, 102–103

Y

-y, 234, 279, 281
-yer, 235, 279, 280
yocto-, 183
yotta-, 183

Z

zepto-, 183
zetta-, 183

Other Books of Interest

The Reading Teacher's Book of Lists, Fourth Edition

Edward B. Fry, Jacqueline E. Kress, and
Dona L. Fountoukidis

Paperback/ 208 pages
ISBN: 0-13-028185-9

This revised and updated Fourth Edition of *The Reading Teacher's Book of Lists* places at your fingertips over 190 of the most used and useful lists for developing instructional materials and planning lessons for elementary and secondary students.

For quick access, the lists are organized into 15 sections, from "Phonics," "Useful Words" and "Vocabulary" to "Literature," "Assessment" and "References," each brimming with examples, key words, teaching ideas and activities that you can use as is or easily adapt to meet your students' needs.

You'll find over 40 new lists in the Fourth Edition, making it even more helpful than previous editions. Moreover, all of the lists are printed in a big 8" × 11" format ready to be photocopied whenever you need them.

Edward B. Fry, Ph.D., is a Professor Emeritus of Education at Rutgers University (New Brunswick, NJ). At Rutgers, Dr. Fry taught graduate and undergraduate courses in reading, curriculum, and other educational subjects. He lives in Laguna Beach, CA.

Jacqueline Kress, Ed.D., is Associate Dean and Director of Graduate Studies at Fordham University's Graduate School of Education (New York, NY) and works with the faculty in the preparation and professional development of educators. She lives in Elizabeth, NJ.

Dona Lee Fountoukidis, Ed.D., is director of Planning, Research, and Evaluation at William Paterson University (Wayne, NJ) where she conducts research on student learning. She lives in Kinnelon, NJ.

Other Books of Interest

The Children's Literature Lover's Book of Lists

Joanna Sullivan

Paperback/ 500 pages
ISBN: 0-7879-6595-2

"Joanna Sullivan has created a wonderful resource for educators who want to enhance the literary development of students in the elementary school. The book's lists and resources are well organized and easy to use."

—Jerry L. Johns, Ph.D.,
Distinguished Teaching Professor Emeritus, Northern Illinois University and Past President, International Reading Association

This book is a unique compendium of lists of quality children's books, related activities, software programs, and videos for teachers, librarians, and parents of children ages 3-12. An indispensable resource and idea generator, this book provides over 200 lists of books, software programs, Web sites, and videos, all organized by theme, genre, topic, and grade level from preschool through grade six. Included are ABC books, concept books, multicultural books, read-alouds, folklore, science and social studies books that relate to state standards, chapter books, fiction and nonfiction, and award winners. A timeline outlining the history of children's literature is also included.

This book is the single, most comprehensive reference to the best children's books, software programs, and videos. The latest volume in the successful "Book of Lists" series, this book will save teachers many hours of preparation time in meeting current content standards, creating curriculum, generating imaginative activities, and matching students' interests and reading levels with "just the right books."

Joanna Sullivan is director of the Family Migrant Literacy Program at Southern Illinois University. She is a former elementary school teacher, and has taught reading, children's literature, and language arts at the college level. She is the author of numerous articles on language and literacy.

Other Books of Interest

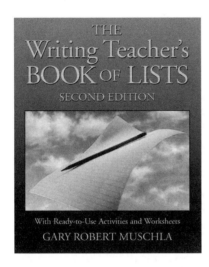

The Writing Teacher's Book of Lists, 2nd Edition

Gary Robert Muschla

Paperback/ 368 pages
ISBN: 0-7879-7080-8

This is the second edition of the unique information source and timesaver for English and language arts teachers. *The Writing Teacher's Book of Lists with Ready-to-Use Activities and Worksheets* includes 90 useful lists for developing instructional materials and planning lessons for elementary and secondary students. In addition, the book includes innovative activities and reproducible black-line masters that help students to improve their writing skills, word usage, and vocabulary.

For quick access and easy use, all of these lists and activities are organized into seven sections and individually printed in a format that can be photocopied as many times as required for individual or group instruction. This handy resource is filled with helpful lists, activities, teaching suggestions, and reproducible worksheets.

Gary Robert Muschla, B.A., M.A.T., taught reading and writing for more than twenty-five years at Appleby School in Spotswood, New Jersey. He is the author of several practical resources for teachers, including *Writing Workshop Survival Kit, English Teacher's Great Books Activities Kit, Reading Workshop Survival Kit,* and three books of *Ready-to-Use Reading Proficiency Lessons and Activities,* 4th, 8th, and 10th Grade Levels, all published by Jossey-Bass.

Other Books of Interest

Grammar Grabbers!

Jack Umstatter

Paperback/ 328 pages
0-13-042592-3

Would you like to make learning grammar more fun for your students? Would you like to have more fun teaching it? *Grammar Grabbers!* is packed with more than 200 creative, titillating, ready-to-use activities that give students the tools they need to use grammar more effectively in their writing and make the writing process more enjoyable. These challenging grammar teaching games are all designed to spark and hold students' interest.

- Identify the functions of main and subordinate clauses as well as prepositional and verbal phrases.
- Help students classify sentences according to structure and purpose.
- Review troublesome usage problems such as double negatives, misplaced modifiers, and incorrect pronouns or verbs.
- Cover common problems in punctuation.

You'll find the 203 ready-to-use activities in *Grammar Grabbers!* give students in grades 4 and up the tools they need to use grammar more effectively in their writings and make the writing process more enjoyable. As your students become more proficient and comfortable with grammar, they will become more eager to write!

Jack Umstatter, a master English teacher with over 25 years' experience, is a multiple winner of the Teacher of the Year award. He currently teaches English in the Cold Spring Harbor School District in New York and education and literature at Dowling College in Oakdale, New York. He is the author of numerous teacher resources such as *Brain Games!, Hooked on English!* and *Words, Words, Words,* all published by Jossey-Bass.